Large-Scale Group Decision-Making

Su-Min Yu · Zhi-Jiao Du

Large-Scale Group Decision-Making

State-to-the-Art Clustering and Consensus Paths

 Springer

Su-Min Yu (ID)
College of Management
Shenzhen University
Shenzhen, Guangdong, China

Zhi-Jiao Du (ID)
Business School
Sun Yat-sen University
Guangzhou, Guangdong, China

ISBN 978-981-16-7891-2   ISBN 978-981-16-7889-9   (eBook)
https://doi.org/10.1007/978-981-16-7889-9

This Springer imprint is published by the registered company Springer Nature Singapore Pte Ltd.
The registered company address is: 152 Beach Road, #21-01/04 Gateway East, Singapore 189721,
Singapore

To our dear daughter Yuxi.

Preface

Decision-making is something that everyone faces on a daily basis. Because real-world decisions usually involve multiple interests and are driven by democratization, the mode of *group decision-making* has been widely adopted. It refers to a decision situation where a group of decision-makers/experts provide their own opinions on the given alternative(s) and achieve the common solution by the aggregation of their opinions. The boom in technologies, such as social networking and e-democracy, has brought three new trends to the world of decision-making: (1) The decision group is usually composed of a large number of decision-makers from different industries and professional fields, who may represent the interests of different groups. (2) Individual opinions are prone to controversies and conflicts. Achieving a highly consensual solution often requires the implementation of a consensus-reaching process. (3) Individual decisions are more likely to be influenced by the preferences of friends or acquaintances in the same social network.

Large-scale group decision-making (LSGDM) is a kind of group decision-making situation in which typically greater than twenty decision-makers participate to select an optimal common solution. Note that in some specific scenarios, the number of decision-makers may be in the hundreds or even thousands. To date, the main topics of theoretical research include three aspects: (1) clustering that uses appropriate measurement rules to classify the original large group into several smaller size subgroups, (2) consensus building that aims to promote the convergence of individual opinions and produce a high-consensus decision outcome, and (3) the management of social networks among decision-makers in an attempt to explore the effect of on the trust relationships on the decision-making process. It can be concluded that all topics share the same goals: to facilitate and enhance interactions among decision-makers, to improve the efficiency of the decision-making process, and to guarantee the quality of decision outcomes.

This book is a collection of the authors' most advanced published research on LSGDM topics. The authors further improve and deepen the research content and findings in order to promote the contributions to be understood by more audiences. The book puts the two measurement attributes of opinion similarity and trust relationship in the same important position and proposes several novel clustering methods to reduce the dimension of decision-makers and solve the scalability challenge of LSGDM models. On this basis, a variety of consensus-reaching models are developed from the perspectives of social network environment, decision-makers' behaviors, and trust loss compensation. We hope that any researcher interested in LSGDM and consensus building in management science, computer science, information management, engineering, and other fields will become a potential reader of this book. It is believed that graduate students engaged in the research on LSGDM and consensus building can also get beneficial inspiration and harvest from this book.

This book consists of nine chapters: Chap. 1 introduces the motivation and structure of the book, Chap. 2 provides the related preliminary knowledge, Chap. 3 puts forward the clustering method based on trust-similarity analysis, Chap. 4 develops a trust-similarity measure-based hierarchical clustering method, Chap. 5 proposes a hierarchical punishment-driven consensus model, Chap. 6 designs the confidence consensus-based model, Chap. 7 combines independent consensus and supervision models, Chap. 8 discusses the role of trust relationships and opinion similarity in consensus building, and finally, Chap. 9 ends the book by giving conclusions and future research directions.

We would like to express special thanks to Prof. Jianqiang Wang and Prof. Xuanhua Xu for their support and suggestions for this book. We also would like to express our sincere thanks to the colleagues in our group, Prof. Xudong Lin, Prof. Hanyang Luo, Prof. Lijun Ma, Assistant Professor Xueyang Zhang, for their contributions and consultation to this book. We would like to thank the anonymous reviewers for their valuable comments and suggestions on the improvement of this book. Equally importantly, we would like to express our deep gratitude to the production team for their support for the publication of this book, especially to Senior Editor Emily Zhang and Project Coordinator Arulmurugan Venkatasalam. This book is supported by the National Natural Science Foundation of China (no. 71901151).

Shenzhen, China   Su-Min Yu
September 2021   Zhi-Jiao Du

Contents

About the Authors

Su-Min Yu is an Assistant professor, Distinguished Associate Research Fellow and Master Supervisor at the College of Management, Shenzhen University. She is also currently a member of the Institute of Big Data Intelligent Management and Decision, Shenzhen University. She received her Ph.D. degree in Management from Central South University, Changsha, China, in 2018. Her research interests include electronic commerce, information management, decision theory and methods, large-scale group decision-making and consensus, big data decision, social network analysis, tourism management, etc. She has presided one project of the National Natural Science Foundation of China. She has published 18 international journal papers in top journals and conference proceedings, including *IEEE Transactions on Fuzzy Systems, Information Fusion, Information Sciences, Knowledge-Based Systems, Applied Soft Computing, Computers and Industrial Engineering, Group Decision and Negotiation, International Transactions in Operational Research*, among others. Her h-index is 9 with more than 570 citations received in Google Scholar. A total of 4 articles were selected into ESI Global High Citation Paper Database, among which 2 articles were selected as hot papers. She serves as a reviewer in many top-tier international journals in related areas to fuzzy soft computing and group decision-making.

Zhi-Jiao Du is a doctoral candidate at the Business School, Sun Yat-Sen University, China. He is IEEE Student Member. He received his B.S. degree in Management from Hainan University, Haikou, China, in 2012, and his M.S. degree in Management from Central south university, Changsha, China, in 2016. He presided over a Special Fund Project of Science and Technology Innovation Cultivation for College Students in Guangdong ("Climbing Plan"). His research interests include supply chain management, decision theory and methods, large-scale group decision-making and consensus, social network analysis, etc. At present, he has published 14 academic articles in top journals and conference proceedings, including *Decision Support Systems, IEEE Transactions on Fuzzy Systems, Information Fusion, Information Sciences, Knowledge-Based Systems, Computers and Industrial Engineering, Group Decision and Negotiation, International Transactions in Operational Research*, among others. One of the articles was selected into ESI Global Database of Highly Cited Papers in Computer Science. His h-index is 6 with more than 340 citations received in Google Scholar. He serves as a reviewer in many top-tier international journals in related areas to large-scale group decision-making, consensus building, supply chain management.

Acronyms

CRP	Consensus-reaching process
DM(s)	Decision-maker(s)
GDM	Group decision-making
HFLTS	Hesitant fuzzy linguistic term set
HPDCM	Hierarchical punishment-driven consensus model
ICRM	Independent consensus-reaching model
JT	Joint threshold
LGSNE	Large-group social network environment
LSGDM	Large-scale group decision-making
MCC	Minimum-cost consensus
MCRM	Mixed consensus-reaching model
OWA	Ordered weighted averaging
PDCRM	Punishment-driven consensus-reaching model
PL-LSGDM	Probabilistic linguistic large-scale group decision-making
PLTS	Probabilistic linguistic term set
SCRM	Supervised consensus-reaching model
SNA	Social network analysis
SN-GDM	Social network group decision-making
TSA	Trust-similarity analysis
TSF	Trust-similarity function
TSS	Trust-similarity score
UTWA	Uninorm trust weighted average

Symbols

$E = \{e_1, e_2, \ldots, e_q\}$	Set of DMs/experts
$X = \{x_1, x_2, \ldots, x_m\}$	Set of alternatives
$A = \{a_1, a_2, \ldots, a_n\}$	Set of attributes/criteria
$V_l = (v_{l,ij})_{m \times n}$	Individual opinion provided by DM e_l
$R_l = (r_{l,ij})_{m \times n}$	Normalized individual opinion
$\overrightarrow{TM} = \left(\overrightarrow{TF_{lh}}\right)_{q \times q}$	Directed sociomatrix
$\overrightarrow{TSM} = \left(\overrightarrow{TSF_{lh}}\right)_{q \times q}$	Trust-similarity matrix
$ATM = (ATS_{lh})_{q \times q}$	Adjusted sociomatrix
$UTSM = (UTSS_{lh})_{q \times q}$	Undirected trust-similarity matrix
TSS_{lh}	Trust-similarity score from DM e_l to DM e_h
SD_{lh}	Similarity degree between R_l and R_h
CD_{lh}	Closeness degree between DM e_l and DM e_h
$UTSS_{kg}$	Undirected trust-similarity score between cluster C_k and cluster C_g
$R_k = (r_{k,ij})_{m \times n}$ or $G_k = (g_{k,ij})_{m \times n}$	The opinion of cluster C_k
w_l	Weight of DM e_l
ω_j	Weight of attribute a_j
$\overline{TS}$	Threshold of trust score
$\overline{SD}$	Threshold of similarity degree
$\overline{TSS}$	Threshold of trust-similarity score
$cohesion(C_k)$	Cohesion of cluster C_k
n_k	Size of cluster C_k
λ_k or η_k	Weight of cluster C_k
GCL^t or GCI^t	Group consensus degree at the tth iteration
pc_k^t	Punishment coefficient
$\overline{AA}_k^{t+1}$	Adjustment amount
$\widehat{AA}_k^{t+1}$	The proportion of adjusted matrix elements
$ARoCI^t$	Attainment rate of the consensus index

$IX\left(G_k^t\right)$ Number of matrix elements that contribute less to consensus

$\alpha_1,\ \alpha_2,\ \beta_1^2,\ \beta_2^2,\ \mu_{WG},\ \nu_{WG}$ Parameters

List of Figures

List of Tables

Chapter 1
Introduction

Abstract This chapter provides a concise introduction to the book by stating the motivation and structural outline. The motivation describes the origin, scope, purpose, expectations of the book. Some useful suggestions are offered to potential readers.

1.1 Motivation

Real-world decision-making is increasingly complex and uncertain, which usually requires the participation of a large number of decision-makers (DMs) with different knowledge structures and areas of expertise. The theoretical exploration and practical application of *Large-scale group decision-making (LSGDM)* has become one of the most attractive research hotspots in the field of decision science. Compared with traditional small-size GDM, the most important feature of LSGDM is that it often involves a large number of DMs (ranging from dozens to hundreds or even thousands). Under such circumstances, the interactions between DMs may be less effective and efficient. To make matters worse, multi-source decision information inevitably leads to divergences and conflicts. Consequently, clustering and consensus building have always been the focus of research on LSGDM. Over the last decades, numerous researchers in the fields of management science, computer science, engineering, neuroscience and other fields have carried out extensive research on the models, methods and decision support systems of LSGDM, and achieved considerable and satisfactory results.

It is an indisputable fact that social relationships are prevalent among DMs and that individual decisions are often influenced by others in the same social network. Opinion similarity and trust relationship are considered to be two important measurement attributes for clustering. Traditional clustering methods usually use a single measurement attribute to divide the original large group, but fail to combine the two measurement attributes and analyze their different roles in the clustering process. The opinion similarity is used to measure the difference degree of individual opinions, while the trust relationship represents the credibility of one DM. Meanwhile, research on the different roles played by trust relationship and opinion similarity in

S.-M. Yu and Z.-J. Du, *Large-Scale Group Decision-Making*,
https://doi.org/10.1007/978-981-16-7889-9_1

the consensus-reaching process is still in its infancy. The consensus level based on opinion similarity is used to assess the current difference degree between individual opinions, while the trust score derived from the trust relationship can guide opinion adjustment. We consider that a DM with a high trust score but a low consensus level can reduce the opinion adjustment amount by losing some trust. In this way, the DM's original opinion can be appropriately preserved.

In our opinions, the following important issues concerning LSGDM need further exploration and discussion:

(1) *The respective roles of trust relationship and opinion similarity in clustering.* This book argues that it is not appropriate to separate the trust relationship and opinion similarity to implement clustering analysis. Therefore, we propose a series of clustering methods based on trust-similarity analysis.

(2) *The moderating effect of trust loss on the consensus-reaching process.* This book holds that a DM with low consensus but high trust can reduce the cost of consensus by sacrificing part of its own trust, because high consensus means that the corresponding individual opinion is accepted by others. This active trust loss may have an impact on the overall consensus cost as well as the consensus-reaching process.

(3) *The management of non-cooperative behaviors in the consensus-reaching process.* Non-cooperative behavior refers to a DM's (or a cluster's) non-cooperative attitude toward adjusting opinions to promote consensus. The structure of DMs in LSGDM problems is complex and as a consequence, it is easy to encounter non-cooperative behaviors due to self-interest or insistence. Non-cooperative behaviors can sometimes seriously impede the consensus-reaching process, which is a major challenge of achieving a reliable decision outcome.

The authors of this book have been focusing on the research of LSGDM since 2013, with particular reference to clustering and consensus building. This book is a collection of the most advanced published research on LSGDM problems by the authors. In order to facilitate different readers to understand the research findings, we have further enriched the research background, added necessary explanations and explanations, adjusted the structure of the writing, and reorganized the research findings. After reading this book, we expect readers to have a deeper and more comprehensive understanding of clustering analysis and consensus building in LSGDM problems. To make it easier and more accurate for potential readers to understand and master the methods and models proposed in this book, we strongly recommend that readers have a good research foundation in fuzzy soft computing, group decision-making, classical clustering algorithms, and social network analysis. In addition, readers should be able to skillfully operate some commonly used statistics, simulation and graphics software, such as MATLAB, Microsoft Excel, CorelDRAW Graphics Suite, etc.

1.2 Chapter Overview

Clustering and consensus building are two key processes of LSGDM problems. The research content of this book is carried out around these two processes. Clustering analysis in LSGDM is implemented in Chaps. 3–4. Chapters 5–8 proposes some new solutions for consensus building in LSGDM. To be specific, Chaps. 5–7 deal with non-cooperative behaviors in the consensus-reaching process, while Chap. 8 focuses on consensus building in LSGDM under a social network environment. The structure of this book is described in Fig. 1.1.

The detailed chapter overview is presented as follows.

- **Chapter** 2: **Preliminary Knowledge**. This foundation-oriented chapter presents the basic knowledge of large-scale group decision-making, social network analysis, and consensus-reaching process.
- **Chapter** 3: **Trust-Similarity Analysis-Based Clustering Method**. This chapter develops a trust-similarity analysis-based clustering method to manage clustering operations in LSGDM problems in the social network context.
- **Chapter** 4: **Trust-Similarity Analysis-Based Hierarchical Clustering Method**. Following the proposed trust-similarity analysis, this chapter presents a hierarchical clustering method for GDM problems in large-scale social network environment.

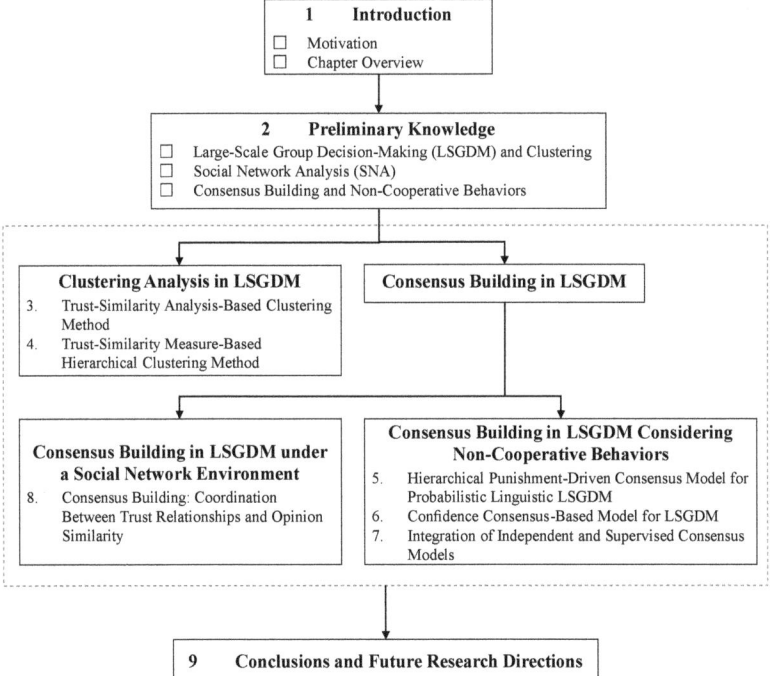

Fig. 1.1 The structure of this book

- **Chapter** 5: **Hierarchical Punishment-Driven Consensus Model for Probabilistic Linguistic LSGDM**. In this chapter, a hierarchical punishment-driven consensus model for LSGDM problems in the context of probabilistic linguistic information is put forward.
- **Chapter** 6: **Confidence Consensus-Based Model for LSGDM**. In this chapter, we present a confidence consensus-based model for LSGDM scenarios that provides a novel approach to addressing non-cooperative behaviors.
- **Chapter** 7: **Integration of Independent and Supervised Consensus Models**. Traditional consensus models dealing with non-cooperative behaviors focus on situations where only one DM modifies its opinion in each consensus iteration. However, some, or even all DMs may adjust their opinions in one iteration, especially at the beginning. In this chapter, a mixed consensus model for managing non-cooperative behaviors is proposed.
- **Chapter** 8: **Consensus Building: Coordination Between Trust Relationships and Opinion Similarity**. This chapter designs a two-dimensional consensus model considering non-cooperative behaviors, and explores the coordination between opinion similarity and trust relationships on the consensus-reaching process.
- **Chapter** 9: **Conclusions and Future Research Directions**. This book ends with some important conclusions and future research directions in the field of LSGDM.

Chapter 2
Preliminary Knowledge

Abstract This chapter introduces the basic knowledge of large-scale group decision-making, social network analysis, and consensus building, which are fundamental to understanding the clustering methods and consensus models presented in this book.

Keywords Large-scale group decision-making (LSGDM) · Clustering · Social network analysis (SNA) · Consensus building · Non-cooperative behaviors

2.1 Large-Scale Group Decision-Making (LSGDM) and Clustering

Group decision-making (GDM) aims to achieve a common solution to a decision problem in which no fewer than two decision-makers (DMs) participate, and it has been paid an increasing amount of attention [2, 11, 13, 68, 94, 98, 120, 138, 158]. Traditional GDM is regarded as a group discussion and decision process that involves a small number of DMs (e.g., three to five people) and the complexity is often not very high (e.g., a vacation travel decision for a family). Driven by current technological developments (especially communication technologies represented by social networks and mobile Internet), new definitions of social relationships, and social demands (e-democracy), a challenging issue in the field of decision-making has recently emerged, namely the decision-making involve a large number of DMs [18, 99, 156]. A *large-scale group decision-making (LSGDM)* scenario is a kind of GDM event in which no fewer than 20 DMs participate to select an optimal solution [38, 110, 159, 185]. Because the background, situation, and difficulty of real LSGDM problems are different, the number of DMs in current studies can range from dozens to thousands [93, 131, 142]. Shi et al. [102], Xu et al. [143, 144], and Zhang et al. [167] argued that a large group should include more than 11 DMs. Gou et al. [38], Li et al. [56], Liu et al. [65], and Zhong et al. [186] held that a group could be considered to be a large group if the number of DMs involved is greater than 20. In some literature (e.g., [84, 127]), the illustrative examples included as many as 50 DMs.

The main topics of LSGDM focus on the following three aspects: (i) clustering used to classify the original large group into several smaller-size subgroups [20, 31, 67, 71, 75, 86, 144, 184]; (ii) consensus building that aims to reduce the differences of opinion, promote convergence of individual opinions, and obtain a high-consensus decision outcome [29, 59, 72, 100, 118, 135]; and (iii) the exploration of the influence of social relationships on the decision-making process [12, 32, 35, 58, 97, 111, 127, 188]. It can be concluded that all topics share the same goals: to promote interaction among DMs, to improve decision satisfaction, and to ensure the smooth implementation of the decision-making process.

With the development of information and communication technology, social networks have become increasingly common in driving the relationships between DMs and the decision-making process in LSGDM problems. Several studies have shown that social networks play an important role in decision-making, such as providing comments [104, 108, 157, 160, 161], sharing recommendations based on trust or recognition [78, 113, 117], and affecting interactions [24, 125, 156]. Social network analysis (SNA) studies the relationships between social entities, such as members of a group, corporations or nations [73, 122].

By incorporating social networks into LSGDM, a new decision-making scenario is established, called LSGDM under social network. It can be summarized as having the following three characteristics [73, 127, 144, 172, 187]: (i) The group involves a large number of DMs (i.e., usually no fewer than 20). (ii) There are differences of opinion among DMs, and achieving a high-consensus solution often requires implementing a consensus reaching process (CRP). (iii) The social relationships that exist between DMs influence interactions and the decision-making process. In some of the chapters that follow, in order to emphasize the existence of social networks in LSGDM, we also call the decision situation after the integration of social networks and LSGDM as GDM in large-group social network environment (LGSNE).

Typically, solving LSGDM events involves three crucial processes: the clustering process, the consensus-reaching process, and the selection process [84, 142, 159]. Fig. 2.1 describes the general procedure of dealing with an LSGDM problem (possibly in a social network environment), as follows:

(1) *Decision information preprocessing.* Individual opinions (and possibly trust relationships) are collected and processed as valid input for the following steps.
(2) *Clustering process.* The DMs in an original large group are divided into several smaller-size subgroups according to certain measurement rules. Opinion similarity and trust relationship can be used as measurement attributes.
(3) *Consensus-reaching process.* A consensus model is adopted to guide the convergence of individual opinions and improve the level of group consensus. The trust relationships among DMs may affect the CRP.
(4) *Selection process.* This process often consists of two steps, including aggregation and exploitation. Clusters' opinions are aggregated into the group opinion, from which the optimal solution is generated.

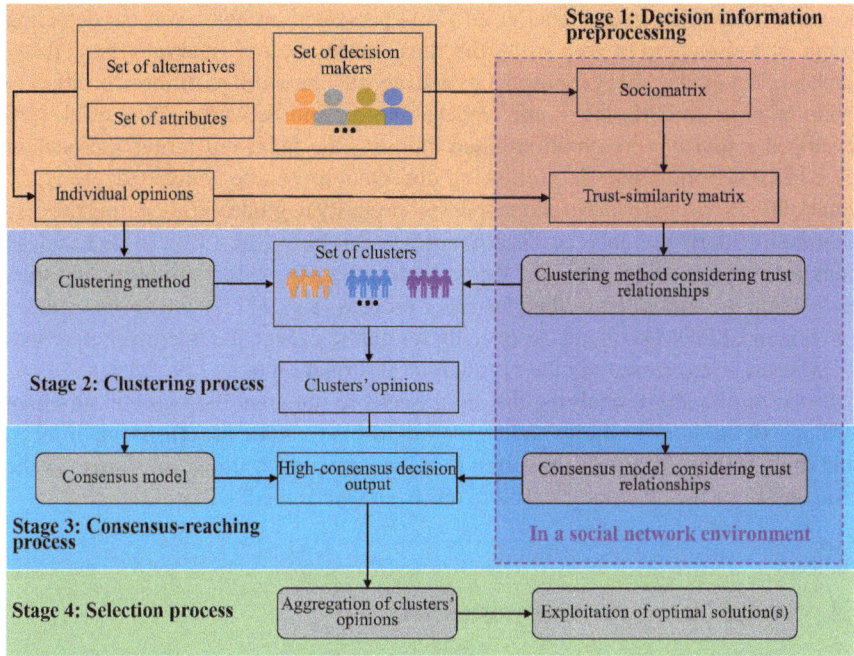

Fig. 2.1 The general procedure of dealing with LSGDM problems (possibly in a social network environment) [99, 154]

Clustering is an effective way to manage large-scale DMs and reduce the dimensionality through which a large group is divided into smaller clusters according to certain rules. Traditional clustering methods are based on the similarity measurement of individual opinions, such as K-means clustering algorithm [51, 131], density-based clustering algorithm [114], hierarchical clustering algorithm [182], and vector space-based clustering method [140, 144]. If two individual opinions are sufficiently similar, the DMs can be assigned to the same cluster. This classification produces a hierarchical structure consisting of a top-down division of the membership structure and a bottom-up aggregation of individual opinions. It takes two steps to produce a group opinion. First, the 'DM to DM' interaction in each cluster forms a unified cluster opinion. Then, the 'cluster to cluster' discussion eventually generates the group opinion. Such bottom-up transmission and aggregation of information can guarantee the orderly and efficient decision-making process.

Most existing clustering methods are based on the similarities of DMs' opinions [152]. Ding et al. [18] presented an overview of LSGDM models, and pointed out that due to the complexity of LSGDM problems, it was not always sensible to cluster DMs by only considering the similarities/distances of opinions. In a social network environment, the social relationships between DMs affect individual opinions and provide a new solution for the classification of DMs. Table 2.1 presents a literature review on clustering in LSGDM problems. Regarding the literature on clustering in the social network context, Tian et al. [111] presented an algorithm for detecting groups in a directed network using the trust information of interval type-2 fuzzy numbers. Wu et al. [133] proposed a two-stage trust network partition algorithm to divide large-scale DMs into some leader–follower sub-networks. Ding et al. [20] developed a sparse representation-based intuitionistic fuzzy clustering approach to solve LSGDM problems. The following observations can be concluded: (i) Traditional LSGDM events usually adopt opinion similarity to guide the clustering process without considering social relationships among DMs (e.g., [84, 142]). (ii) In LSGDM scenarios under a social network, the two attributes of opinion similarity and trust relationship are separated in the clustering process (e.g., [111]). (iii) Some studies hold that in LSGDM problems, especially for public events, the interest preferences of DMs can be expressed via their evaluation information (e.g., [19, 20]).

Based on the above analysis, this book seeks to integrate the two measurement attributes of opinion similarity and trust relationship to guide the clustering process. This study follows Xu et al.'s research [144] in terms of regarding the cluster as the basic unit once the clustering structure has been determined.

2.2 Social Network Analysis (SNA)

In today's era of big data, social networks continually exert a huge influence on people's lives. From a sociological perspective, humans are social creatures whose individual decisions are influenced to various degrees by those with whom they are closely related or socially connected [24, 55, 160]. GDM is also influenced by social relationships among the participants [125]. A positive social relationship can be reflected as a trust relationship between two DMs, which makes one DM vulnerable to the influence of another DM he/she trusts [19]. Social network analysis (SNA) is a theoretical tool for studying relationships between social entities, such as individuals, groups, organizations, or nations [73, 123, 158]. This book aims to investigate the clustering and consensus building of large-scale DMs connected via a network in which they explicitly express opinions in the form of trust and distrust statements.

SNA studies the relationships between social entities, such as members of organizations, corporations, or nations [73, 116]. It can be used to examine structural and locational properties, including centrality, prestige, and structural balance [122]. As a direct and reliable social relation, trust has been extensively studied. The trust-propagation operator and the trust score–induced aggregation operator were first proposed to apply SNA to GDM problems [113, 123]. Ureña et al. [112] presented a review on trust propagation and opinion dynamics in social networks and GDM frameworks. For GDM events in LGSNE, Wu et al. [125] and Tian et al. [111] used community detection technology to reduce the dimension of the social trust network with large-scale DMs. Wu et al. [128] and Zhang et al. [169] applied network partition technology based on leadership to generate subnetworks. Lu et al. [74] proposed an expert clustering method by combining trust degree and relationship strength. Dong et al. [21] and Ding et al. [17] investigated opinion dynamics in social networks.

Table 2.1 Summary of articles written about clustering in LSGDM problems

Article author	Publication year	Being in a social network context	Clustering based entirely on opinion similarity	Considering trust relationships among DMs in clustering
Xu and Chen [140]	2005	No	Yes	No
Palomares et al. [84]	2014	No	Yes	No
Palomares et al. [85]	2014	No	Yes	No
Quesada et al. [93]	2015	No	–	–
Xu et al. [144]	2015	No	Yes	No
Liu et al. [62]	2016	No	–	–
Zhang et al. [167]	2017	No	Yes	No
Dong et al. [28]	2018	No	Yes	No
Gou et al. [38]	2018	No	Yes	No
Labella et al. [54]	2018	No	Yes	No
Wu and Xu [131]	2018	No	Yes	No
Xu et al. [146]	2018	No	Yes	No
Liu et al. [71]	2018	Yes	No	Yes
Wu et al. [127]	2018	No	Yes	No
Ding et al. [20]	2019	Yes	Yes	Yes
Tian et al. [111]	2019	Yes	No	Yes
Li et al. [56]	2019	No	Yes	No
Ding et al. [19]	2019	Yes	Yes	Yes
Liu et al. [73]	2019	Yes	–	–
Wu et al. [133]	2019	Yes	No	Yes
Tang et al. [110]	2020	No	Yes	No
Yu et al. [155]	2020	No	Yes	No
Du et al. [33]	2020	No	Yes	No
Gou et al. [39]	2021	No	Yes	No
Chen et al. [14]	2021	No	Yes	No
This book	–	Yes	Yes	Yes

Note The indicator "–" represents that the corresponding item is not considered

To deal with consensus issues, Wu et al. [125] developed a consensus model based on a minimum adjustment cost feedback mechanism. Liu et al. [69] proposed a self-confidence-based consensus model for social network GDM using the dynamic importance degree of experts and a trust-based feedback mechanism. Gai et al. [34] proposed a joint feedback strategy framework to promote consensus among large-scale DMs by combining social network context and feedback behavior. Zhang et al. [172] focused on the management of non-cooperative behaviors in consensus-based multiple-attribute GDM and suggested that the trust scores of non-cooperative DMs should be lowered.

Based on the above-mentioned literature on the application of SNA in GDM, we can observe the following: (i) Trust is an effective basis for reducing the dimensionality of large-scale DMs for GDM problems in LGSNE. However, how to set the roles played by trust relationships and opinion similarity in the clustering process needs further analysis. (ii) Most studies on the influence of trust on CRP have focused on weight assignment for DMs [124, 125] and recommendations for adjusting opinions [24, 64]. Moreover, the trust reduction proposed in [172] is a passive operation. We aim to address these issues in two ways. First, opinion similarity and trust relationship are taken into account as important factors in the clustering process. Second, we explore a consensus-reaching process in which the cluster can lower the amount of opinion adjustment by taking the initiative to reduce the trust score.

Generally, there are three notational schemes in SNA: the set of actors, the relations themselves, and the actors' attributes. Different representation schemes in SNA are presented as follows.

- Sociometric: $A = \begin{pmatrix} 0 & 1 & 0 & 0 \\ 0 & 0 & 0 & 1 \\ 1 & 0 & 0 & 1 \\ 1 & 0 & 0 & 0 \end{pmatrix}$

- Directed graph:

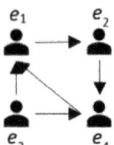

- Algebraic: $e_1 Re_2$, $e_2 Re_4$, $e_3 Re_1$, $e_3 Re_4$, $e_4 Re_1$, whre $e_l Re_h$ represents the trust e_l assigns to e_h.

However, the presented sociomatrix is a binary relationship, which may not be suitable for modeling the uncertainty associated with the relationship representation in the social network [123]. Hence, this book follows one type of social network—namely, a trust network—in which users explicitly express their opinions, such as trusting someone "very much" or "more or less", rather than "trusting" and "not trusting."

Definition 2.1 [123] A tuple $\lambda = (t, d)$ with the first component t being a trust degree and the second component d being a distrust degree, such that $t, d \in [0, 1]$, is referred to as a trust function.

Following the above, Wu et al. [125] defined the trust score as $TS(\lambda) = (t - d + 1)/2$. Clearly, $0 \leq TS(\lambda) \leq 1$. A trust score represents the normalized dominance the trust value has over the corresponding distrust value of a trust function. Meanwhile, the order relation of trust functions was defined [64], which can be used to calculate the weights of DMs in terms of trust and guide the aggregation of individual opinions.

Definition 2.2 [124] Let $TM = (t_{lh}, d_{lh})_{q \times q}$ be a sociomatrix, where (t_{lh}, d_{lh}) is the trust function from DM e_l to DM e_h. Then, we can obtain the trust score of DM e_h as

$$TS_h = \frac{1}{q-1} \sum_{l=1, l \neq h}^{q} \frac{t_{lh} - d_{lh} + 1}{2}. \tag{2.1}$$

Clearly, $0 \leq TS_h \leq 1$. TS_h represents the average of trust scores from other DMs to DM e_h.

For simplicity, the sociomatrix can be written as $TM = (TS_{lh})_{q \times q}$. Zhang et al. [172] defined another format of sociomatrix by introducing only trust statements.

Definition 2.3 [172] A fuzzy sociometrix $TM = (td_{lh})_{q \times q}$ on E is a relation in $E \times E$ with membership function $\mu_{TM} : E \times E \rightarrow [0, 1]$, and $\mu_{TM}(e_l, e_h)$, where td_{lh} denotes the trust degree that DM e_l assigns to DM e_l.

For notation simplicity, fuzzy sociometrix will be herein referred to as sociometrix in the book. The relationships can be divided into three types [19, 73], as shown in Fig. 2.2.

- *Direct relationship.* As the top path in Fig. 2.2 shows, there is an edge from A to B in the social network. This indicates that A has a direct relationship with B. In this case, A might have a good interaction with B.
- *Indirect relationship.* As the middle path in Fig. 2.2 shows, there is no edge from A to B in the social network, but A can build a new edge to B through mediator C. We can think of A as having an indirect relationship with B. In this case, A does not typically know B, but we can obtain reliable relationship information from A to B by the direct relationship information between their mediator
- *Irrelevant relationship.* As the bottom path in Fig. 2.2 shows, there is neither a direct nor indirect relationship between A and B. A is considered to have an irrelevant relationship with B.

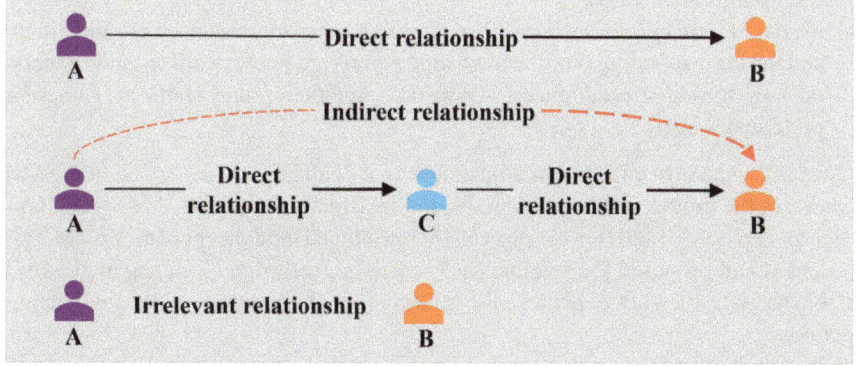

Fig. 2.2 An example of a social network used to illustrate types of relationships

Any social network has at least one of the three types of relationships mentioned above. Note that the irrelevant relationship requires special attention. It must be quantified before it can be applied to the decision-making process, but it cannot be solved by trust propagation.

2.3 Consensus Building and Non-cooperative Behaviors

2.3.1 Consensus Building

Consensus building is another important issue that needs to be solved; it is an iterative process of group discussion and consensus improvement [30, 84, 143, 144, 177, 185]. To ensure that the final decision result is widely accepted, it is preferable for experts to reach a sufficiently high level of consensus before applying the selection process. Traditionally, consensus is defined as a state of unanimous agreement among members of a group regarding all the alternatives. However, a complete agreement is often costly and unnecessary in practice and, as a consequence, the concept of soft consensus is introduced, which requires most (but perhaps not all) experts to agree on the most important alternatives [45]. A consensus-reaching process (CRP) is a dynamic process in which dispersed experts' preferences are converged through multiple rounds of group discussions. The general scheme of a CRP is illustrated below, as depicted in Fig. 2.3.

(1) *Gathering opinions.* The opinions provided by DMs are gathered.
(2) *Computing the degrees of consensus.* According to distance measures or similarity measures, individual consensus degrees and group consensus degree are calculated. Palomares et al. [84] classified consensus measures into two categories: the distances to the collective opinion and the distances among experts.
(3) *Consensus control.* If the obtained consensus degree is greater than a given consensus threshold, the selection process is entered; otherwise more rounds of discussions are needed.
(4) *Feedback process.* Preferences that contribute less to consensus are identified, and the corresponding modification suggestions are put forward to guide experts on how to adjust preferences. Afterwards, another round starts by gathering preferences again.

In CRPs, the cost of opinion adjustment is a challenge that must be addressed because of the limited resources available for decision making [168, 176, 180]. Ben-Arieh and Easton [7] and Ben-Arieh et al. [8] introduced the concept of minimum-cost consensus and proposed the original MCC models. Accordingly, Zhang et al. [165] established a framework to achieve the minimum-cost consensus under aggregation operators.

Definition 2.4 Let $(o_1, \ldots, o_q)$ be the original numerical opinions given by a set of DMs E, $\bar{o}_1, \ldots, \bar{o}_q$ be the modified opinions after the CRP, $\bar{\pi}$ be the collective opin-

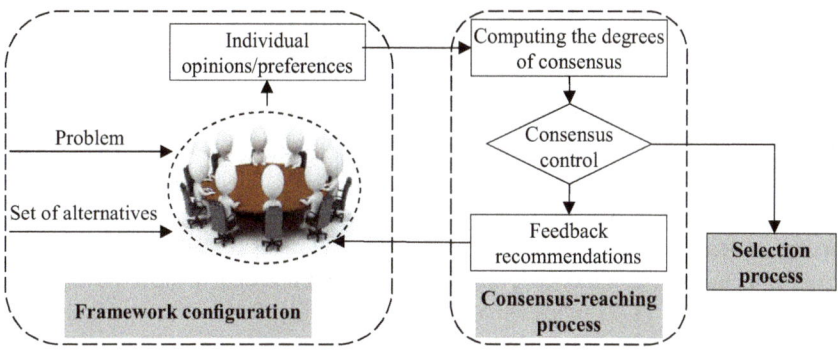

Fig. 2.3 General scheme of a CRP [54, 154]

ion, and $(c_1, \ldots, c_q)$ be the cost of moving each DM's opinion 1 unit, respectively. The parameter ϵ is the maximum acceptable distance of each DM to the collective opinion. The MCC model based on a linear cost function is given as follows:

$$\min \sum_{l=1}^{q} c_l \cdot |\overline{o}_l - o_l|$$
$$s.t. \quad \begin{cases} \overline{\pi} = F(\overline{h}_1, \ldots, \overline{h}_q) \\ |\overline{o}_l - \overline{\pi}| \leq \epsilon, l = 1, 2, \ldots, q \end{cases} \tag{2.2}$$

where F is an aggregation function.

Later, some new MCC models were proposed. Gong et al. [36] presented two types of MCC models with regard to all the individuals and one particular individual. Zhang et al. [171] generalized the MCC models in Ben-Arieh and Easton [7] and Gong et al. [36] with uncertain opinions. Wu et al. [125] developed a minimum adjustment cost feedback mechanism to improve the group consensus in SN-GDM events. Nevertheless, all of these models automatically modify DMs' opinions without considering the interaction among DMs. They include only a consensus measure, that is, the distance of each DM to collective opinion, ignoring the minimum agreement among all DMs. Labella et al. [53] proposed a comprehensive MCC model that considered the distance to collective opinion and consensus degree, as follows:

$$\min \sum_{l=1}^{q} c_l \cdot |\overline{o}_l - o_l|$$
$$s.t. \quad \begin{cases} \overline{\pi} = F(\overline{h}_1, \ldots, \overline{h}_q) \\ |\overline{o}_l - \overline{\pi}| \leq \epsilon, l = 1, 2, \ldots, q \\ consensus(\overline{o}_1 \ldots, \overline{o}_q) \geq \alpha \end{cases} \tag{2.3}$$

where $consensus(\cdot)$ represents the obtained consensus degree, and $\alpha \in [0, 1]$ is a consensus threshold fixed a prior.

Currently, the research on consensus reaching in GDM events under social network has attracted much attention. Wu et al. [123] put forward a trust based consensus model for social network in an incomplete linguistic information context. Liu et al. [64] developed a trust induced recommendation mechanism to generate personalized advice for inconsistent experts to reach higher consensus degree. Wu et al. [124] proposed a visual interactive method for consensus in social network GDM. Dong et al. [21] presented a consensus reaching process in opinion dynamics based on the concept of leadership. Liu et al. [69] and Ding et al. [17] studied the influence of expert's/agent's self-confidence level on the consensus reaching in the social network GDM. Zhang et al. [172] proposed a consensus reaching framework based on SNA to manage different patterns of non-cooperative behaviors.

It can be seen from the above literature review that trust, as an effective decision-making attribute, plays an important role in the CRP. However, there are few studies on how a DM with high trust and low consensus reduce the amount of preference adjustment by sacrificing part of his/her own trust. This book attempts to develop a consensus model that allows qualified DMs to reduce the amount of opinion/preference adjustment through voluntary trust loss.

2.3.2 Non-cooperative Behaviors

In an LSGDM problem, it is often the case that several DMs or clusters adopt non-cooperative behaviors and are unwilling to adjust their opinions to promote consensus [141, 144]. Non-cooperative behaviors may have negative or even obstructing effects on the consensus-reaching process and ultimately reduce the decision-making quality. In an extreme scenario, some DMs refuse to adjust opinions, and the consensus-reaching process becomes deadlocked. Naturally, a high consensus decision result will not be achieved. Thus, it is necessary and important to detect and manage non-cooperative behaviors before entering the selection process. Non-cooperative decision-makers can be divided into the following four categories [142]: (1) a domain expert or an experienced person whose opinion is usually considered reasonable and unselfish, (2) a leader whose opinion is considered authoritative but may be somewhat private, (3) a maverick person who provides a view that is often out of the ordinary and insists that his or her opinion is constructive, and (3) a stakeholder with private interests. In this study, we focus on the first category of decision-makers. Currently, there are two main approaches to dealing with non-cooperative behaviors: opinion punishment and weight punishment [27, 32, 142]. The former refers to the forced adjustment of individual opinions while the latter aims to reduce the importance of non-cooperative individual opinions in the group. Finally, we can identify four main approaches to addressing non-cooperative behaviors:

(1) *No punishment:* The weight of a non-cooperative DM will not be reduced, and non-cooperative opinions will not be forced to adjust. This approach can be used as a benchmark (for comparative analysis) because it requires DMs to adjust their

opinions according to their own subjective will without any coercive measures (see [23]).
(2) *Weight punishment:* This only forces a reduction in the weight of a non-cooperative DM. However, opinion adjustment can be made according to the individual's subjective wishes (see [142]).
(3) *Opinion punishment:* This imposes a greater degree of opinion adjustment but does not reduce the weight of a non-cooperative DM.
(4) *Full punishment:* Weight punishment and opinion punishment are both involved in the CRP (see [144]).

Note that opinion punishment and opinion adjustment are not the same thing. As an example, consider that the adjustment coefficient given by one DM is 0.3, which is lower than the required adjustment degree of 0.5. Thus, this DM is judged to hold a non-cooperative behavior. If the opinion punishment approach is applied, the DM should use a coefficient greater than 0.3 to adjust the opinion; if the weight punishment approach is implemented, the DM can adjust the opinion using 0.3.

We can conclude that few studies have investigated the role of trust relationships in dealing with non-cooperative behaviors. When a DM with a high trust score holds the opinion that deviates the most from that of the group, its opinion will be asked to adjust to promote consensus. However, the DM might hold a non-cooperative attitude toward opinion adjustment. In that case, the DM will be punished through, for example, opinion punishment or weight punishment. Since the DM has a high trust score, it is meaningful to explore whether the DM can reduce the degree of opinion punishment by lowering the trust score. Moreover, a high trust score indicates that other DMs have sufficient trust in the DM's opinion.

Chapter 3
Trust-Similarity Analysis-Based Clustering Method

Abstract Opinion similarity and trust relationship are considered to be two important measurement attributes for implementing clustering. Traditional clustering methods often use a single attribute to divide the original large group without requiring a combination of the above two attributes. However, these two attributes play different roles in the clustering process, insofar as opinion similarity is used to measure the level of difference among individual opinions, whereas the trust relationship represents the trustworthiness of decision makers. This chapter proposes a trust-similarity analysis (TSA)-based clustering method to implement clustering in LSGDM events under a social network context. First, the trust-similarity matrix is established to collectively describe the decision information. Second, all measurement attribute values are mapped to a trust-similarity plot from which the joint threshold can be calculated. Finally, a TSA-based clustering method is proposed that considers the attributes of opinion similarity and trust relationship and that allocates their importance to achieve specific clustering objectives. The numerical experiment and comparative analysis reveal the feasibility and advantages of the proposed method.

Keywords Large-scale group decision-making (LSGDM) · Trust-similarity analysis (TSA) · Clustering · Social network analysis (SNA) · Trust relationship · Opinion similarity

3.1 Introduction

Real-world decision-making is increasingly complicated and marked by uncertainty, which requires the participation of a large number of decision-makers (DMs) with different knowledge structures and interests [28, 38, 56]. Meanwhile, the rapid development of communications technology and social networks promotes the interactions among people. As stated in Sect. 2.1, large-scale group decision-making (LSGDM) refers to a group decision-making scenario in which no fewer than 20 DMs participate [19, 38, 184] to select an optimal solution. Clustering is a basic means of analyzing and managing large-scale opinions. According to certain clustering principle or algorithm, reducing the dimensionality of large-scale DMs can make the internal structure of the large group hierarchical and easy to analyze [84, 144]. The outer layer is the interaction among subgroups, and the inner layer is the discussion among the internal members of each subgroup. Clustering in LSGDM events is typically based on the similarity measures of DMs' opinions [38, 110, 159]. If the opinions of certain DMs are sufficiently similar (i.e., over a preset consensus threshold), these DMs can be assigned to the same subgroup.

The development of social media to drive the relationships among DMs in LSGDM problems has become increasingly common. Several studies show that social networks play an important role in decision-making, such as providing comments and references [107, 108, 158, 160, 162], sharing recommendations based on trust [78, 113, 117], and affecting interactions [24, 125, 156]. The GDM under a social network takes advantage of the information related to the interactions among DMs in the process of opinion evolution. Social network analysis (SNA) studies the relationships between social entities, such as members of a group, corporations or nations [73, 122]. This chapter focuses on clustering analysis for a group of DMs connected via a network in which they explicitly express opinions in the form of trust and distrust statements, which are referenced herein as the "trust network" [124] and "trust/distrust values " [123], respectively. As a special kind of social relationship, trust is perceived as the basis for decision-making in many contexts and as the motivation for maintaining cooperation in GDM [123, 125] and LSGDM problems [109, 111, 133, 145, 181].

For LSGDM problems under a social network, this chapter holds that two measurement attributes should be taken into account in clustering, namely, opinion similarity and trust relationship. The former aims to measure the similarity among individual opinions, while the latter is based on DMs' subjective judgments of trust. Although these measurement attributes are important for clustering, they are independent of each other and are sometimes contradictory. Hence the core issue is to address the following challenge for LSGDM problems in the social network:

- How to design a clustering method that takes opinion similarity and trust relationship as two important measurement attributes to guide the clustering.

The above issue can be further decomposed into four sub-aspects: how to calculate the similarity of individual opinions, how to measure the trust relationships among DMs, what roles the two attributes play respectively in clustering, and how to integrate the two attributes to manage the clustering process. In this chapter, we propose a trust-similarity analysis (TSA)-based clustering method, which consists of two stages. In Stage 1, DMs are required to provide two aspects of decision information: individual evaluation matrices and trust relationships among DMs. The trust-similarity matrix is then established, which combines the above information into a tuple of the form (trust relationship, opinion similarity). All the decision information is mapped to a two-dimensional coordinate system that divides the measurement attributes into four quadrants. In Stage 2, four algorithms of the TSA-based clustering method are designed according to different clustering purposes, and visual clustering operations are implemented.

The remainder of this chapter is organized as follows. Section 3.2 presents the TSA-based decision information processing. In Sect. 3.3, a TSA-based clustering method in LSGDM events under a social network context is proposed. Section 3.4 provides a numerical experiment to illustrate the feasibility of the proposed clustering method. A simulation experiment to further analyze the characteristics of the TSA-based clustering method is conducted in Sect. 3.5. Section 3.6 discusses the advantages of the TSA-based clustering method through a comparative experiment. This chapter ends with the conclusions in Sect. 3.7.

3.2 TSA-Based Decision Information Processing

Consider an LSGDM event under a social network context. Let $X = \{x_1, x_2, \ldots, x_m\}$ be a set of alternatives, $A = \{a_1, a_2, \ldots, a_n\}$ be a set of criteria, and $E = \{e_1, e_2, \ldots, e_q\}(q \geq 20)$ be a set of DMs. The DMs are required to provide two aspects of decision-making information, including the evaluation matrices and the statements of trust relationships. Let $V_l = (v_{l,ij})_{m \times n}$ be the individual evaluation matrix of DM e_l, where $v_{l,ij}$ is a crisp number, interpreting the evaluation of alternative $x_i \in X$ with respect to criterion $a_j \in A$. Through normalizing the individual evaluation matrices using the method in Xu et al. [136], the standardized evaluation matrices are obtained as $R_l = (r_{l,ij})_{m \times n}, l = 1, 2, \ldots, q$. In the following, the individual evaluation matrix is also called individual opinion. DMs use the trust and distrust statements to explicitly express their social relationships with each other. The directed sociomatrix is obtained as $\overrightarrow{TM} = (\overrightarrow{TF}_{lh})_{q \times q}, l \neq h$, where $\overrightarrow{TF} = (\overrightarrow{t}, \overrightarrow{d})$ is a tuple [123] representing the directed trust function from DM e_l to DM e_h.

Remark 3.1 In real LSGDM events, some DMs are sometimes unable to accurately evaluate others they do not know. In this way, there are likely to be indirect or irrelevant relationships. However, the clustering operation requires a complete trust network among DMs in this chapter. There should be a two-way trust relationship between any two DMs. For indirect relationships, trust can be propagated and improved via an indirect chain of trusted third partners [73]. If there is neither a direct nor indirect relationship between two DMs, the trust degree and distrust degree between them can be set to 0.5. The value of 0.5 indicates a neutral attitude toward trust.

As previously mentioned, clustering is an effective means to address large-scale DMs. In terms of individual opinions, if the similarity between the opinions of two DMs reaches a certain level, these DMs can be clustered into the same subgroup. Therefore, we first introduce the concept of similarity degree. Here, the Euclidean distance in [103] is used to measure the distance between R_l and R_h .

Definition 3.1 [103] Let $R_l = (r_{l,ij})_{m \times n}$ and $R_h = (r_{h,ij})_{m \times n}$ be two normalized evaluation matrices, then the similarity degree between them is defined as

$$SD_{lh} = 1 - d(R_l, R_h) = 1 - \sqrt{\frac{1}{m \times n} \sum_{i=1}^{m} \sum_{j=1}^{n} (r_{l,ij} - r_{h,ij})^2}. \qquad (3.1)$$

Clearly, $SD_{lh} = SD_{hl}$, $0 \le SD_{lh} \le 1$, $l, h = 1, 2, \ldots, q$. The higher the value of SD_{lh}, the more similar R_l and R_h are.

3.2.1 Establishment of the Trust-Similarity Matrix

Restate that clustering in an LSGDM event under a social network context involves two measurement attributes, i.e., opinion similarity and trust relationship. Similar to the representation schemes in the SNA, the attributes can be characterized by the following three formats: graphically, algebraically, and as a trust-similarity matrix.

- Graphically, as in Fig. 3.1, the network is viewed as a set of nodes joined by lines.
- The algebraic format can be used to distinguish directed and undirected relationships and to represent combinations of relationships. The corresponding algebraic representation of Fig. 3.1 would be as follows:
  $e_1 \overrightarrow{SD_{12}} e_2$, $e_1 \overrightarrow{SD_{13}} e_3$, $e_1 \overrightarrow{SD_{14}} e_4$, $e_2 \overrightarrow{SD_{21}} e_1$, $e_2 \overrightarrow{SD_{23}} e_3$, $e_2 \overrightarrow{SD_{24}} e_4$, $e_3 \overrightarrow{SD_{31}} e_1$,
  $e_3 \overline{SD_{32}} e_2$, $e_3 \overrightarrow{SD_{34}} e_4$, $e_4 \overline{SD_{41}} e_1$, $e_4 \overline{SD_{42}} e_2$, $e_4 \overline{SD_{43}} e_3$,
  where $e_l \overrightarrow{SD_{lh}} e_h$ represents a directed edge from node e_l to node e_h, and $e_l \overline{SD_{lh}} e_h$ means there is no directed relationship from e_l to e_h.
- The trust-similarity matrix presents relational data in a matrix as follows:

$$\begin{pmatrix} (0, SD_{11}) & (1, SD_{12}) & (1, SD_{13}) & (1, SD_{14}) \\ (0, SD_{21}) & (0, SD_{22}) & (0, SD_{23}) & (0, SD_{24}) \\ (1, SD_{31}) & (1, SD_{32}) & (0, SD_{33}) & (1, SD_{34}) \\ (0, SD_{41}) & (1, SD_{42}) & (0, SD_{43}) & (0, SD_{44}) \end{pmatrix}$$

Analogously, to overcome the limitations of binary trust relationships, this chapter adopts the trust network to characterize the social relationships by which the DMs explicitly express their views as trust and distrust statements. Inspired by the defn of trust function in [123], we propose the concept of trust-similarity function, which integrates the information about trust degree and similarity degree.

Definition 3.2 (Trust-similarity function (TSF)). A tuple $\theta = \{(t, d), SD\}$ with t being a trust degree, d a distrust degree, and SD a similarity degree such that $t, d, SD \in [0, 1]$, will be referred to as a trust-similarity function. The set of trust-similarity functions (TSFs) is denoted by $\Theta = \langle \theta = \{(t, d), SD\} | t, d, SD \in [0, 1] \rangle$.

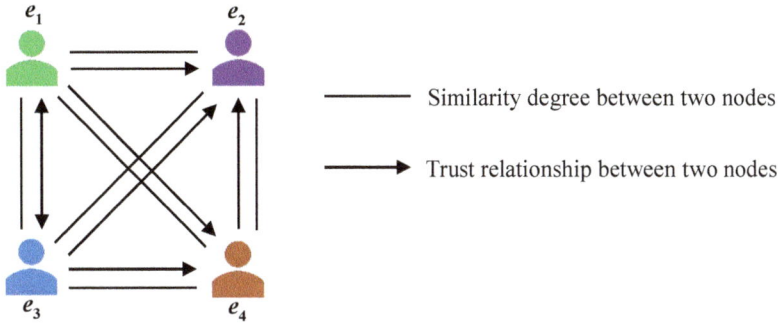

Fig. 3.1 Graphical representation of a trust-similarity matrix

By applying the TSF to the GDM problem, the trust-similarity matrix is established, denoted as $\overrightarrow{TSM} = (\overrightarrow{TSF}_{lh})_{q \times q}$, where $\overrightarrow{TSF}_{lh} = (\overrightarrow{TF}_{lh}, SD_{lh})$ is the TSF from DM e_l to DM e_h. The first component $\overrightarrow{TF}_{lh}$ is the trust function from DM e_l to DM e_h, and the second component is the similarity degree between R_l and R_h. Through calculating the trust score [124], the trust-similarity matrix is simplified to $\overrightarrow{TSM} = (\overrightarrow{TS}_{lh}, SD_{lh})_{q \times q}$, where $\overrightarrow{TS}_{lh}$ is referred to as the trust score from DM e_l to DM e_h.

The trust relationship is a social attribute that always occurs among DMs. If DM A trusts DM B to a low degree and yet B has a high degree of trust in A, it does not mean that there is a strong trust relationship between them. Thus, the aggregated trust function is used to measure the average trust among multiple DMs.

Definition 3.3 [129] Let $\{\lambda_i = (t_i, d_i)\}$ be a collection of $m(m \geq 2)$ trust functions and $w = (w_1, w_2, \ldots, w_m)^T$ be a weight vector such that $w_i \in [0, 1]$ and $\sum_{i=1}^{m} w_i = 1$. The uninorm trust weighted average (UTWA) is computed as

$$UTWA_w(\lambda_1, \lambda_2, \ldots, \lambda_m) =$$
$$\begin{cases} \left(\dfrac{\prod_{i=1}^{m} (t_i)^{w_i}}{\prod_{i=1}^{m} (t_i)^{w_i} + \prod_{i=1}^{m} (1-t_i)^{w_i}}, \dfrac{\prod_{i=1}^{m} (d_i)^{w_i}}{\prod_{i=1}^{m} (d_i)^{w_i} + \prod_{i=1}^{m} (1-d_i)^{w_i}} \right) & \lambda_i \notin \{(0, 1), (1, 0)\} \\ (0, 0), & otherwise \end{cases} \quad (3.2)$$

The UTWA operator needs to precompute the associated weights, which can be calculated through the trust scores of DMs [124]. For two DMs e_l and e_h, trust functions are established about each other, denoted as $\overrightarrow{TF}_{lh}$ and $\overrightarrow{TF}_{hl}$. Through using the UTWA operator, the aggregated trust function is obtained, which represents the trust function of this pair of DMs. In this way, the two directed trust functions are converted to an aggregated trust function.

Definition 3.4 Let $\overrightarrow{TM} = (\overrightarrow{TF}_{lh})_{q \times q}, l \neq h$ be a complete directed sociomatrix; the aggregated sociomatrix is defined as $TM = (TF_{lh})_{q \times q}$, where

$$T F_{lh} = T F_{hl} = U T W A_w(\overrightarrow{T F}_{lh}, \overrightarrow{T F}_{hl}) \qquad (3.3)$$

To simplify, the aggregated sociomatrix can be denoted as $T M = (T S_{lh})_{q \times q}$, where $T S_{lh}$ is the aggregated trust score for $T F_{lh}$. The aggregated trust-similarity matrix is obtained as $T S M = (T S F_{lh})_{q \times q}$, where $T S F_{lh} = (T S_{lh}, S D_{lh})_{q \times q}$ is the aggregated trust-similarity function.

Example 3.1 A company invites a set of DMs $\{e_1, e_2, e_3, e_4\}$ to select the most appropriate cloud service supplier. Suppose the complete trust-similarity matrix is presented as

$$\overrightarrow{TSM} = \begin{pmatrix} - & \{(0.2, 0.8), 0.5\} & \{(0.4, 0.6), 0.1\} & \{(0.2, 0.4), 0.3\} \\ \{(0.5, 0.2), 0.5\} & - & \{(0.7, 0.3), 0.5\} & \{(0.3, 0.4), 0.2\} \\ \{(0.3, 0.1), 0.1\} & \{(0.9, 0.1), 0.5\} & - & \{(0.3, 0.2), 0.1\} \\ \{(0.1, 0.5), 0.3\} & \{(0.2, 0.4), 0.2\} & \{(0.6, 0.4), 0.1\} & - \end{pmatrix}.$$

By using the trust score, the trust-similarity matrix can be simplified as

$$\overrightarrow{TSM} = \begin{pmatrix} - & (0.2, 0.5) & (0.4, 0.1) & (0.4, 0.3) \\ (0.65, 0.5) & - & (0.7, 0.5) & (0.45, 0.2) \\ (0.6, 0.1) & (0.9, 0.5) & - & (0.55, 0.1) \\ (0.3, 0.3) & (0.4, 0.2) & (0.6, 0.1) & - \end{pmatrix}.$$

By using the UTWA operator in Definition 3.3, the aggregated trust-similarity matrix is obtained as

$$TSM = \begin{pmatrix} - & (0.5976, 0.5) & (0.5774, 0.1) & (0.3731, 0.3) \\ (0.5976, 0.5) & - & (0.8653, 0.5) & (0.435, 0.2) \\ (0.5774, 0.1) & (0.8653, 0.5) & - & (0.5888, 0.1) \\ (0.3731, 0.3) & (0.435, 0.2) & (0.5888, 0.1) & - \end{pmatrix}.$$

It should be pointed out that the weight vector of the UTWA operator can be obtained by using Yager's Ordered Weighted Averaging (OWA)-based procedure [123, 148].

3.2.2   Construction of the TSA Plot

Through dividing each one of the two dimensions (i.e., trust score and similarity degree) into two levels, the measurement attributes are classified into four quadrants (or categories). Then, a TSA plot is designed to implement the trust-similarity analysis (see Fig. 3.2), in which the X-axis and Y-axis represent the trust score and similarity degree, respectively. All aggregated trust-similarity functions are mapped to the two-dimensional coordinate system (please see the black dots in Fig. 3.2). The detailed description of the four quadrants in Fig. 3.2 is as follows.

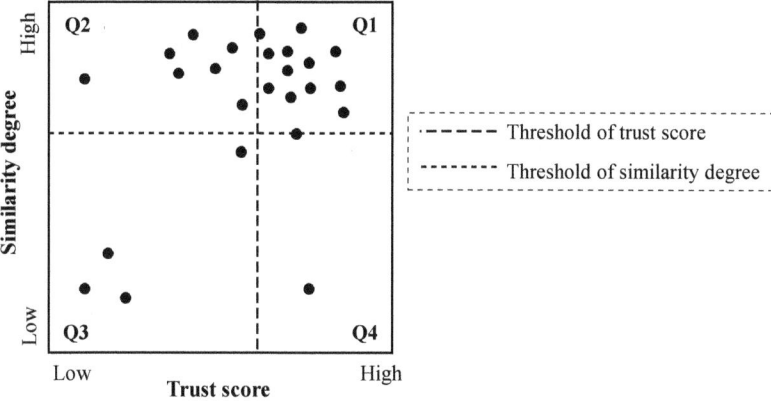

Fig. 3.2 An example of TSA plot

(1) Quadrant 1 (Q1) is described as the '*ideal area*'. The TSF located in Q1 has a high trust score and a high similarity degree, which indicates that the two relevant DMs have a high level of trust relationship and very similar opinions. Thus, such DMs are considered to belong to the same cluster.

(2) Quadrant 2 (Q2) is described as the '*similarity-priority area*'. The TSF located in Q2 has a low trust score but a high similarity degree. Thus, the corresponding DMs can be classified into a same cluster if a similarity-priority strategy is adopted.

(3) Quadrant 3 (Q3) is described as the '*most isolated area*'. The TSF located in Q3 has a low trust score and a low similarity degree, which means that the related DMs have a low trust relationship and significantly different opinions. Thus, it is better for these DMs to remain independent than to form a cluster.

(4) Quadrant 4 (Q4) is described as the '*trust-priority area*'. In contrast to the similarity-priority area, the TSF located in Q4 has a high trust score but a low similarity degree. Thus, the corresponding DMs can be allocated to a cluster if a trust-priority strategy is adopted.

3.2.3 Determination of Crosshair Placement

The two thresholds acting on the trust score and similarity degree in the TSA plot are collectively referred to as the crosshair, denoted as $(\overline{TS}, \overline{SD})$, where $\overline{TS}$ and $\overline{SD}$ are the thresholds of trust score and similarity degree, respectively. Herein, three basic methods are presented to calculate the crosshair placement, i.e., the scale-centered method, the data-centered method, and the method based on clustering simulation.

- *Scale-centered method.* The midpoint of the scale is used to divide each of the two attributes into two levels. For example, if all data belong to the interval [0, 1], then

0.5 (that is, the midpoint of the interval) is taken as the dividing point. However, since the trust-similarity functions are usually unevenly distributed (such as concentrated in one area), the scale-centered method will cause most of them to fall into the same area, which is not conducive to clustering.

- *Data-centered method.* The means, medians or midpoints of the values concerning trust score and similarity degree are used for distinguishing the two levels of the two measurement attributes. This method takes advantage of the characteristics of the data.
- *Method based on clustering simulation.* The larger the number of clusters, the smaller the number of DMs typically contained within each cluster, because the total number of DMs is fixed. In this method, multiple rounds of clustering simulation are implemented to detect the appropriate crosshair that can generate the predetermined number of clusters. It is generally considered reasonable for the number of DMs within a cluster to be equal to or greater than 3. Hence, the number of clusters can be set as $K = INF(q/3)$, where $INF(q/3)$ is an integer-valued function of q divided by 3. For example, if $q = 20$, then the number of clusters can be set as $K = INF(20/3) = 6$.

The first two methods directly use the original data to calculate the crosshair placement, while the last method first determines the number of clusters and then implements the clustering simulation. Section 3.5.2 will analyze the influence of different methods for calculating the crosshair placement on the clustering results.

3.3 TSA-Based Clustering Algorithm

Clustering is usually based on the similarity among data objects through distance measures. The most common distance measure is the Euclidean distance, which can be defined as

$$d(i, j) = \sqrt{|X_{i1} - X_{j1}|^2 + |X_{i2} - X_{j2}|^2 + \cdots + |X_{iq} - X_{jq}|^2} \qquad (3.4)$$

where $i = (X_{i1}, X_{i2}, \ldots, X_{iq})$ and $j = (X_{j1}, X_{j2}, \ldots, X_{jq})$ are two q-dimensional data objects. If each variable is given a weight according to its importance, the weighted Euclidean distance is obtained as

$$d(i, j) = \sqrt{w_1|X_{i1} - X_{j1}|^2 + w_2|X_{i2} - X_{j2}|^2 + \cdots + w_q|X_{iq} - X_{jq}|^2} \quad (3.5)$$

where $0 \leq w_l \leq 1, l = 1, 2, \ldots, q$, and $\sum_{l=1}^{q} w_l = 1$. The use of weighted Euclidean distance in clustering reflects the different importance of variables in the data.

Herein, the weighted Euclidean distance is used to calculate the closeness degree between two DMs. The closeness degree refers to the weighted aggregation of trust score and similarity degree, which is utilized to quantify whether two DMs can be assigned to the same subgroup. Because of the social nature of the trust relationship, the aggregated trust score is used to measure the level of trust between two DMs.

Definition 3.5 *(Closeness degree)* Let $TSF_{lh} = (TS_{lh}, SD_{lh})$ be the aggregated trust-similarity function, as above. The closeness degree between DM e_l to DM e_h can be calculated as

$$CD_{lh} = \sqrt{\alpha_1 \cdot TS_{lh}^2 + \alpha_2 \cdot SD_{lh}^2} \tag{3.6}$$

where α_1 and α_2 are the importance weights of trust score and similarity degree, respectively, such that $0 \le \alpha_1, \alpha_2 \le 1$ and $\alpha_1 + \alpha_2 = 1$.

Once all the trust-similarity functions are mapped to a TSA plot to realize a visualization of the clustering process, the closeness degree is changed to

$$CD_{lh} = \sqrt{\beta_1^2 \cdot TS_{lh}^2 + \beta_2^2 \cdot SD_{lh}^2} \tag{3.7}$$

where β_1^2 and β_2^2 are the importance of trust score and similarity degree, respectively, such that $0 \le \beta_1^2, \beta_2^2 \le 1$ and $\beta_1^2 + \beta_2^2 = 1$. Clearly, $0 \le CD_{lh} \le 1$. If $\beta_1^2 = 0$, then the closeness degree reduces to similarity degree; if $\beta_1^2 = 1$, then the closeness degree reduces to aggregated trust score. The closeness degree matrix can be established as $CDM = (CD_{lh})_{q \times q}$, $l \ne h$, where CD_{lh} represents the closeness degree between DM e_l and DM e_h in terms of the fusion of trust score and similarity degree.

Remark 3.2 The parameters β_1^2 and β_2^2 play an important role in the calculation of closeness degree. If $\beta_1^2 > 0.5$, it indicates that the trust score has greater importance when weighing the closeness degree. Conversely, if $\beta_2^2 > 0.5$, it means that the similarity degree has greater influence on the measure of closeness degree. If $\beta_1^2 = \beta_2^2 = 0.5$, trust score and similarity degree are considered equally important in the closeness degree. In the following, the closeness degree will be used as a threshold to guide the clustering process. The simulation and analysis of the effects of the above parameters on clustering will be presented in Sect. 3.5.1.

Definition 3.6 (Order Relation of TSFs). Let $\theta_1 = (TS_1, SD_1)$ and $\theta_2 = (TS_2, SD_2)$ be any two aggregated TSFs, and let CD_1 and CD_2 be the associated closeness degrees. We have the following:

(1) If $CD_1 < CD_2$, then θ_1 is smaller than θ_2, denoted by $\theta_1 \prec \theta_2$;
(2) If $CD_1 > CD_2$, then θ_1 is greater than θ_2, denoted by $\theta_1 \succ \theta_2$; and
(3) If $CD_1 = CD_2$, then:

  (a) Setting that similarity degree takes precedence. If $SD_1 < SD_2$, then θ_1 is smaller than θ_2, denoted by $\theta_1 \prec \theta_2$; if $SD_1 > SD_2$, then is greater than θ_2, denoted by $\theta_1 \succ \theta_2$; if $SD_1 = SD_2$, then θ_1 is equal to θ_2, denoted by $\theta_1 = \theta_2$.

(b) Setting the trust score is a priority. If $TS_1 < TS_2$, then θ_1 is smaller than θ_2, denoted by $\theta_1 \prec \theta_2$; if $TS_1 > TS_2$, then θ_1 is greater than θ_2, denoted by $\theta_1 \succ \theta_2$; if $TS_1 = TS_2$, then θ_1 is equal to θ_2, denoted by $\theta_1 = \theta_2$.

(c) When there is no preference for similarity degree and trust score, θ_1 is equal to θ_2, denoted by $\theta_1 = \theta_2$.

Thus, when comparing two TSFs, the one with higher closeness degree is ordered first, and in case of equal closeness degrees, which of the trust score and similarity degree is the priority should be determined in advance. Through using the order relation of pairs of TSFs, the DMs with the highest closeness degree can be distinguished from a group, which is useful in guiding the clustering and aggregation of individual evaluation information.

3.3.1 Definition of the Joint Threshold

As we hold that opinion similarity and trust relationship are both important measurement attributes for clustering, the concept of joint threshold (JT) is proposed. The setting of JT is inspired by the TSA plot. Figure 3.3 presents an improved TSA plot, with $\beta_1 \cdot TS$ and $\beta_2 \cdot SD$ being the X-axis and Y-axis, respectively. All aggregated trust-similarity functions are mapped to the coordinate system, namely, the black dot, denoted as $(\beta_1 \cdot TS, \beta_2 \cdot SD)$. An arc is drawn, centered at the origin, with the weighted quadratic mean of thresholds of trust score and similarity degree $\sqrt{(\beta_1 \cdot \overline{TS})^2, (\beta_2 \cdot \overline{SD})^2}$ as the radius, where $0 \leq \beta_1^2, \beta_2^2 \leq 1$ and $\beta_1^2 + \beta_2^2 = 1$. This arc is called the joint threshold arc (see the red line in Fig. 3.3). In this manner, the TSA plot is redivided into two areas. The dots in the upper right area of the arc meet the joint threshold, while the dots in the lower left area fail.

Definition 3.7 Let $(\overline{TS}, \overline{SD})$ be the crosshair as above; the basic joint threshold is calculated as

$$BJT = \sqrt{(\beta_1 \cdot \overline{TS})^2 + (\beta_2 \cdot \overline{SD})^2} \qquad (3.8)$$

where β_1^2 and β_2^2 are defined in the same way as Eq. (3.7). Clearly, $0 \leq BJT \leq 1$. The crosshair is used to evaluate the values of trust score and similarity degree, while the basic joint threshold is used to assess closeness degree.

Remark 3.3 In keeping with the definition of closeness degree that reflects the importance of trust score and similarity degree, the abscissa and ordinate values of all dots in the following TSA plot are multiplied by the coefficients β_1 and β_2, respectively.

It is called the basic joint threshold in Definition 3.7 because the following four categories of joint thresholds can be obtained by combining the crosshair (also see Table 3.1).

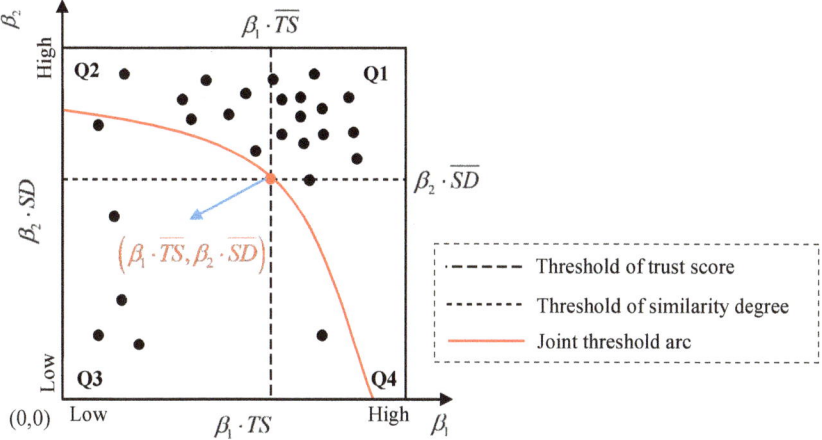

Fig. 3.3 The setting of joint threshold based on the TSA plot

(1) *Basic JT.* Instead of considering the measurement attributes separately, the DMs only need to determine whether the closeness degree satisfies the joint threshold.

(2) *Trust-priority JT.* This threshold is denoted as $\sqrt{(\beta_1 \cdot \overline{TS})^2, (\beta_2 \cdot \overline{SD})^2} \wedge \beta_1 \cdot \overline{TS}$, where the symbol "$\wedge$" means that the left and right conditions must be satisfied simultaneously. Not only should the closeness degree meet the basic joint threshold, but the trust score must also be greater than the threshold of trust.

(3) *Similarity-priority JT.* This threshold is denoted as $\sqrt{(\beta_1 \cdot \overline{TS})^2 + (\beta_2 \cdot \overline{SD})^2} \wedge \beta_2 \cdot \overline{SD}$. Not only should the closeness degree meet the basic joint threshold, but the similarity degree must also be greater than the threshold of similarity.

(4) *Strong JT.* This threshold is denoted as $\sqrt{(\beta_1 \cdot \overline{TS})^2 + (\beta_2 \cdot \overline{SD})^2} \wedge \beta_1 \cdot \overline{TS} \wedge \beta_2 \cdot \overline{SD}$. Not only should the closeness degree meet the basic joint threshold, but each measurement attribute must also be greater than the corresponding threshold.

Example 3.2 Let the crosshair be $(\overline{TS}, \overline{SD}) = (0.8, 0.6)$, the aggregated trust-similarity function be $TSF_{lh} = (0.7, 0.8)$, and the parameters be $\beta_1^2 = \beta_2^2 = 0.5$. The basic joint threshold can be obtained as $BJT = 0.7071$. If using the basic JT, as $CD_{lh} = 0.8921 > BJT$, the related two DMs e_l and e_h can be classified into the same cluster. If using the trust-priority JT, as $CD_{lh} > BJT$ and $0.7 \cdot \beta_1 < \beta_1 \cdot \overline{TS}$, the two DMs cannot be grouped into the same cluster. Consequently, if the four types of joint thresholds are adopted in turn, the results as to whether the two DMs can be placed in a cluster are as follows: Yes, No, Yes, No.

If both the crosshair and joint threshold arc are considered, the two-dimensional plot is further subdivided into six areas (see Fig. 3.4). The areas Q1 and Q3 remain unchanged, while Q2 and Q4 are split into two parts according to the joint threshold

Table 3.1 Four categories of joint thresholds

Joint threshold	Mathematical expression	Area that satisfies the threshold in Fig. 3.4
Basic JT	$\sqrt{\beta_1^2 \cdot \overline{TS}^2 + \beta_2^2 \cdot \overline{SD}^2}$	$Q1 \cup A \cup C$
Trust-priority JT	$\sqrt{\beta_1^2 \cdot \overline{TS}^2 + \beta_2^2 \cdot \overline{SD}^2} \wedge \beta_1 \cdot \overline{TS}$	$Q1 \cup C$
Similarity-priority JT	$\sqrt{\beta_1^2 \cdot \overline{TS}^2 + \beta_2^2 \cdot \overline{SD}^2} \wedge \beta_2 \cdot \overline{SD}$	$Q1 \cup A$
Strong JT	$\sqrt{\beta_1^2 \cdot \overline{TS}^2 + \beta_2^2 \cdot \overline{SD}^2} \wedge \beta_1 \cdot \overline{TS} \wedge \beta_2 \cdot \overline{SD}$	$Q1$

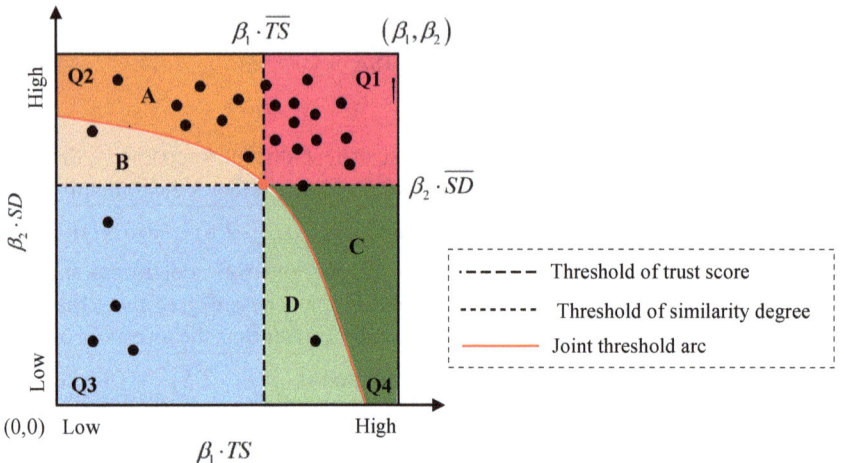

Fig. 3.4 Division of areas on the TSA plot

arc. In this manner, if the trust-priority JT is used, only the dots in Q1 and C need to be examined, rather than all the dots in Q1 and Q4 (see Table 3.1).

3.3.2 Algorithm Design of the TSA-Based Clustering Method

Based on different categories of joint thresholds, four algorithms of the TSA-based clustering method are presented by improving the algorithm in Xu and Chen's research [140].

Case A. *Use the basic JT as the measurement standard by which to determine whether two DMs can be clustered into the same cluster.*

In this case, only the elements in areas Q1, A and C of the TSA plot need to be examined.

If Algorithm 3.1 is adopted, it is generally impossible to guarantee that the internal structures of all the clusters perform well on the two measurement attributes of trust score and similarity degree. For example, one cluster has a high level of trust score among the members and a low degree of similarity, while another one has the opposite result. If we require high trust scores and high similarity degrees among DMs, new constraints need to be added. The clustering algorithm based on the basic JT is the most basic algorithm. By adding different constraints on it, the following three clustering algorithms are obtained to realize different clustering requirements.

Algorithm 3.1 TSA-based clustering method using the basic JT

Input: Normalized individual evaluation matrices R_l, $l = 1, 2, \ldots, q$, complete directed socioma-trix $\overline{TSM}$, the basic joint threshold BJT, and parameters β_1^2, β_2^2.

Output: Clusters $C_1, \ldots, C_K$.

1: All the DMs are formed into a set U, which is randomly ordered and marked as $1, 2, \ldots, q$. Then, a temporary set T is constructed. Initialize the cluster counter as $k = 1$.

2: Use Eq. (3.3) to compute the aggregated sociomatrix TSM, and use Eq. (3.7) to conclude the closeness degree matrix CDM.

3: Pay attention to the elements in areas Q1, A and C, and then select the maximum closeness degree (denoted as $CD_{l^*h^*}$). If $CD_{l^*h^*} \geq BJT$, then take the corresponding DMs out of U and put them into cluster C_k. Let $n_k = n_k + 2$, and proceed to the next step. If $CD_{l^*h^*} < BJT$, proceed to Step 8.

4: Aggregate the individual evaluation matrices and trust scores in cluster C_k via a linear combi-nation:

$$G_k = \frac{1}{n_k} \sum_{l=1}^{n_k} R_l, \tag{3.9}$$

$$TS_k = \frac{1}{n_k(n_k - 1)} \sum_{l=1}^{n_k} \sum_{h=1}^{n_k} TS_{lh}, \quad l \neq h, \tag{3.10}$$

where G_k is the collective evaluation matrix, and TS_k is the aggregated trust score.

5: Calculate the closeness degree between C_k and each of the rest DMs in U, and obtain the closeness degree matrix as $CDM = (CD_{kh})_{(q-n_k) \times (q-n_k)}$, where $CD_{kh} = (TS_{kh}, SD_{kh})$, such that $TS_{kh} = (1/n_k) \sum_{l=1}^{n_k} TS_{lh}$, $e_l \in C_k$, and $SD_{kh} = 1 - d(G_k, R_h)$ by Eq. (3.1).

6: Select the maximum closeness degree. If $CD_{lh} \geq BJT$, then take e_h out of U, and put it into cluster C_k. Let $n_k = n_k + 1$, and return to Step 4. If $CD_{lh} < BJT$, proceed to Step 7.

7: If the set U is not null, return to Step 2; otherwise, proceed to the next step.

8: Output the clusters $C_1, \ldots, C_K$.

Case B. *Use the trust-priority JT as the measurement standard by which to determine whether two DMs can be clustered into the same cluster.*

The new algorithm of the TSA-based clustering method using the trust-priority JT is inherited from Algorithm 3.1, and the following changes need to be made.

(1) Add the trust-priority JT into the Input, i.e., BJT and $\overline{TS}$.

(2) Step 3→ Step 3^B. Pay attention to the elements in areas Q1 and C, and then arrange the values of closeness degree in the upper triangle region of the close-

ness degree matrix in descending order. Select the first largest closeness degree (denoted as CD_{l*h*}) and determine if the condition $CD_{l*h*} \geq BJT \wedge TS_{l*h*} \geq \overline{TS}$ is true. If it is true, then take the related DMs out of U and put them into cluster C_k. Let $n_k = n_k + 2$, and proceed to the next step. Otherwise, select the second-largest closeness degree, and repeat the above operations. If no closeness degree satisfies the condition, then proceed to Step 8.

(3) Step 6→ Step 6^B. Arrange the values of closeness degree in descending order. Determine whether the condition $CD_{lh} \geq BJT \wedge TS_{lh} \geq \overline{TS}$ is true in order. If so, then take e_h out of U, and put it into cluster C_k. Let $n_k = n_k + 2$, and return to Step 4. If all the remaining trust-similarity functions cannot satisfy the above condition, then proceed to Step 7.

Case C. *Use the similarity-priority JT as the measurement standard by which to determine whether two DMs can be clustered into the same cluster.*

The new algorithm of the TSA-based clustering method using the similarity-priority JT comes from the clustering algorithm by using the trust-priority JT, and the following changes are made.

(1) Add the similarity-priority JT into the Input, i.e., BJT and $\overline{SD}$.
(2) Step 3^B →Step 3^C. Pay attention to the elements in areas Q1 and A, and change the condition $CD_{lh} \geq BJT \wedge TS_{lh} \geq \overline{TS}$ to $CD_{lh} \geq BJT \wedge SD_{lh} \geq \overline{SD}$.
(3) Step 6^B →Step 6^C. Change the condition $CD_{kh} \geq BJT \wedge TS_{kh} \geq \overline{TS}$ to $CD_{kh} \geq BJT \wedge SD_{kh} \geq \overline{SD}$.

Case D. *Use the strong JT as the measurement standard by which to determine whether two DMs can be clustered into the same cluster.*

The new algorithm of the TSA-based clustering method using the strong JT comes from the clustering algorithm by using the trust-priority JT, and the following changes are made.

(1) Add the strong JT into the Input, i.e., BJT, $\overline{TS}$ and $\overline{SD}$.
(2) Step 3^B →Step 3^D. Pay attention to the elements in area Q1, and change the condition $CD_{lh} \geq BJT \wedge TS_{lh} \geq \overline{TS}$ to $CD_{lh} \geq BJT \wedge TS_{lh} \geq \overline{TS} \wedge SD_{lh} \geq \overline{SD}$.
(3) Step 6^B →Step 6^D. Change the condition $CD_{kh} \geq BJT \wedge TS_{kh} \geq \overline{TS}$ to $CD_{kh} \geq BJT \wedge TS_{kh} \geq \overline{TS} \wedge SD_{kh} \geq \overline{SD}$.

Fig. 3.5 presents the clustering process using the TSA-based clustering method.

According to the majority principle, the larger the number of DMs a cluster contains, the more weight it should be given [38, 167]. Let λ_k represent the weight of cluster C_k. Without loss of generality, the weight of cluster C_k is calculated as

$$\lambda_k = \frac{(n_k)^2}{\sum_{k=1}^{K}(n_k)^2} \tag{3.11}$$

where n_k is the number of DMs in cluster C_k.

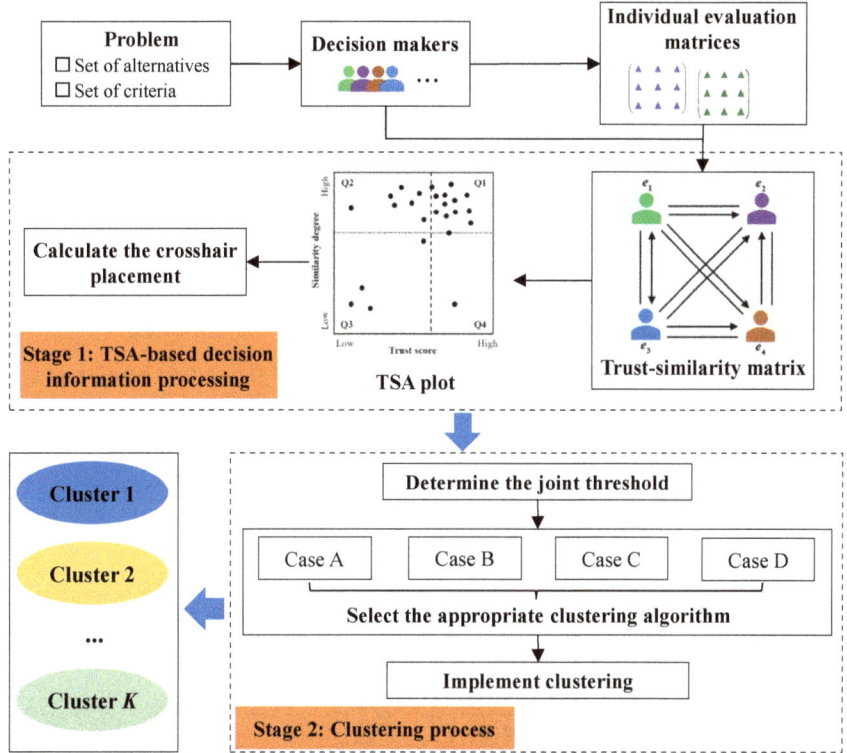

Fig. 3.5 Visual clustering process by using the TSA-based clustering method in LSGDM under a social network context

For an LSGDM event under a social network context, when trying to collect the individual opinions within each cluster, the calculation of DMs' weights needs to be reconsidered instead of setting the weights of DMs in the same cluster equal as in [167]. This is because the DMs have two measurement attributes associated with assigning weights, i.e., trust relationship and opinion similarity. Trust among DMs in a group plays an important role in the GDM process; thus, it should be considered as a reliable source for assigning importance to the DMs.

Definition 3.8 Given the cluster C_k including $n_k(n_k > 1)$ DMs, the trust score of DM e_l is defined as

$$T S_l = \frac{1}{n_k - 1} \sum_{h=1, l \neq h}^{n_k} \overrightarrow{TS}_{hl} \tag{3.12}$$

where $e_l, e_h \in C_k, h \neq l$. Clearly, $0 \leq T S_l \leq 1, l = 1, \ldots, n_k$.

Equally important, the given evaluation information contains all the views of the DMs on the decision problem, so it should be considered in the weight calculation.

According to the majority principle, the higher the degree of similarity with the collective opinion, the more weight the corresponding DM should be given.

Definition 3.9 Given a cluster C_k including n_k DMs, the similarity score of DM e_l is defined as

$$SS_l = \frac{1}{n_k - 1} \sum_{h=1, l \neq h}^{n_k} SD_{hl} \tag{3.13}$$

where $e_l, e_h \in C_k, h \neq l$. Clearly, $0 \leq SS_l \leq 1, l = 1, \ldots, n_k$. The similarity score aims to measure the average similarity between one DM and all others.

Definition 3.10 (Comprehensive score) Let the scores TS_l and SD_l be the same as above. The comprehensive score of DM e_l can be calculated as

$$CS_l = \sqrt{\beta_1^2 \cdot TS_l^2 + \beta_2^2 \cdot SD_l^2} \tag{3.14}$$

where β_1^2 and β_2^2 are the same as Eq. (3.7).

By using Yager's OWA-based procedure [123, 148], DMs' weights within cluster C_k are obtained as follows:

$$w_{\sigma(l)} = Q\left(\frac{CS(\sigma(l))}{CS(\sigma(n_k))}\right) - Q\left(\frac{CS(\sigma(l-1))}{CS(\sigma(n_k))}\right) \tag{3.15}$$

where $CS(\sigma(l)) = \sum_{h=1}^{l} CS_{\sigma(h)}$, σ is a permutation such that $CS_{\sigma(h)}$ is the h-th largest value of set $\{CS_1, \ldots, CS_{n_k}\}$, and Q is a Basic Unit-interval Monotone (BUM) membership function of the fuzzy quantifier to implement the mapping operation: $Q : [0, 1] \to [0, 1]$ such that $Q(0) = 0, Q(1) = 1$ and if $x > y$ then $Q(x) \geq Q(y)$. According to the previous order, we can find the weight of corresponding DM backward.

Note that the weights of DMs within each cluster should be normalized before calculating the opinions of clusters through aggregating the individual opinions.

Remark 3.4 If the number of DMs within a certain cluster exceeds one, then Eqs. (3.12)–(3.15) are effective for the calculation of weights. If there is only one DM in a cluster, the DM's opinion is just the cluster's opinion. In this case, the weight of the DM is set to equal the weight of the cluster. Without loss of generality, the weight can be denoted as $w_l = \lambda_k$, where e_l is the only DM in cluster C_k.

3.3.3   Time Complexity Analyses

The proposed clustering method is divided into four clustering algorithms based on different constraints. The time complexity of each clustering algorithm is investigated below.

The implementation of the TSA-based clustering method using the basic JT consists of two key steps: (1) combining the two DMs with the largest closeness degree into a new cluster, and (2) recalculating the closeness degrees between the new cluster and other remaining DMs. Suppose the total number of DMs involved is q. It will take $O(q)$ time to calculate the closeness between all the pairs of DMs. Once a new cluster is determined, it takes time to calculate the closeness of the new cluster to other DMs. It can be seen that the TSA-based clustering method needs to be carried out with q iterations, and each iteration needs to update and store the closeness degree matrix, such that the time complexity is the cubic order of the number of DMs, i.e., $O(q^3)$. Therefore, we can summarize the time complexity of the TSA-based clustering method using the basic JT as Theorem 3.1.

Theorem 3.1 *The time complexity of the TSA-based clustering method using the basic JT is $O(q^3)$.*

Compared with the basic JT, the clustering method using the trust-priority JT adds another step: checking whether the trust score corresponding to the maximum closeness degree meets the requirement. This step requires calculating the trust score between the new cluster and each other DM. Therefore, the time cost of this step is $O(q)$. Considering the time cost of the first two steps, the time complexity of the TSA-based method using the trust-priority JT is calculated as $O(q^4)$. It is easy to know that the same time complexity can be obtained by using the similarity-priority JT. As the strong JT requires both trust priority and similarity priority, the corresponding time complexity is $O(q^5)$. Hence, the time complexities of the TSA-based clustering method using the other three types of JTs are concluded as Theorem 3.2.

Theorem 3.2 *The time complexities of the TSA-based method using the trust-priority JT, similarity-priority JT, and strong JT are $O(q^4)$, $O(q^4)$ and $O(q^5)$, respectively.*

It can be seen that adding a constraint increases the time complexity by an order of magnitude. Although the TSA clustering method can effectively manage clustering in the presence of multiple constraints, the time complexity is relatively high. Therefore, important research in the future will focuses on reasonably reducing the time complexity by some means.

3.4 Numerical Experiment

Suppose an LSGDM problem involves three benefit attributes $A = \{a_1, a_2, a_3\}$, five alternatives $X = \{x_1, x_2, x_3, x_4, x_5\}$, and twenty DMs $E = \{e_1, e_2, \ldots, e_{20}\}$. The initial evaluation matrices and complete sociomatrix are randomly generated by using MATLAB software. The individual evaluation matrices are expressed in the form of crisp numbers within the interval [0, 1]. The sociomatrix is established in strict accordance with the requirements of Definition 3.4. The basic JT is used as the measurement standard to manage the clustering process. Hence, Algorithm 3.1 is applied to implement the clustering operation.

Table 3.2 Clustering process using the basic JT

Number of counts	DMs (and Cluster) involved	Closeness degree	Direction of assignment
1	e_2, e_3	0.914	Assigned to C_1
2	C_1, e_8	0.8548	Assigned to C_1
3	C_1, e_{12}	0.8634	Assigned to C_1
4	C_1, e_5	0.8446	Assigned to C_1
5	C_1, e_{18}	0.8376	Assigned to C_1
6	C_1, e_1	0.7673	Assigned to C_1
7	C_1, e_4	0.7726	Assigned to C_1
8	C_1, e_{20}	0.7583	–
9	e_9, e_{17}	0.8719	Assigned to C_2
10	C_2, e_{15}	0.779	Assigned to C_2
11	C_2, e_{20}	0.7664	Assigned to C_2
12	C_2, e_{10}	0.7643	Assigned to –
13	e_7, e_{19}	0.8389	Assigned to C_3
14	C_3, e_{14}	0.7879	Assigned to C_3
15	C_3, e_{16}	0.7601	–
16	e_2, e_{16}	0.8378	Assigned to C_4
17	C_4, e_{10}	0.7458	–
18	e_{10}, e_{13}	0.7864	Assigned to C_5
19	C_5, e_{11}	0.6647	–
20	e_{11}	–	Assigned to C_6

Input: Normalized individual evaluation matrices R_l, $l = 1, 2, \ldots, 20$, directed sociomatrix $\overrightarrow{TM}$, basic joint threshold $BJT = 0.7651$ (setting $\overline{TS} = 0.755$, $\overline{SD} = 0.78$, $\beta_1^2 = 0.6$, $\beta_2^2 = 0.4$).

Note that the determination of joint threshold and relevant parameters will be discussed in Sect. 3.5.1. The clustering process and result are presented in Table 3.2 and Table 3.3, respectively.

The following presents a visualization of the clustering process using the basic JT. Each trust-similarity function is mapped to a two-dimensional TSA plot, with the trust score as the abscissa and the similarity degree as the ordinate. Figure 3.6 shows the crosshair distributions using different methods. This illustrative experiment adopts the method based on clustering simulation to calculate the thresholds of trust score and similarity degree.

We define a clustering phase to be completed when a cluster is formed until no new DMs are included. Figure 3.7 shows the first three clustering phases. Each phase displays two graphs, that is, one at the beginning of the phase and one at the end of the phase. A clustering phase will be terminated when all the remaining dots fall into the lower left area of the joint threshold arc. The detailed description is as follows.

Table 3.3 Clustering results using the basic JT

Cluster	Number of DMs included	DM included	Weight of cluster	Weight of DM with each cluster
C_1	8	$e_2, e_3, e_8, e_{12}, e_5,$ e_{18}, e_1, e_4	0.6531	$w_2 = 0.0751,$ $w_3 = 0.0633,$ $w_8 = 0.0536,$ $w_{12} = 0.2435,$ $w_5 = 0.0452,$ $w_{18} = 0.0979,$ $w_1 = 0.0361,$ $w_3 = 0.0384$
C_2	4	$e_9, e_{17}, e_{15}, e_{20}$	0.1633	$w_9 = 0.0359,$ $w_{17} = 0.0229,$ $w_{15} = 0.0163,$ $w_{20} = 0.0882$
C_3	3	e_7, e_{19}, e_{14}	0.0918	$w_7 = 0.0201,$ $w_{19} = 0.0157,$ $w_{14} = 0.056$
C_4	2	e_6, e_{16}	0.0408	$w_6 = 0.0089,$ $w_{16} = 0.0319$
C_5	2	e_{10}, e_{13}	0.0408	$w_{10} = 0.031,$ $w_{13} = 0.0097$
C_6	1	e_{11}	0.0102	$w_{11} = 0.0102$

Note Set the BUM function as $Q(r) = r^{1/2}$.

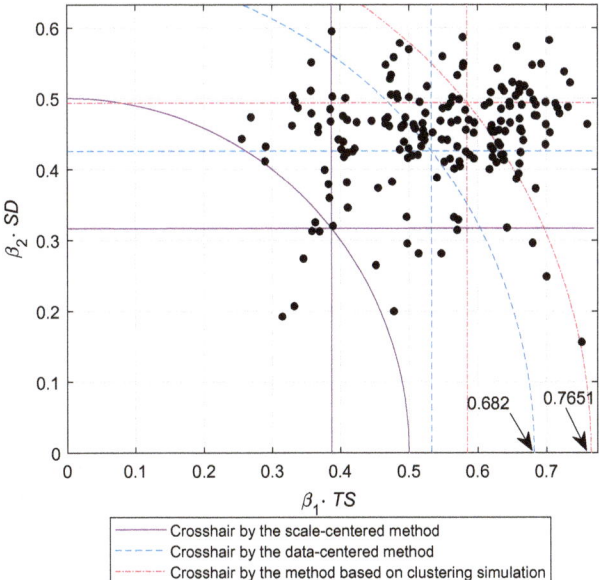

Fig. 3.6 Distributions of individual trust-similarity functions and crosshairs

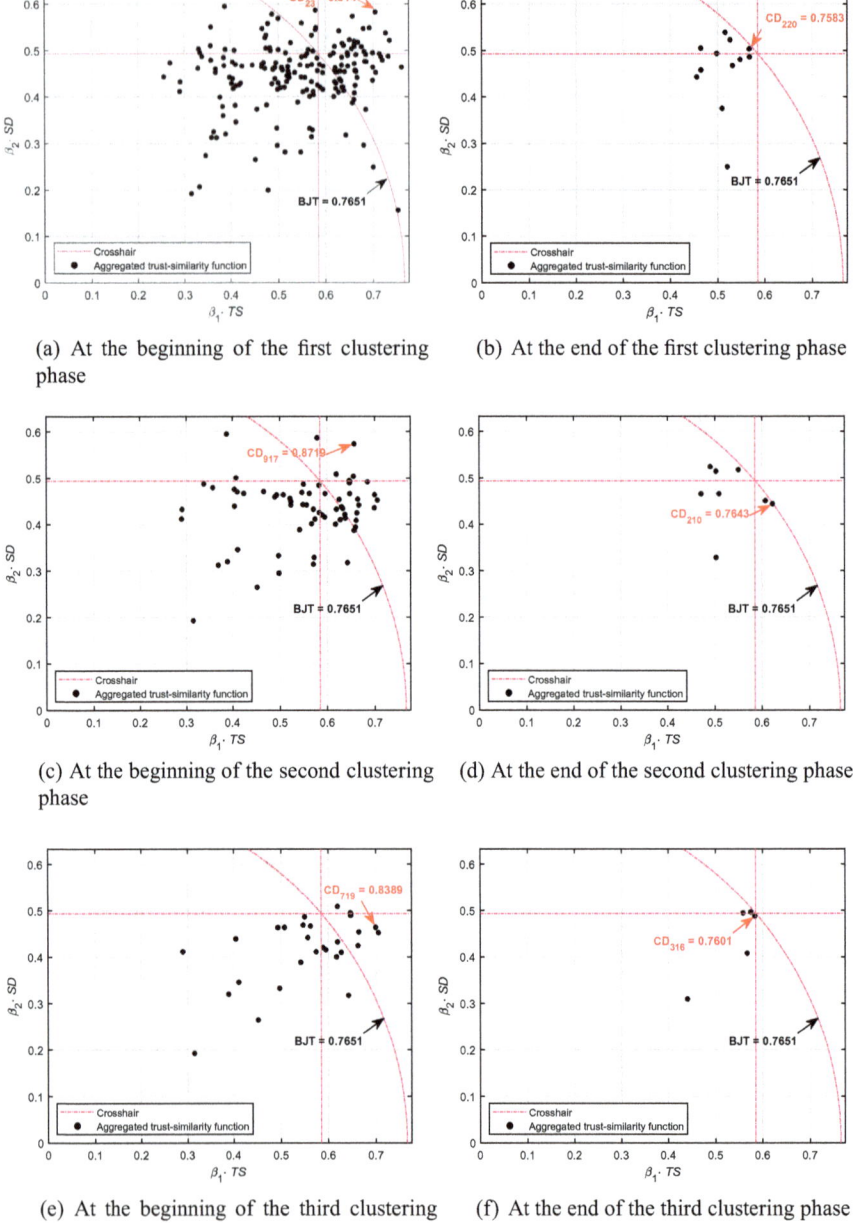

(a) At the beginning of the first clustering phase

(b) At the end of the first clustering phase

(c) At the beginning of the second clustering phase

(d) At the end of the second clustering phase

(e) At the beginning of the third clustering phase

(f) At the end of the third clustering phase

Fig. 3.7 Visualization of the clustering process in the first three clustering phases

(1) The beginning of the first clustering phase. The trust-similarity functions of all DMs are mapped to the TSA plot (see Fig. 3.7a). Since the aggregated trust-similarity matrix is a symmetric matrix, only the elements in the upper triangular region (excluding the main diagonal) are listed (the total number of dots is $(20 * 19)/2 = 190$). The maximum closeness degree is marked, i.e., $CD_{23} = 0.914$. As $CD_{23} > BJT$, the DMs e_2 and e_3 are assigned to the same cluster (denoted by C_1).

(2) The end of the first clustering phase. Figure 3.7b presents the trust-similarity functions between cluster and the remaining DMs. Because the maximum closeness degree is smaller than the basic joint threshold, i.e., $CD_{120} = 0.7583 < BJT$, the first clustering phase ends.

(3) The beginning of the second clustering phase. Figure 3.7c presents the trust-similarity functions of the remaining DMs. The number of dots in the TSA plot decreases to $(12 * 11)/2 = 66$. The maximum closeness degree is marked, i.e., $CD_{917} = 0.8719$. As $CD_{917} > JT$, the DMs e_9 and e_{17} are assigned to the same cluster (denoted by C_2).

The remaining clustering process will execute the above loop until the final remaining dots are located in the lower left area of joint threshold arc.

3.5 Further Analysis of the TSA-Based Clustering Method

In this section, in order to demonstrate the characteristics of the proposed method and provide the guidance for practical application, the analysis will be implemented through the following aspects: calculation of the joint threshold and simulation in different situations.

3.5.1 Calculation of the Joint Threshold

A basic joint threshold involves four parameters, including the threshold of trust score $\overline{TS}$, the threshold of similarity degree $\overline{SD}$, and importance weights of the above two β_1^2, β_2^2. Clearly, $\overline{TS}$, $\overline{SD}$, β_1^2, β_2^2. The threshold $\overline{TS}$ is used to determine whether the trust score between two DMs is sufficiently high. If the aggregated trust score is greater than $\overline{TS}$, it indicates that the related DMs can be assigned to the same cluster in terms of the trust relationship. Likewise, the threshold $\overline{SD}$ measures whether the opinions of two DMs are similar enough. If the similarity degree is larger than $\overline{SD}$, it means that the DMs can be grouped into the same cluster in terms of opinion similarity. These two parameters $\overline{TS}$ and $\overline{SD}$ play a central role in the calculation of the joint threshold; as such, they are called "core parameters". The other two parameters, called "auxiliary parameters", are used to adjust the importance of the core parameters. Hence, the core parameters should be quantified first.

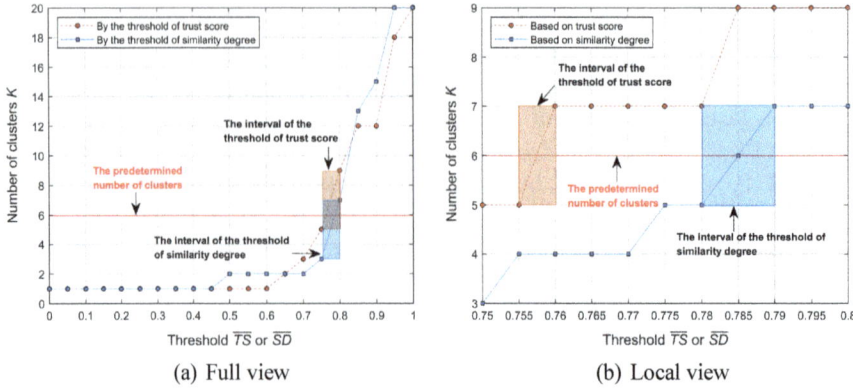

Fig. 3.8 Simulation results of the number of clusters using trust score and similarity degree, respectively

Take Algorithm 3.1 to implement the clustering operation. The simulation results regarding the number of clusters by using trust score and similarity degree are obtained, respectively (see Fig. 3.8). Note that the clustering here adopts only the threshold of trust score or the threshold of similarity degree and does not involve the association between them. Let $\overline{TS}$ (or $\overline{SD}$) increase from 0 to 1 with a step size of 0.1, and observe the change of the number of clusters. Suppose the value of K is preset to $K = INF(20/3) = 6$. Typically, the larger clustering threshold, the greater the number of clusters, even up to the total number of DMs. From Fig. 3.8a, if the number of clusters is fixed at 6, we can set $\overline{TS} \in [0.75, 0.8]$ and $\overline{SD} \in [0.75, 0.8]$. By further refining the above interval, Fig. 3.8b shows the change in the number of clusters when $\overline{TS}$ (or $\overline{SD}$) increases from 0.75 to 0.8 with a step length of 0.05. We can narrow the ranges to $\overline{TS} \in [0.755, 0.76]$ and $\overline{SD} \in [0.78, 0.79]$. Since the joint threshold is usually more severe than the single threshold, the=0.755 core parameters can eventually be set as $\overline{TS}$ and $\overline{SD} = 0.78$ (namely, selecting the left endpoint values of two intervals).

Based on the above obtained core parameters, the next thing is to calculate the auxiliary parameters. When the value of β_1^2 changes, the basic joint threshold will change; furthermore, the results of the number of clusters will be different. Let β_1^2 increase from 0 to 1 with a step size of 0.1, and observe the change in the number of clusters using different categories of joint thresholds (see Fig. 3.9).

Here, the basic JT is used as an example to illustrate how to calculate auxiliary parameters. The following steps are involved.

Step 1:   Set the initial conditions: $\overline{TS} = 0.755$, $\overline{SD} = 0.78$, $K = 6$.

Step 2:   Preliminarily determine the value range of β_1^2. As shown in Fig. 3.9, to ensure that the number of clusters is 6, the value of β_1^2 should be belong to the interval $[0.1, 0.6]$.

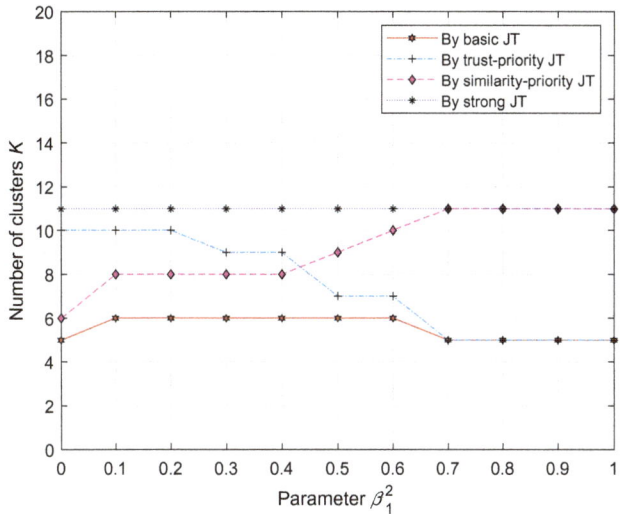

Fig. 3.9 Simulation results of the number of clusters using different categories of JTs

Step 3: Prioritize opinion similarity and trust relationship. The DMs consider the trust relationship to be more important than the opinion similarity in clustering, i.e., $\beta_1^2 > \beta_2^2$. Since $\beta_1^2 + \beta_2^2 = 1$, it is appropriate to set $\beta_1^2 \in (0.5, 0.6]$.

Step 4: Based on the above membership interval, the DMs determine the accurate value of β_1^2 through discussion, such as setting $\beta_1^2 = 0.6$.

Section 3.5.3 will analyze how to assign the importance of trust score and similarity degree in the clustering in terms of different decision situations. Moreover, the following observations can be made from Fig. 3.9.

(1) Let the auxiliary coefficient β_1^2 be fixed. Different types of JTs may produce different numbers of clusters. As shown in Fig. 3.9, for $\beta_1^2 = 0.3$, if using strong JT, the number of clusters is 11; if using trust-priority JT, the number drops to 9. This is because different categories of JTs have different clustering constraints. The more stringent the clustering constraints, the more likely to produce a greater number of clusters. Given two DMs e_l and e_h. If using the basic JT, the DMs can be grouped into a cluster as long as the condition $CD_{lh} \geq \sqrt{\beta_1^2 \cdot \overline{TS}^2 + \beta_2^2 \cdot \overline{SD}^2}$ is true. Yet, the trust-priority JT requires the following two conditions to be true simultaneously: $CD_{lh} \geq \sqrt{\beta_1^2 \cdot \overline{TS}^2 + \beta_2^2 \cdot \overline{SD}^2}$ and $TS_{lh} \geq \overline{TS}$.

(2) When β_1^2 increases from 0 to 1, the change trajectories of the clustering number generated by different types of JTs are different. Adopting the strong JT will always produce the maximum number of clusters, while the basic JT will result in the minimum number of clusters. If using the trust-priority JT, the number will reduce from 10 to 5, as β_1^2 increases from 0 to 1. Using the similarity-priority

JT causes the number of clusters to continuously increase from 6 to 11. All of the above differences arise for the following two reasons: (i) As previously mentioned, different categories of JTs have different clustering constraints; (ii) The calculation of JT is influenced by several parameters, including the thresholds of trust score and similarity degree, and two auxiliary parameters. When β_1^2 increases from 0 to 1, the closeness degree may be either greater than or less than the value of basic joint threshold. This change is reflected in the fact that the number of clusters may fluctuate with the change of β_1^2. Furthermore, due to the different clustering constraints, different types of JTs produce different trajectories of the number of clusters.

The above observations bring some useful enlightenments to the determination of the JT. The DMs should first determine which type of JT to use for clustering. According to the simulation results of the number of clusters shown in Fig. 3.9, the membership interval of auxiliary coefficient β_1^2 can be obtained. Sometimes there may be more than one membership interval that meets the requirement. In this case, the final membership interval can be obtained by determining the relative importance of trust score and similarity degree.

3.5.2 Simulation with Different Methods for Calculating the Crosshair Placement

Section 3.2.3 has presented three methods for determining the crosshair placement (i.e., the scale-centered method, the data-centered method, and the method based on clustering simulation). Figure 3.6 shows the crosshair distributions using the above methods. The scale-centered method is the easiest to calculate because it chooses the midpoint of the scale as the threshold. However, the irregularity of the data may cause the values of trust scores and similarity degrees between the DMs to be higher than the midpoint, and the majority of trust-similarity functions may be classified into the Q1 area. As shown in Fig. 3.6, most of the dots are placed in Q1 if the scale-centered method is adopted. The data-centered method uses the means of trust score and similarity degree to calculate the crosshair, which also faces the problem of uneven distributions caused by irregular data. The third method performs clustering analysis on decision information based on the single measurement attribute. According to the specific clustering purpose, the value range of the crosshair can be obtained. The method based on clustering simulation has the highest ability of data identification, but the exact value of the crosshair still needs to be determined subjectively by the DMs. Table 3.4 presents the clustering results using the basic JT when different methods are used to calculate the crosshair placement. The following observations and discussions can be provided.

(1) First, there are significant differences in the number of clusters. When using the method based on clustering simulation, six clusters are obtained. The scale-centered method allows all DMs to be assigned to the same cluster. This occurs

Table 3.4 Clustering results using the basic JT when different methods are adopted to calculate the crosshair placement

	Scale-centered method	Data-centered method	Method based on clustering simulation
Basic joint threshold	0.5	0.682	0.7651
Clustering structure	$\{e_2, e_3, e_8, e_{12}, e_5, e_{18},$ $e_1, e_{20}, e_{17}, e_{13}, e_9, e_7,$ $e_6, e_{16}, e_{15}, e_{19}, e_{10},$ $e_{14}, e_{11}\}$	$\{e_2, e_3, e_8, e_{12}, e_5, e_{18},$ $e_1, e_{20}, e_{17}, e_{13}, e_9,$ $e_7, e_6, e_{16}, e_{15}, e_{19},$ $e_{10}, e_{14}\}, e_{11}$	$\{e_2, e_3, e_8, e_{12}, e_5,$ $e_{18}, e_1, e_4\},$ $\{e_9, e_{17}, e_{15}, e_{20}\},$ $\{e_7, e_{19}, e_{14}\},$ $\{e_6, e_{16}\}, \{e_{10}, e_{13}\},$ $\{e_{11}\}$

Note Set $\beta_1^2 = 0.6$, $\beta_2^2 = 0.4$.

because of the irregularity of the decision data; the basic joint threshold obtained by the scale-based method is 0.5, which is less than the closeness degrees of all DMs.

(2) Since in Algorithm 3.1, a new cluster is formed by selecting the DMs corresponding to the maximum closeness degree, the ordinal number of each DM assigned to a certain cluster may differ. If the data-centered method is used, DM e_9 is the 11th to be pulled into a cluster, whereas if the method based on clustering simulation is adopted, its serial number is the 9th.

(3) There is a substantial difference in the internal structure of the cluster. If the scale-centered method is used, DM e_7 and DM e_8 can be assigned to the same cluster. If the method based on clustering simulation is used, these DMs belong to different clusters.

All the differences observed above are due to the fact that different methods of calculating the crosshairs will result in different basic joint thresholds. The method based on clustering simulation is recommended, especially for irregular decision data, because it establishes a direct relationship between the crosshair and the subsequent clustering processes.

This chapter presents four categories of JTs: the basic JT, the trust-priority JT, the similarity-priority JT, and the strong JT. Following the settings in Sect. 3.5.2, such that $\overline{TS} = 0.755$, $\overline{SD} = 0.78$, $\beta_1^2 = 0.6$ and $\beta_2^2 = 0.4$, Table 3.5 shows the clustering results using different types of JTs. The differences are reflected in the number of clusters and the members within each cluster. As the threshold with the weakest constraint, the basic JT produces the minimum number of clusters (i.e., 6). Using the strong JT, the number of clusters will increase to 11. This is because the basic JT only considers the fusion of the thresholds of trust score and similarity degree, not any of them alone. Since the trust-priority JT and similarity-priority JT have different emphases on trust relationship and opinion similarity, they may lead to different clustering results. As shown in Table 3.5, if using the trust-priority JT, DM e_1 and DM e_{13} are assigned to the same cluster, while these DMs are assigned to different clusters under the similarity-priority JT.

Table 3.5 Clustering results using different categories of joint thresholds

	By basic JT	By trust-priority JT	By similarity-priority JT
Number of clusters	6	7	10
Clustering structure	$\{e_2, e_3, e_8, e_{12}, e_5, e_{18}, e_1, e_4\}$, $\{e_9, e_{17}, e_{15}, e_{20}\}$, $\{e_7, e_{19}, e_{14}\}$, $\{e_6, e_{16}\}$, $\{e_{10}, e_{13}\}$, $\{e_{11}\}$	$\{e_2, e_3, e_8, e_{12}, e_5, e_{18}\}$, $\{e_1, e_{13}, e_6, e_7, e_{16}\}$, $\{e_9, e_{17}, e_{15}, e_{20}\}$, $\{e_{10}, e_{14}\}$, $\{e_4\}$, $\{e_{11}\}$, $\{e_{19}\}$	$\{e_2, e_3, e_8, e_{12}, e_5, e_{18}\}$, $\{e_1, e_4\}$, $\{e_9, e_{17}\}$, $\{e_{16}, e_{20}\}$, $\{e_6, e_{10}\}$, $\{e_7\}$, $\{e_{11}\}$, $\{e_{13}\}$, $\{e_{14}\}$, $\{e_{15}\}$, $\{e_{19}\}$

Note Set $\overline{TS} = 0.755$, $\overline{SD} = 0.78$, $\beta_1^2 = 0.6$, $\beta_2^2 = 0.4$.

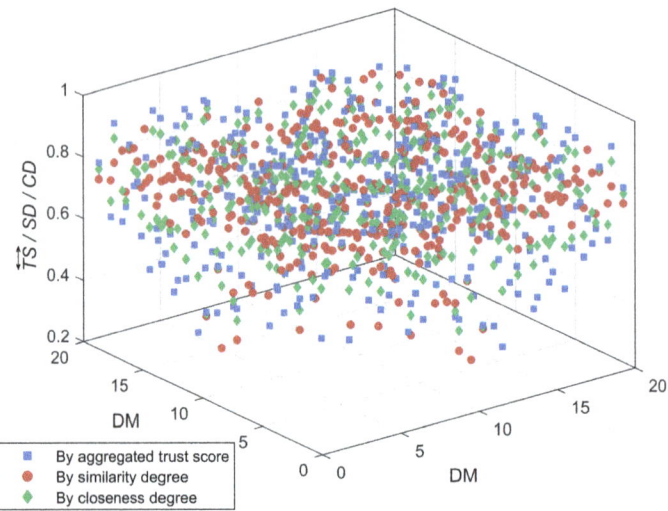

Fig. 3.10 Distribution of measurement results using different measurement attributes

3.5.3 Simulation with Different Measurement Attributes

The trust score measures the trust relationships between DMs, while the similarity degree calculates the differences between individual opinions. Because these measurement attributes focus on different objects, the clustering results obtained by using them will be different. The distributions of data using different measurement attributes are elaborated upon in Fig. 3.10. It can be intuitively seen that the distributions obtained by three different measurement attributes are almost completely different, which can result in different clustering results, as shown in Table 3.6. It is worth noting that no matter which measurement attribute is adopted, there may always be two DMs who are drawn into the same cluster from beginning to end. (e.g., e_2 and e_3). This is the best case for promoting opinion-gathering and consensus-building. If two DMs have a high trust score and if their opinions are significantly similar, they are considered easy to consolidate into a unified opinion. In fact, the trust-similarity function corresponding to the DMs belongs to the 'ideal area' (namely Q1).

Table 3.6 Clustering results using different measurement attributes

Clustering method	Based on similarity degree	Based on trust score	Based on closeness degree
Our method	$\{e_9, e_{13}, e_{17}, e_{18}, e_1,$ $e_5, e_6, e_8, e_{18}, e_{16},$ $e_{15}, e_2, e_3, e_7, e_{12},$ $e_4, e_{20}\}, \{e_{10}\}, \{e_{14}\},$ $\{e_{11}\}, \{e_{19}\}$	$\{e_3, e_{15}, e_{20}, e_8, e_5,$ $e_2, e_{12}, e_{18}\}, \{e_1, e_{13},$ $e_6, e_7, e_{10}, e_{16}\},$ $\{e_4, e_{11}\}, \{e_{14}, e_{19}\},$ $\{e_9, e_7\}$	$\{e_2, e_3, e_8, e_{12}, e_5,$ $e_{18}, e_1, e_4\}, \{e_9, e_{17},$ $e_{15}, e_{20}\}, \{e_7, e_{19}, e_{14}\},$ $\{e_6, e_{16}\}, \{e_{10}, e_{13}\},$ $\{e_{11}\}$

Note Set $\overline{TS} = 0.755$, $\overline{SD} = 0.78$, $\beta_1^2 = 0.6$, $\beta_2^2 = 0.4$.

Table 3.7 The effects of three core issues on assigning the importance of trust score and similarity degree

	Trust score is more important	Similarity degree is more important
Involving participants' own private interests	↓	↑
Frequent interactions	↑	↑
Tight decision-making time	↑	↓

There are two main difficulties in using TSA to implement clustering: (i) how to determine the crosshair placement; and (ii) how to assign the importance of trust score and similarity degree for clustering. This chapter holds that the following three core issues need to be addressed: whether the decision problem involves the interests of participants, whether the decision process values the interaction of DMs, and whether the decision time is urgent. The effects of the issues on assigning the importance of trust score and similarity degree are presented in Table 3.7. The symbol "↑" (or "↓") indicates that the related measurement attribute should be given priority (or not be given priority).

The following viewpoints are summarized.

(1) If the decision problem involves personal interests of multiple participants, the trust relationships between DMs may hinder the formation of a group opinion. Individual interests can enhance the importance of the trust relationship in opinion convergence and induce some DMs to form an alliance. In this case, the emphasis on opinion similarity can overcome the influence of some small-interest alliances on the decision process to some extent.

(2) When faced with an LSGDM event that requires frequent interactions among DMs, the trust relationship plays an equally important role as opinion similarity. For example, multiple rounds of feedback are often necessary for complex decisions involving public interests. Similar opinions are more likely to form a decision outcome upon which the majority agrees. On the other hand, a strong trust relationship can promote the transformation of different opinions into similar or even identical ones. Moreover, the better the trust relationship is, the more the convergence of opinions will accelerate.

Table 3.8 Clustering results using different clustering methods

	K-means method	Xu and Chen's method [140]	TSA-based clustering method
Clustering structure	$\{e_9, e_{13}, e_{17}, e_{18}\}$, $\{e_2, e_7, e_{12}\}$, $\{e_3, e_8\}$, $\{e_4, e_{14}, e_{20}\}$, $\{e_1, e_5, e_{15}\}$, $\{e_6, e_{10}, e_{11}\}$, $\{e_{16}, e_{19}\}$	$\{e_1, e_2, e_3, e_4, e_5,$ $e_7, e_8, e_{12}, e_{16}, e_{17},$ $e_{18}, e_{20}\}$, $\{e_6, e_{10}\}$, $\{e_9, e_{13}\}$, $\{e_{11}\}$, $\{e_{14}\}$, $\{e_{15}\}$, $\{e_{19}\}$	$\{e_1, e_5, e_6, e_9, e_{13},$ $e_{17}, e_{18}\}$, $\{e_2, e_3, e_4, e_7, e_8,$ $e_{12}, e_{16}, e_{20}\}$, $\{e_{10}\}$, $\{e_{11}\}$, $\{e_{14}\}$, $\{e_{15}\}$, $\{e_{19}\}$

Note Set $\overline{SD} = 0.78$ for Xu and Chen's method [140] and the proposed clustering method.

(3) For a time-critical LSGDM event, the most important goal is to make decisions quickly and within a limited time. Certainly, quick decisions may not be nearly perfect, but they must be made and carried out in a timely manner, and they can be improved during implementation. In this case, the trust relationship will take precedence over opinion similarity. Because DMs can rely on trust to find the authoritative conclusions or senior expert opinions to form a common output. Multiple consensus iterations are conducive to the good performance of opinion similarity but may consume a lot of time and delay the optimal decision time.

3.6 Comparison with Other Clustering Methods

The proposed clustering method aims to realize the effective clustering of DMs in LSGDM under a social network context, which involves two measurement attributes—namely, the trust relationship and opinion similarity. In Sect. 3.6.1, we compare the proposed method with the K-means clustering method and Xu and Chen's method [140]. In Sect. 3.6.2, a comparative analysis is conducted between our method and the network partition method.

3.6.1 Comparison with the K-Means Clustering Method and Xu and Chen's Method [140]

To ensure comparability, the clustering operation in this section takes opinion similarity as the unique measurement attribute. The clustering results using different clustering methods are elaborated upon in Table 3.8. Clearly, there are differences in the number of clusters and the internal structures of the clusters.

The K-means clustering method is an iterative algorithm of unsupervised learning starting with K centers of mass. There are two main disadvantages of the K-means clustering method: the parameter selection of K, and if the similarity degree is required to reach a certain threshold, unsupervised learning may fail. As shown in

Table 3.8, DM e_{16} and DM e_{19} are assigned to the same cluster, but their similarity degree is less than 0.78, i.e., $SD_{1619} < \overline{SD}$. Although the value of K or the current center of mass can be adjusted, there is no guarantee that the similarity between DMs in each cluster meets the threshold. The TSA-based clustering method first observes the relationship between the threshold of similarity degree and the number of clusters through the clustering simulation. Only the DMs whose similarity degree is greater than the threshold can be classified into a cluster. Therefore, the proposed method can not only divide a large group into a specified number of clusters, but more importantly, it can ensure that the minimum similarity degree between DMs in each cluster is greater than the threshold.

The TSA-based clustering method extends Xu and Chen's research [140] to LSGDM events under a social network context and makes effective improvements. The biggest drawback of the latter method is that the DMs are randomly ranked at the beginning of each clustering phase. The DM whose serial number is 1 is selected as the core, and the similarities with other DMs are measured successively to determine whether they can be grouped with the first DM. In this manner, the initial order of DMs has a significant impact on the clustering result. As shown in Table 3.8, DM e_1 is set to be the core, so DM e_2 is first identified and placed in a cluster with e_1. This is because the similarity between DMs e_1 and e_2 is higher than that between any other DM and e_1. However, in fact, the similarity between DMs e_2 and e_3 is the highest. The proposed method takes the DMs with the maximum similarity degree as the core of the new cluster, which can eliminate the uncertainty caused by random ordering.

It should be noted that the above analysis is based on the premise that only the measurement attribute of opinion similarity is used for clustering, without considering the trust relationships between DMs. If two measurement attributes are considered simultaneously (e.g., trust-priority JT), the K-means clustering method and Xu and Chen's method [140] must be improved. This study has been emphasizing that the two attributes of opinion similarity and trust relationship should be given equal importance in the clustering process in LSGDM under a social network context. The proposed method can solve the clustering issue well for an LSGDM event in the context of a social network. It prompts clustering analysis from two measurement attributes and puts forward four categories of joint thresholds to meet different clustering purposes. Based on the above analysis, Table 3.9 details a comparison of the advantages and disadvantages of the three clustering methods in LSGDM under a social network context.

3.6.2 Comparison with Dong et al.'s Method [21] and Ding et al.'s Method [17]

To highlight the advantages of the proposed clustering method, a comparative analysis is conducted between our method and another technique (namely, the network partition method based on leadership presented in [17, 21]). The concept of network

Table 3.9 Comparison of the advantages and disadvantages of the three clustering methods mentioned above

Clustering method	Detailed description
K-means clustering method	**Advantage**: The convergence rate of individual opinions is fast, and K clusters are rapidly formed **Disadvantages/difficulties**: (a) The determination of the value of K (b) The choice of K initial centers of mass (c) If the DMs within the cluster are required to satisfy other measurement attributes, such as how much opinion similarity is reached, it is difficult to automatically implement. Although the value of K or the initial center of mass can be adjusted continuously, it is not guaranteed to meet the above requirements
Xu and Chen's method [140]	**Advantage**: Easy to manipulate and merely includes continuous distance-based measures **Disadvantages/difficulties**: (a) The initial order of DMs has a significant impact on the clustering result (b) The clustering operation is based on the similarity measure of individual opinions, without considering the potential social relationships among DMs (c) The determination of clustering threshold
TSA-based clustering method	**Advantage**: (a) The clustering result is not affected by the initialization of the center of mass (b) The individual opinions within the cluster can meet different measurement attribute requirements (c) Providing a method for determining the clustering threshold **Disadvantages/difficulties**: (a) Selecting the DMs with the best threshold conditions to form the initial cluster is more likely to form a local optimal (b) It is likely to produce a chain-like cluster structure. Some clusters may contain only one DM (c) High time complexity

partition aims to divide an original unrecognized social network into several subnetworks, each of which consists of at least one leader and some relevant followers. This operation is similar to the clustering, the purpose of which is to divide the original large group into several clusters. However, there are significant differences between our method and the network partition method.

(1) *Required input information*. In Dong et al.'s method [21] and Ding et al.'s method [17], a directed social network with an attached adjacency matrix and the self-confidences of all DMs are necessary inputs. The self-confidence represents the value of a DM's trust in his or her own opinion. The method in this paper needs two aspects of input information: the DMs' evaluation matrices and a directed sociomatrix (in which each element is expressed as a couple of trust/distrust values).

(2) *The basis of the clustering operation (or network partition)*. Dong et al.'s method [21] and Ding et al.'s method [17] emphasize the importance of leadership in opinion dynamics. There are two statements: (a) all DMs can form a consensus if there are opinion leaders under a social network context, and (b) the consensus opinion is a linear combination of the original opinions of all opinion leaders. The clustering operation in this paper is based on the measure of opinion similarity and trust relationship. Both of the two measurement attributes are put in the important positions in the clustering process.

(3) *The clustering process and result (or network partition process)*. In Dong et al.'s method [21] and Ding et al.'s method [17], an important task is to identify the leaders and followers according to the directed paths in a social network. Any sub-network consists of at least one leader at the core and some associated followers. Such a leader-follower structure facilitates the formation of consensus, but the DMs' opinions in the same network partition may be quite different. The main workload of the proposed clustering method is to determine which kind of joint threshold to adopt and to calculate its value. The method considers two measurement attributes at the beginning, which can make each cluster perform well with regard to trust score and opinion similarity.

Based on the above comparison results, the most significant feature and advantage of the proposed method over the network partition method can be summarized as follows: the two measurement attributes of opinion similarity and trust relationship are considered simultaneously in the clustering operation. Both the individual opinions and the trust relationships among DMs are the core elements for the LSGDM problem in a social network environment. The proposed method can obtain the ideal clustering structure, that is, the DMs within each cluster have high trust relationships and sufficiently similar opinions. The network partition method relies solely on the leadership (derived from the trust relationships among DMs) and does not examine the similarity among the DMs' opinions.

3.7 Conclusions

In this age of information overload and mobile Internet popularization, the LSGDM scenario becomes increasingly complex, which combines the characteristics of large-group participation and social networks. In this paper, a TSA-based clustering method is developed to classify large-group DMs. The major contributions of this chapter are as follows:

(1) Two measurement attributes related to clustering in LSGDM problems under a social network context are explored. The trust score is a measure of the trust relationships among DMs, while similarity degree is a measure of the differences among DMs' opinions. Both of these attributes are afforded important positions in the clustering process.

(2) Trust-similarity analysis is well defined and implemented. Firstly, the trust-similarity matrix is established by fusing trust scores and similarity degrees. Then, a two-dimensional coordinate system (namely, the TSA plot) is designed to divide the measurement attributes into four quadrants. The determination of crosshair placement and different categories of joint thresholds are analyzed.

(3) A TSA-based clustering method is developed that includes four clustering algorithms to satisfy different clustering purposes. Simulation experiments reveal the characteristics and application conditions of the method, and a visualization of the clustering process is presented.

In some real-world LSGDM events involving a huge number of DMs, many DMs may not have a direct trust relationship with each other, and they may even be unrelated. In this case, the guiding utility of two-dimensional measurement attributes for clustering will decrease. Thus, the use of TSA-based clustering methods has a certain boundary for the number of participants. Moreover, this boundary depends on the number of irrelevant relationships as a percentage of all relationships. Reducing the time complexity of the TSA-based clustering method is also an important direction of future research.

Chapter 4
Trust-Similarity Measure-Based Hierarchical Clustering Method

Abstract Group decision-making (GDM) in large-group social network environment (LGSNE) has attracted considerable attention in the field of decision science. Social relationships exist among decision-makers, and individual decisions are often influenced by others they are connected with. In this chapter, we first describe the characteristics of GDM problems in LGSNE. Two measurement attributes—trust relationship and opinion similarity—are identified as important factors throughout the decision-making process. Then, we propose a hierarchical clustering method based on the trust-similarity measure. A weight-determining method for clusters is presented that considers the internal and external features of a cluster.

Keywords Large-group social network environment (LGSNE) · Trust-similarity measure · Hierarchical clustering · Weight-determining method · Group decision-making (GDM) · Social network analysis (SNA)

4.1 Introduction

By combining social networks with large-scale group decision-making (LSGDM), a new decision-making scenario is established, called GDM in large-group social network environment (LGSNE). It is summarized as having the following three characteristics [18, 38, 144, 154]:

- The group involves a large number of decision-makers (DMs) (i.e., no fewer than 20).
- Opinion differences exist, and achieving a high-consensus solution usually necessitates the implementation of a consensus-reaching process (CRP).
- There are social relationships among DMs that affect consensus convergence.

Table 4.1 summarizes the literature on GDM problems. Regarding the research on clustering, we find that traditional clustering methods are typically based on similarities among DMs' opinions [28, 38, 65, 144]. However, this classification fails to examine the trust relationships among DMs. If two DMs without a good trust relationship are assigned to a subgroup, it might not be conducive to consensus. Therefore, trust relationships should be taken into account in the clustering of GDM

Table 4.1 Summary of articles on GDM problems

Article	Year of publication	Involves large-scale DMs	Involves LGSNE	Clustering based on opinion similarity	Considers trust relationships in clustering
Palomares et al. [84]	2014	Yes	No	Yes	No
Xu et al. [147]	2015	Yes	No	Yes	No
Wu and Liu [128]	2016	Yes	No	Yes	No
Dong et al. [26]	2016	No	No	–	–
Rodríguez et al. [99]	2018	Yes	No	Yes	No
Wu and Xu [131]	2018	Yes	No	Yes	No
Wu et al. [127]	2018	Yes	Yes	No	Yes
Gou et al. [38]	2018	Yes	No	Yes	No
Shi et al. [102]	2018	Yes	No	Yes	No
Zhang et al. [167]	2018	Yes	No	Yes	No
Liu et al. [69]	2019	Yes	No	Yes	No
Wu et al. [133]	2019	Yes	Yes	No	Yes
Tang et al. [110]	2020	Yes	No	Yes	No
Zhong and Xu [184]	2020	Yes	No	Yes	No
This chapter	–	**Yes**	**Yes**	**Yes**	**Yes**

events in LGSNE. The clustering of nodes in a social network is called community detection or network partition [16, 133]. Wu et al. [127] and Tian et al. [111] focused on community detection and made full use of the trust relationships among DMs. Dong et al. [21] and Wu et al. [133] designed network partition algorithms based on leadership. It should be emphasized that opinion similarity is also important for clustering, as seen in the traditional clustering methods. Hence, we hold that opinion similarity and trust relationship are both important for the clustering of GDM problems in LGSNE.

Based on the above analysis, we can identify the following issues that need to be further addressed:

(1) Few studies have used trust relationship and opinion similarity as measurement attributes to guide the clustering process. Most clustering methods are based entirely on either trust relationship [111, 133] or on opinion similarity [84, 144]. We hold that both measurement attributes should be taken into account in clustering. Opinion similarity is used to measure the difference among DMs' opinions whereas trust relationship represents the level of trust among DMs.

(2) Most studies have simply used the number of DMs in a cluster as the standard to calculate the weights of clusters [74, 97, 144]. Other important internal and external structural characteristics of a cluster, such as inter-cluster consensus level and intra-cluster structure, are not considered. Therefore, we need to develop a weight-determining method involving consensus levels and trust scores within and outside a cluster.

The contributions of this chapter are summarized as follows:

(1) We analyze the characteristics of GDM problems in LGSNE. Two measurement attributes are determined: trust relationship and opinion similarity. Both attributes are considered important in the decision-making process.
(2) A trust-similarity matrix is obtained by integrating a similarity matrix and a sociomatrix. The condition where two DMs are divided into a subgroup in terms of trust relationship is analyzed. The concept of an undirected trust-similarity matrix is defined as the basis for clustering.
(3) A trust-similarity measure-based hierarchical clustering method is proposed that takes into account four categories of clustering constraints. The visualization of clustering process is presented. The internal and external characteristics of a cluster are analyzed, and a weight-determining method for clusters is developed.

4.2 Problem Configuration and Decision Information Preprocessing

For a GDM problem in LGSNE, DMs within a network are required to evaluate alternatives with attributes to obtain a high-consensus outcome. Formally, the main elements found in any GDM scenario in LGSNE are set as follows:

(1) Let $E = \{e_1, e_2, \ldots, e_q\}$ be a DM set. Usually, if the number of DMs exceeds 20, the group can be regarded as a large group [18, 38]. Let $w = (w_1, w_2, \ldots, w_q)^T$ bet the weight of DMs such that $w_l \geq 0 (1, 2, \ldots, q)$ and $\sum_{l=1}^{q} w_l = 1$.
(2) Let $X = \{x_1, x_2, \ldots, x_m\}$ and $A = \{a_1, a_2, \ldots, a_n\}$ be the set of alternatives and the set of attributes, respectively. Let $\omega = (\omega_1, \omega_2, \ldots, \omega_n)^T$ be the weight vector of attributes such that $\omega_j \geq 0$ ($j = 1, 2, \ldots, n$) and $\sum_{j=1}^{n} \omega_j = 1$.
(3) DMs are required to provide decision information in two aspects: individual trust functions about other DMs and individual opinions. Let the individual opinion be $V_l = (v_{l,ij})_{m \times n}$, where $v_{l,ij}$ is a crisp number, representing the evaluation of DM e_l on alternative $x_i \in X$ with respect to attribute $a_j \in A$. By using the concept of trust score to simplify the trust function, a sociomatrix is obtained as $TM = (TS_{lh})_{q \times q}$, such that $l \neq h, l, h = 1, 2, \ldots, q$, where TS_{lh} represents the trust score from DM e_l to DM e_h.

In general, GDM problems have benefit attributes and cost attributes. To unify the dimensions of all attributes, individual opinion $V_l = (v_{l,ij})_{m \times n}$ should be normalized into the standardized opinion $R_l = (r_{l,ij})_{m \times n}$, where [136]:

$\frac{x_{l,ij} - min_i\{v_{l,ij}\}}{max_i\{v_{l,ij}\} - min_i\{v_{l,ij}\}}$, for benefit attribute a_j, $i = 1, 2, \ldots, m, j = 1, 2, \ldots, n, l = 1, 2, \ldots, q$, and

$\frac{max_i\{v_{l,ij}\} - x_{l,ij}}{max_i\{v_{l,ij}\} - min_i\{v_{l,ij}\}}$, for cost attribute a_j, $i = 1, 2, \ldots, m, j = 1, 2, \ldots, n$, $l = 1, 2, \ldots, q$.

Similarity measure is one basis for the clustering operation. If two DMs' opinions are sufficiently similar, they can be assigned to a subgroup. A similarity matrix is denoted as $SM = (SD_{lh})_{q \times q}$, such that $l \neq h$, $l, h = 1, 2, \ldots, q$, where SD_{lh} represents the similarity degree between R_l and R_h, such as [136]

$$SD_{lh} = 1 - \frac{1}{m \times n} \sum_{i=1}^{m} \sum_{j=1}^{n} |r_{l,ij} - r_{h,ij}|. \tag{4.1}$$

Clearly, $SD_{lh} = SD_{hl}$, $0 \leq SD_{lh} \leq 1$, $l \neq h$, $l, h = 1, 2, \ldots, q$.

Definition 4.1 (Trust-Similarity Score, TSS) Given trust score TS_{lh} and similarity degree SD_{lh}, the trust-similarity score from e_l to e_h can be defined as:

$$TSS_{lh} = \alpha \cdot TS_{lh} + (1 - \alpha) \cdot SD_{lh}, \tag{4.2}$$

where $\alpha \in [0, 1]$ is the weight parameter. Therefore, the trust-similarity matrix can be obtained as $TSM = ((TS_{lh}, SD_{lh}))_{q \times q}$. For simplicity, the matrix is written as $TSM = (TSS_{lh})_{q \times q}$.

Remark 4.1 As discussed in Sect. 2.2, there are three types of relationships among DMs in a social network. An indirect relationship can be quantified through trust propagation [124]. However, for an irrelevant relationship, trust propagation fails. In this case, we use the trust aggregation operator [123] to calculate the average of the trust functions corresponding to all of the existing direct relationships. This average value can be used as the measure of the irrelevant relation.

It should be pointed out that the trust scores mentioned above are directional. That is, the values of TS_{lh} and TS_{hl} are not necessarily equal. For example, DM e_l trusts DM eh very much, but DM e_h does not trust DM e_l as much. This raises the question of whether these two DMs can be assigned to a subgroup. From the perspective of DM e_l, the answer is yes, but for DM e_h, the answer may be the opposite. Since DM e_h distrusts DM e_l, he/she is reluctant to allow the opinion of DM e_l to be reflected in the collective opinion. We hold that only when two DMs trust each other enough can they be grouped together. Thus, we define the adjusted sociomatrix.

Definition 4.2 Given a directed sociomatrix $TM = (TS_{lh})_{q \times q}$, the adjusted socioma-trix is denoted as $ATM = (ATS_{lh})_{q \times q}$, where

$$ATS_{lh} = min\{TS_{lh}, TS_{hl}\}, l \neq h, h = 1, 2, \ldots, q \tag{4.3}$$

Clearly, $ATS_{lh} = ATS_{hl}$. Equation (4.2) transforms a directed sociomatrix into an undirected one. In the following, we refer to the sociomatrix adjusted by Eq. (4.2) as the undirected sociomatrix. Eventually, an undirected trust-similarity matrix is obtained as $UTSM = ((ATS_{lh}, SD_{lh}))_{q \times q}$, which can also be written as $UTSM = (UTSS_{lh})_{q \times q}$ for simplicity. $UTSS_{lh}$ is the undirected trust-similarity score computed by

$$TSS_{lh} = \alpha \cdot ATS_{lh} + (1 - \alpha) \cdot SD_{lh}, \tag{4.4}$$

where α is already presented in Definition 4.1.

Remark 4.2 The directed sociomatrix is usually used to calculate the weights of DMs, while the undirected sociomatrix is used as a constraint to guide the clustering.

4.3 Agglomerate Hierarchical Clustering Method with Given Constraints

Clustering is widely used to analyze and manage large-scale DMs. By dividing a large group into several small subgroups, a hierarchical structure is generated. Agglomerate hierarchical clustering is a bottom-up clustering operation that initially treats each data sample as a cluster. By calculating the distance between each pair of clusters, the clusters that satisfy the given constraints are continuously identified. Here, we first use the undirected trust-similarity score as the measurement standard. The minimum undirected trust-similarity score between DMs belonging to the two different clusters is defined as the undirected trust-similarity score between these clusters. In this way, we can ensure that the undirected trust-similarity score between any pair of DMs within the fused cluster satisfies the measurement standard.

Definition 4.3 Given two clusters C_k and C_g, the undirected trust-similarity score between them can be calculated by

$$UTSS_{kg} = min\{UTSS_{lh} | e_l \in C_k, e_h \in C_g, l = 1, \ldots, n_k, j = 1, \ldots, n_g\} \tag{4.5}$$

where n_k and n_g are the number of DMs in clusters C_k and C_g, respectively.

Analogously, the undirected trust score and similarity degree between clusters C_k and C_g can be obtained as $ATS_{kg} = min\{ATS_{lh}\}$ and $SD_{kg} = min\{SD_{lh}\}$, respectively. We hold that trust score and similarity degree are both crucial measurement attributes for GDM events in LGSNE. Therefore, three constraints on clustering are concluded-trust-similarity threshold $\overline{TSS}$, trust threshold $\overline{TS}$, and similarity threshold $\overline{SD}$, such that $0 \le \overline{TS}, \overline{SD}, \overline{TSS} \le 1$. Since trust relationship and opinion similarity should be considered in the clustering process, the trust-similarity threshold is regarded as the most basic constraint. Through the permutation and combination of the other two constraints and the basic constraint, four types of clustering constraints are obtained (see Table 4.2).

In the following, we add the four types of clustering constraints to the agglomerate hierarchical clustering method to achieve different clustering purposes.

Table 4.2 Four types of constraints on clustering for GDM problems in LGSNE

Constraint type	Description	Mathematical expression
Type A	Trust-similarity score only	$1^{st} : \overline{TSS}$
Type B	Trust priority	$1^{st} : \overline{TSS}; 2^{nd} : \overline{TS}$
Type C	Similarity priority	$1^{st} : \overline{TSS}; 2^{nd} : \overline{SD}$
Type D	No bias between trust relationship and opinion similarity	$1^{st} : \overline{TSS}; 2^{nd} : \overline{TS}$ and $\overline{SD}$

4.3.1 Only the Constraint of the Trust-Similarity Score (Type A)

The trust-similarity threshold is the basic clustering constraint. This is because it only considers the combination of trust score and similarity degree, and does not involve each single measurement attribute. Therefore, the distance measure in traditional hierarchical clustering methods can be transformed into the measure of the trust-similarity score. Algorithm 4.1 presents the hierarchical clustering method with the constraint of the trust-similarity score.

Algorithm 4.1 Hierarchical clustering method with the constraint of the trust-similarity score

---

Input: Undirected trust-similarity matrix $UTSM$ and clustering constraint $\overline{TSS}$.

Output: Clusters $C_1, \ldots, C_K$.

1: Treat each DM as a cluster, and thus generate u initial clusters.

2: Select the maximum UTSS, denoted as $UTSS_{k^*g^*}$. If $UTSS_{k^*g^*} \geq \overline{TSS}$, then merge C_{k^*} and C_{g^*} to form a new cluster. Otherwise, proceed to Step 5.

3: Add the new cluster obtained in Step 2, delete clusters C_{k^*} and C_{g^*}, and recalculate the UTSS between each pair of clusters using Eq. (4.5).

4: Repeat Steps 2 and 3 until all UTSSs are less than the constraint (i.e., $UTSS_{kg} < \overline{TSS}$ for any C_k, C_g, or until the current number of clusters is equal to $INT(q/3)$.

5: Output the clusters $C_1, \ldots, C_K$.

Remark 4.3 $INT(q/3)$ is the bracket function of q divided by 3. Song and Yang [106] suggested that two to five DMs tend to form a unified opinion. Without loss of generality, we set this number to 3. Thus, the designated number of clusters is set as $K = INT(q/3)$. If the current number of clusters is smaller than $INT(q/3)$, it indicates that the merger is excessive.

4.3.2 Trust Priority or Similarity Priority Constraint (Type B or Type C)

Introducing the trust priority (or similarity priority) is intended to make clustering more focused on the single measurement attribute. Trust priority means the clustering involves two constraints: trust-similarity threshold $\overline{TSS}$ and trust threshold $\overline{TS}$. Analogously, similarity priority contains trust-similarity threshold TSS and similarity threshold $\overline{SD}$. The procedure for the hierarchical clustering method with the constraint of trust priority is shown in Algorithm 4.2. Note that when the similarity priority constraint is used, the clustering algorithm is semblable. All we need to do, then, is replace the trust score in Algorithm 4.2 with the similarity degree.

Algorithm 4.2 Hierarchical clustering method with trust priority constraint

Input: Undirected trust-similarity matrix $UTSM$ and clustering constraint $\overline{TSS}, \overline{TS}$.
Output: Clusters $C_1, \ldots, C_K$.
1: Regard each DM as a cluster, and thus generate q initial clusters.
2: Rank the trust-similarity scores in descending order.
3: Select the first-largest UTSS, denoted as $UTSS_{k^*g^*}$. If $UTSS_{k^*g^*} \geq \overline{TSS}$ and $ATS_{k^*g^*} \geq \overline{TS}$, then merge C_{k^*} and C_{g^*} to form a new cluster and proceed to Step 4. If $UTSS_{k^*g^*} \geq \overline{TSS}$ and $ATS_{k^*g^*} < \overline{TS}$, then select the remaining TSSs in order and repeat the comparison of ATS. If no UTSS is greater than $\overline{TSS}$, proceed to Step 6.
4: Add the new cluster obtained in Step 3, delete clusters C_{k^*} and C_{g^*}, and recalculate the UTSS and ATS between each pair of clusters.
5: Repeat Steps 2–4 until at least one of $UTSS_{kg} < \overline{TSS}$ and $ATS_{kh} < \overline{TS}$ for any C_k, C_g is true or the current number of clusters is $INT(q/3)$.
6: Output the clusters $C_1, \ldots, C_K$.

4.3.3 Constraint with No Bias Between Trust Relationship and Opinion Similarity (Type D)

No bias between trust relationship and opinion similarity is the strictest constraint. This not only takes into account the aggregation of trust score and similarity degree, but also extracts each as a separate threshold. Type D has one more constraint than Type B. We need to modify the input and Steps 3–5 in Algorithm 4.2 to obtain the procedure for the hierarchical clustering method with an unbiased constraint on trust and similarity.

(1) Add similarity threshold $\overline{SD}$ to the input.
(2) Let Steps 1, 2, and 6 be the same as in Algorithm 4.2.
(3) Let Step 3^D replace Step 3 in Algorithm 4.2.
    Step 3^D: Select the first-largest $UTSS$, denoted as $UTSS_{k^*g^*}$. If $UTSS_{k^*g^*} \geq \overline{TSS}$, $ATS_{k^*g^*} \geq \overline{TS}$ and $SD_{k^*g^*} \geq \overline{TSS}$, but $ATS_{k^*g^*} \geq \overline{SD}$, merge C_{k^*} and

C_{g^*} to form a new cluster and then proceed to Step 4^D. If $UTSS_{k^*g^*} < \overline{TS}$ or $SD_{k^*g^*} < \overline{SD}$, then select the remaining UTSSs in order and repeat the comparison of ATS and SD. If no UTSS is greater than $\overline{TSS}$, then proceed to Step 6.

(4) Let Step 4^D replace Step 4 in Algorithm 4.2.

Step 4^D: Add the new cluster obtained in Step 3^D, delete clusters C_{k^*} and C_{g^*}, and recalculate the UTSS, ATS, and SD between each pair of clusters.

(5) Let Step 5^D replace Step 5 in Algorithm 4.2.

Step 5^D: Repeat Steps 2, 3^D, and 4^D until at least one of $UTSS_{kg} < \overline{TSS}$, $ATS_{kg} < \overline{TS}$ and $SD_{kg} \geq \overline{SD}$ for any C_k true or the current number of clusters is $INT(q/3)$.

Different clustering algorithms will lead to different time complexities. When Type-A constraint is adopted, the key clustering steps are as follows: (1) Calculate the trust-similarity score between each pair of clusters, find the two clusters with the largest trust-similarity score, and then merge them into a new cluster. (2) Recalculate the trust-similarity score between the newly generated cluster and each of the other clusters. We can know that the cost of the former step is $O(q^2)$, and the cost of the latter is $O(q)$. Therefore, the overall time complexity is $O(q^3)$. If Type B is used (i.e., adding another constraint TS), we need to traverse the trust scores after calculating the trust-similarity scores between the clusters. This step takes $O(q)$ of time. To summarize, the time complexity is $O(q^4)$ under Type B. Similarly, Type C has the same time complexity as Type B. Since Type D adds another constraint to Type B, this results in the time complexity of $O(q^5)$ that even with the constraint of Type A, the time complexity of the clustering method is high. Therefore, the proposed clustering method is more suitable for processing data samples that are not particularly large.

4.4   Visualization of Clustering Process

The proposed clustering method establishes a hierarchical nested clustering tree by calculating the trust-similarity scores among clusters. The original clusters are the lowest layer of the tree, and the top layer is the root node of a certain cluster. Fig. 4.1 shows the clustering tree using Type-A constraint based on the data in Sect. 4.6.

The main contribution of the proposed clustering method is that it summarizes four types of clustering constraints related to GDM problems in LGSNE and applies them as measurement attributes to the hierarchical clustering method. Type A is regarded as the basic clustering constraint, which contains only the constraint of the trust-similarity score. To achieve different purposes, three other types of constraints are proposed. The clustering tree provides a visual representation of the clustering process (answering where to start and where to end). More importantly, the effect of changes in clustering constraints on the number of clusters and the internal structures of clusters can be illustrated visually.

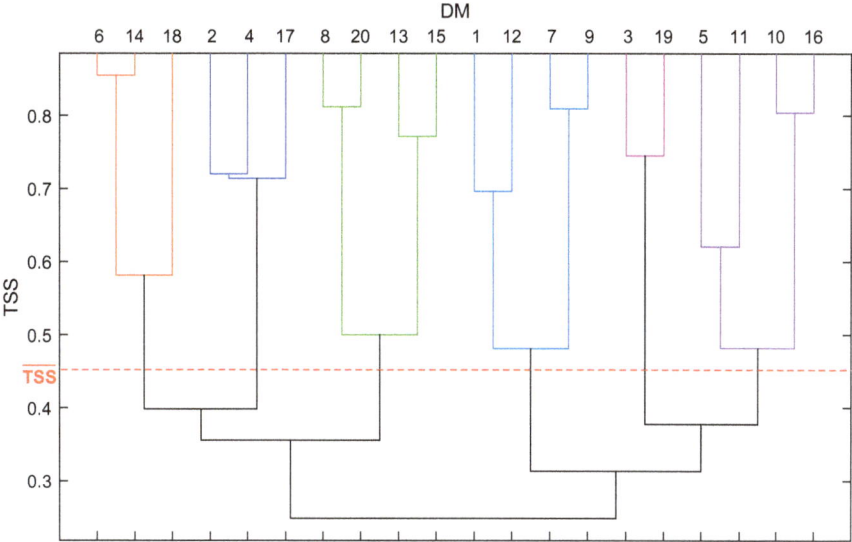

Fig. 4.1 Visualization of the clustering process using Type-A constraint

Table 4.3 Four factors related to the weight assignment for clusters

Factor	Description
Intra-cluster consensus level	Average consensus level of DMs' opinions within a cluster
Intra-cluster trust score	Average trust score of DMs within a cluster
Inter-cluster consensus level	Consensus level between one cluster's opinion and other clusters' opinions within a large group
Inter-cluster trust score	Average trust score of a cluster from other clusters within a large group

4.5 Generation of the Weights and Opinions Regarding Clusters

As mentioned before, trust relationship and opinion similarity are both important for GDM events in LGSNE. Therefore, we consider that both of the above attributes should be taken into account when calculating the weights of clusters. Specifically, four factors related to weight assignment—intra-cluster consensus level, intra-cluster trust score, inter-cluster consensus level, and inter-cluster trust score – are presented (see Table 4.3).

Intra-cluster consensus level is used to measure the similarity of DMs' opinions within a cluster. Two ways of measuring the consensus level have been commonly used: the first is based on the distance to the collective opinion, and the second is based on the distances between DMs' opinions [33, 131, 167, 186]. Xu et al. [142] provided a detailed comparison of the two measures. This chapter adopts the second consensus measure because it is completely based on the differences between DM's opinions without considering the influence of DMs' weights.

Definition 4.4 Given cluster C_k, which contains n_k DMs, the intra-cluster consensus level can be computed by

$$CCL_{k,Intra} = \begin{cases} \frac{1}{n_k(n_k-1)} \sum_{h=1,h\neq l}^{n_k} \sum_{l=1}^{n_k} SD_{lh} & n_k > 1 \\ 1 & n_k = 1 \end{cases}, \qquad (4.6)$$

where $e_h, e_l \in C_k$. Clearly, $0 \leq CCL_{k,Intra} \leq 1$, $k = 1, 2, \ldots, K$. The higher the intra-cluster consensus level, the more similar the opinions of the internal DMs. This is conducive to the formation of a unified cluster's opinion. More importantly, the aggregated cluster opinion reflects the opinions of all internal members to a large extent. From the viewpoint of internal cohesion, the cluster should be given a greater weight. Therefore, we conclude that intra-cluster consensus level has a positive effect on the weight assignment.

The intra-cluster trust score is designed to quantify the average trust score of DMs within a cluster.

Definition 4.5 Given an undirected sociomatrix $ATM = (ATS_{lh})_{n_k \times n_k}$ regarding the DMs in cluster C_k, the intra-cluster trust score is defined as

$$CTS_{k,Intra} = \begin{cases} \frac{1}{n_k(n_k-1)} \sum_{h=1,h\neq l}^{n_k} \sum_{l=1}^{n_k} ATS_{lh} & n_k > 1 \\ 1 & n_k = 1 \end{cases}, \qquad (4.7)$$

where $e_h, e_l \in C_k$. Clearly, $0 \leq CTS_{k,Intra} \leq 1$, $k = 1, 2, \ldots, K$. A higher trust score indicates that the DMs are more willing to obtain a unified cluster opinion through discussion and negotiation as opposed to being forced to aggregate. In this way, the aggregated cluster's opinion is easily accepted by the majority, which supports the subsequent consensus convergence. Therefore, the corresponding cluster can be assigned a greater weight. We consider that the intra-cluster trust score has a positive effect on the weight assignment.

The inter-cluster consensus level is used to calculate the average difference between one cluster's opinion and other opinions.

Definition 4.6 Given K clusters' opinions $R_k(k = 1, 2, \ldots, K)$, the inter-cluster consensus level of cluster C_k can be computed by

$$CCL_{k,Inter} = 1 - \frac{1}{K-1} \cdot \frac{1}{m \times n} \sum_{g=1,k\neq g}^{K} \sum_{i=1}^{m} \sum_{j=1}^{n} |r_{k,ij} - r_{g,ij}|. \qquad (4.8)$$

Clearly, $0 \leq CCL_{k,Inter} \leq 1$. The higher the inter-cluster consensus level, the smaller the difference between the cluster's opinion and other opinions. In terms of promoting consensus, we consider that inter-cluster consensus level has a positive effect on the weight assignment.

The inter-cluster trust score indicates the average degree to which a cluster can be trusted by others.

Definition 4.7 Given a directed sociomatrix $TM = (TS_{lh})_{q \times q}$, the inter-cluster trust score of cluster C_k is defined as

$$CTS_{k,Inter} = \frac{1}{n_k} \cdot \frac{1}{q - n_k} \sum_{l=1,e_l \in C_k}^{n_k} \sum_{e_h \notin C_k} TS_{hl}. \tag{4.9}$$

Clearly, $0 \le CTS_{k,Inter} \le 1$. The higher the inter-cluster trust score, the more the cluster is trusted by other clusters. Naturally, we conclude that inter-cluster trust score has a positive effect on the weight assignment.

Based on the above statements, the following proposition can be obtained.

Proposition 4.1 *All the four related factors, including intra-cluster consensus level, intra-cluster trust score, inter-cluster consensus level, and inter-cluster trust score, have a positive effect on the weight assignment.*

By gathering the aforementioned four factors, we define the overall score of a cluster.

Definition 4.8 The overall score of cluster C_k can be described by the following mapping $f : n_k, q, CCL_{k,Intra}, CTS_{k,Intra}, CCL_{k,Inter}, CTS_{k,Inter} \to OS_k (OS_k \in [0, 1])$.

Definition 4.9 A weighted geometric averaging operator is used to materialize the mapping f, such that

$$OS_k = \frac{n_k}{q} \cdot (CCL_{k,Intra})^{\delta_1} \cdot (CTS_{k,Intra})^{\delta_2} \cdot (CCL_{k,Inter})^{\delta_3} \cdot (CTS_{k,Inter})^{\delta_4}, \tag{4.10}$$

where δ_i is the weight parameter, satisfying that $0 \le \delta_1, \delta_2, \delta_3 \le 1$, $\sum_{i=1}^{4} \delta_i = 1$. The more important a factor is to the weight assignment, the smaller the value assigned to the associated δ_i. Clearly, $0 \le \delta_i \le 1$. The greater the value of OS_k, the greater the weight that should be assigned to cluster C_k.

Therefore, the weight of cluster C_k can be obtained as

$$\eta_k = \frac{OS_k}{\sum_{k=1}^{K} OS_k}. \tag{4.11}$$

Clearly, $0 \le \eta_k \le 1 (k = 1, 2, \ldots, K)$ and $\sum_{k=1}^{K} \eta_k = 1$.

To better understand the calculation of the overall score, we analyze the properties of Eq. (4.10). A function of x and y is abstracted as $f(x, y) = x^y$, where $x(0 < x \le$

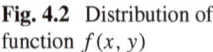

Fig. 4.2 Distribution of function $f(x, y)$

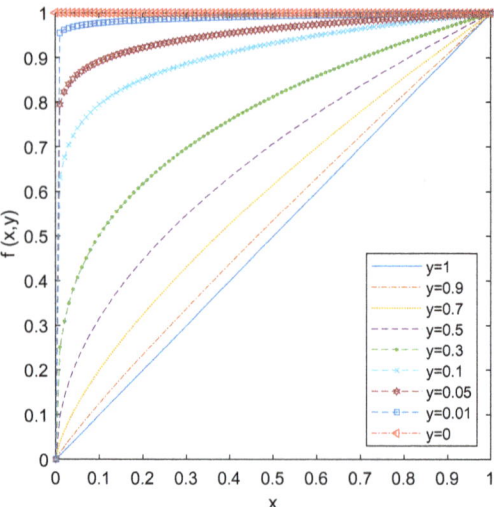

1) corresponds to the value of one of the four factors (e.g., $CCL_{k,Intra}$), and $y(0 \leq y \leq 1)$ corresponds to the importance δ_i. The first derivative of $f(x, y)$ regarding x is $f'_x(x, y) = yx^{y-1} \geq 0$, and the second derivative is $f''_{xx}(x, y) = y(y-1)x^{y-2} \leq 0$. Therefore, we know that $f(x, y)$ is a convex function. The following three properties can be concluded (see Fig. 4.2): (1) When $x = 1$, the maximum value of $f(x, y)$ is obtained as $f(1, y) = 1$. (2) If y is fixed, the larger the value of x is, the larger the value of $f(x, y)$ is. (3) If x is fixed, the smaller the vale of y is, the larger the value of $f(x, y)$ is. (4) Given that $y \neq 0$ and $y \neq 1$, then as x increases from 0 to 1, the slope of the curve decreases.

These properties are consistent with the statement in Proposition 4.1. We chose the geometric average operator to construct the formula for the overall score mainly because we use the fourth property. As x increases, $f(x, y)$ becomes less sensitive to changes in x. In practical decision-making, these four factors need to be sufficiently large (e.g., to reach a certain threshold). If the value of a certain factor does not meet the requirement, its influence on the weight assignment will be greatly reduced.

We have emphasized that trust relationship and opinion similarity are both important for GDM problems in LGSNE. Therefore, we use the trust-similarity score to assign importance weights to DMs.

Definition 4.10 Let $e_l \in C_k$. Then, the trust-similarity score of DM e_l within cluster C_k is defined as

$$TSS_{l,k} = \frac{1}{n_k - 1} \sum_{h=1, h \neq l}^{n_k} TSS_{hl} \tag{4.12}$$

where $e_h \in C_k$. Clearly, $0 \leq TSS_{l,k} \leq 1$.

The trust-similarity score represents the average value of fusing trust scores and similarity degrees between one DM and others in the same cluster. The higher the trust-similarity score, the more weight the corresponding DM should be given. By using Yager's OWA-based procedure guided by the trust-similarity score, the weight of the DM within cluster C_k can be calculated as [123, 149]

$$w_{\sigma(h),k}^{TSS} = Q\left(\frac{T(\sigma(h))}{T(\sigma(n_k))}\right) - Q\left(\frac{T(\sigma(h-1))}{T(\sigma(n_k))}\right), \tag{4.13}$$

where $T(\sigma(h)) = \sum_{l=1}^{h} TSS_{\sigma(l),k}$, σ is permutation such that $TSS_{\sigma(l)k}$ is the kth largest value of set $\{TSS_{1,k}, \ldots, TSS_{n_k,k}\}$ and Q is a basic unit-interval monotone (BUM) membership function of the fuzzy linguistic quantifier to implement in the aggregation process: $Q : [0, 1] \rightarrow [0, 1]$ such that $Q(0) = 0$, $Q(1) = 1$ and if $x > y$ then $Q(x) > Q(y)$. Hence the weight of DM e_l is obtained as $w_{l,k} = w_{\sigma(h),k}^{TSS}$, where $TSS_{\sigma(h),k}$ is the hth largest value of set $\{TSS_{1,k}, \ldots, TSS_{n_k,k}\}$. Clearly, $0 \le w_{l,k} \le 1$, $l = 1, 2, \ldots, n_k$ and $\sum_{l=1}^{n_k} w_{l,k} = 1$, $k = 1, 2, \ldots, K$.

Eventually, the cluster opinion can be obtained as $R_k = (r_{k,ij})_{m \times n}$, where $r_{k,ij} = \sum_{l=1}^{n_k} r_{l,ij} w_{l,k}$. Similarly, the group opinion is denoted as $R_c = (r_{c,ij})_{m \times n}$, where $r_{c,ij} = \sum_{k=1}^{K} r_{k,ij} \eta_k$.

4.6 Numerical Experiment

ABC, a manufacturer of electronic circuit boards, maintains a database to assess the quality of suppliers of raw materials. Copper cladding is the basic material of the electronic circuit board. The company decides to reexamine the sustainability of its five existing copper cladding suppliers. The triple-button principle is adopted for the sustainability assessment, including three benefit attributes, such as economic, environmental, and social bottom lines (denoted by a_1, a_2, a_3). The weight vector of the attributes is set as $\omega = (0.4, 0.35, 0.25)^T$. In addition to the weights given subjectively by DMs, the weights of the attributes can also be obtained through certain calculation rules based on the decision information itself [157, 163, 167]. Twenty heads and experts from various departments are called together to form a review committee. To solve this problem, the following steps are required.

Input: Initial normalized individual opinions $R_l^0 (l = 1, 2, \ldots, 20)$, socioma-trix TM, the weight vector of the attributes ω, and consensus threshold $\overline{GCL} = 0.85$.

Stage 1: Decision information preprocessing.

Step 1.1: Use Eq. (4.1) to calculate the similarity matrix SM and use Eq. (4.3) to obtain the adjusted sociomatrix ATM.

Step 1.2: Compute the undirected trust-similarity matrix $UTSM$ via Eq. (4.4).

Stage 2: Clustering process.

Table 4.4 Clustering results using Algorithm 4.1

C_k	n_k	e_l	η_k^0	$CTS_{k,Intra}^0$	$CCL_{k,Intra}^0$	$CTS_{k,Inter}^0$	$CCL_{k,Inter}^0$
C_1	4	e_1, e_7, e_9, e_{12}	0.19	0.5537	0.6468	0.5293	0.8042
C_2	4	e_2, e_4, e_{17}	0.1569	0.9044	0.5862	0.5307	0.7972
C_3	2	e_3, e_{19}	0.0953	0.6154	0.7242	0.4464	0.7755
C_4	4	$e_5, e_{10}, e_{11}, e_{16}$	0.1905	0.5378	0.6758	0.5206	0.8148
C_5	3	e_6, e_{14}, e_{18}	0.1607	0.7906	0.7022	0.5367	0.8278
C_6	4	$e_8, e_{13}, e_{15}, e_{20}$	0.2066	0.7178	0.7185	0.5035	0.8203

Note Set the BUM function as $Q = r^{2/3}$.

Set the clustering constraints $\overline{TS} = 0.2$, $\overline{SD} = 0.7$, and $\overline{TSS} = 0.45$. Table 4.4 presents the clustering results based on Algorithm 4.1. Fig. 4.1 visualizes the clustering process. To save space, some relevant information generated during the decision-making process is presented in the supplementary materials, such as the undirected trust-similarity matrix, clusters' opinions and group opinion, etc. The determination of clustering constraints will be analyzed in Sect. 4.7.1.

4.7 Comparative Analysis and Discussions

Section 4.7.1 analyzes the proposed trust-similarity measure-based hierarchical clustering method in the context of different types of clustering constraints. Determining the weights of the clusters is covered in Sect. 4.7.2. Note that the data used for the comparative analysis come from Sect. 4.6.

4.7.1 Analysis of the Determination of Clustering Constraints

Three clustering constraints need to be determined: trust threshold $\overline{TS}$, similarity threshold $\overline{SD}$, and trust-similarity threshold $\overline{TSS}$. This section analyzes the clustering threshold of Type A (i.e., trust-similarity threshold). Similar analysis can be applied to other types. In Eq. (4.4), we defined the trust-similarity score as a linear combination of trust score and similarity degree. Trust score and similarity degree are considered to be two core factors for calculating the trust-similarity score while parameter α plays an auxiliary role. Hence, the thresholds $\overline{TS}$ and $\overline{SD}$ should be computed first. The following steps are involved.

Step 1: Use Algorithm 4.1 to implement clustering with $\overline{TS}$ (or $\overline{SD}$) as the constraint.
First, we set the designated number of clusters as $K = INT(20/3) = 6$. Let $\overline{TS}$ (or $\overline{SD}$) increase from 0 to 1, and observe the change in the number of clusters. As shown in Fig. 4.3a, to satisfy the requirement of $K = 6$,

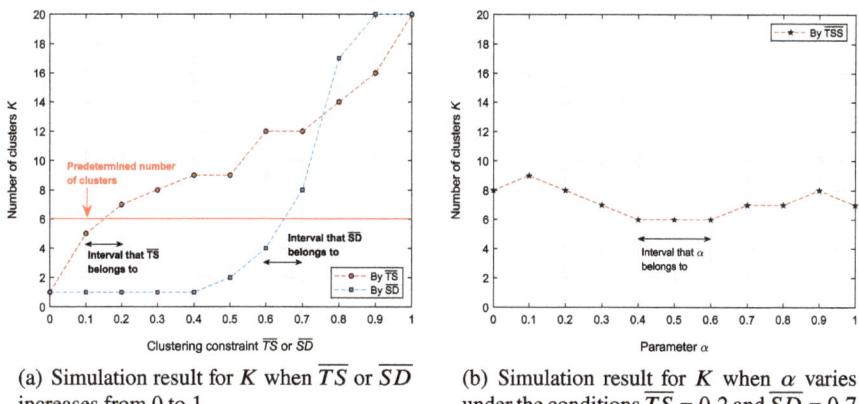

(a) Simulation result for K when $\overline{TS}$ or $\overline{SD}$ increases from 0 to 1

(b) Simulation result for K when α varies under the conditions $\overline{TS} = 0.2$ and $\overline{SD} = 0.7$

Fig. 4.3 Simulation results of the number of clusters using trust score and similarity degree, respectively

> let $\overline{TS} \in [0.1, 0.2]$ and $\overline{SD} \in [0.6, 0.7]$. Specifically, we assign the right endpoints of the above two intervals to $\overline{TS}$ and $\overline{SD}$ respectively (i.e., $\overline{TS} = 0.2$ and $\overline{SD} = 0.7$).

Step 2: Given $\overline{TS}$ and $\overline{SD}$ as above, Fig. 4.3b shows the simulation results when α increases from 0 to 1. We find that setting $\alpha \in [0.4, 0.6]$ can ensure that the number of clusters is identical to 6. Without loss of generality, let $\alpha = 0.5$. Finally, the trust-similarity threshold is calculated as $\overline{TSS} = 0.5 * 0.2 + 0.5 * 0.7 = 0.45$.

4.7.2 Comparison of Clustering Results with Different Types of Constrains

Different types of clustering constraints have different degrees of strictness, which will inevitably affect the clustering results. Table 4.5 presents the clustering results using the trust-similarity measure-based hierarchical clustering method with different types of constraints. Type D has three constraints and thus produces the maximum number of clusters (i.e., $K = 12$), while Type A has only one constraint and thus obtains the minimum number (i.e., $K = 6$).

As we have emphasized throughout this study, trust relationship and opinion similarity should be accounted for when implementing clustering. We therefore use two dimensions to describe the internal structure of a cluster (i.e., intra-cluster trust score and intra-cluster consensus level). The most perfect cluster is one in which both dimensions are sufficiently high. This indicates that the DMs have a positive trust relationship with each other, and the opinion differences are small. Positive internal trust relationships are conducive to the rapid formation of a unified cluster opinion.

Table 4.5 Clustering results using different types of clustering constraints

Type A	Type B	Type C	Type D
$\{e_1, e_7, e_9, e_{12}\}$, $\{e_2, e_4, e_{17}\}$, $\{e_3, e_{19}\}$, $\{e_5, e_{10}, e_{11}, e_{16}\}$, $\{e_6, e_{14}, e_{18}\}$, $\{e_8, e_{13}, e_{15}, e_{20}\}$	$\{e_1, e_7, e_9, e_{12}\}$, $\{e_2, e_4, e_{17}\}$, $\{e_3, e_{19}\}$, $\{e_5, e_{10}, e_{11}, e_{16}\}$, $\{e_6, e_{14}, e_{18}\}$, $\{e_8, e_{13}, e_{15}, e_{20}\}$	$\{e_1\}$, $\{e_2, e_4, e_{17}\}$, $\{e_3\}$, $\{e_5, e_8\}$, $\{e_6, e_{14}\}$, $\{e_7, e_9\}$, $\{e_{10}, e_{16}\}$, $\{e_{11}\}$, $\{e_{12}\}$, $\{e_{13}, e_{15}, e_{20}\}$, $\{e_{18}\}$, $\{e_{19}\}$	$\{e_1\}$, $\{e_2, e_4, e_{17}\}$, $\{e_3\}$, $\{e_5, e_8\}$, $\{e_6, e_{14}\}$, $\{e_7, e_9\}$, $\{e_{10}, e_{16}\}$, $\{e_{11}\}$, $\{e_{12}\}$, $\{e_{13}, e_{15}, e_{20}\}$, $\{e_{18}\}$, $\{e_{19}\}$

Note Set $\overline{TS} = 0.2$, $\overline{SD} = 0.7$, and $\overline{TSS} = 0.45$.

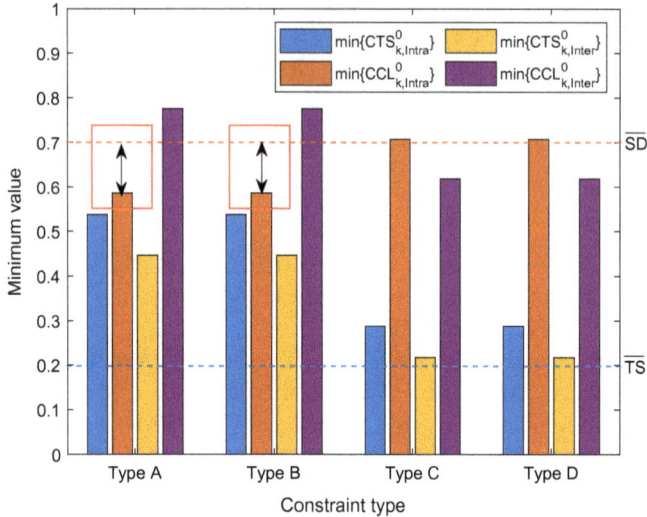

Fig. 4.4 Minimum values of the four factors using different types of clustering constraints

Small opinion differences mean that the aggregated cluster opinion can largely reflect the individual opinions of each internal member. Conversely, the worst clustering result is one in which DMs with very low trust relationships or significant opinion differences are assigned to a cluster. Therefore, we suggest that attention should be paid to both of the above dimensions when making decisions in a social network environment. Fig. 4.4 presents the minimum values of four factors (two concern internal structures and the other two external structures) associated with the results in Table 4.3.

We can observe the following:

(1) Different types of clustering constraints will lead to different clustering results, which are reflected in the number of clusters and the distribution of DMs within each cluster. As shown in Table 4.5, if the clustering constraint of Type A is used, six clusters are obtained, while if Type B is used, seven are obtained. DM e_3 and DM e_{13} are gathered into the same cluster if adopting Type B. However, these DMs belong to different clusters if adopting Type D. Since the proposed

clustering method provides three clustering constraints, the results of whether two DMs can be assigned to a cluster may differ due to the different constraint strengths.

(2) Using Type D produces the clusters with the best internal structures. As shown in Fig. 4.4, the intra-cluster trust score and intra-cluster consensus level both satisfy the defined clustering constraints. Type A usually results in the worst internal cluster structure. The DMs can decide which type of clustering constraint to adopt according to the characteristics of real decision problems. For example, for time-critical GDM events, trust relationship may take precedence over opinion similarity. Since the most important goal is to make a decision quickly within a limited time, the DMs can rely on trust scores to find authoritative opinions.

4.7.3 Comparison with Other Clustering Methods

To highlight the features of the presented clustering method, we compare it with three other commonly used clustering methods: K-means based clustering [133], vector space-based clustering [140], and density-based spatial clustering of applications with noise (DBSCAN) [57]. These three methods are described in the supplementary materials. To ensure comparability, we set the precondition that the clustering operation is implemented under the constraint of Type A. Table 4.6 shows the comparison of the clustering results. The following observations can be made:

(1) The four clustering methods provide different results about the number of clusters. K-means based clustering must determine the value of K in advance while the other three methods do not. Because of this, the number of clusters obtained by using any of the other three methods may vary when different trust-similarity thresholds are set. As shown in Fig. 4.4(b), the value of K fluctuates when $\overline{TSS}$ changes using this study's proposed method.

(2) Even though the results for the value of K obtained by different methods are the same, the internal structure of a cluster may be different. As shown in Table 4.6, if K-means-based clustering is adopted, DM e_1 and DM e_3 are classified into a cluster, but they belong to different clusters if vector space-based clustering is adopted.

(3) Given the large differences in cluster structures, the scores for some important indicators are bound to be different in the four clustering methods (see Table 4.7). As a consequence, setting the consensus threshold is affected because of differences in the initial group consensus level. For example, according to the proposed clustering method, we have that $GCL^0 = 0.8066$. Therefore, it makes sense to implement CRP only if setting $\overline{GCL} > 0.8066$. However, if using K-means-based clustering, the necessity of CRP can only be guaranteed if we set $\overline{GCL} > 0.8136$. We can conclude that the clustering results will directly affect the subsequent CRP.

Table 4.6 Comparison of clustering results using different clustering methods under the constraint of Type A

Clustering method	Cluster structure
K-means based clustering method [133]	$C_1 = \{e_1, e_3, e_{12}\}$, $C_2 = \{e_4, e_8, e_{19}\}$, $C_3 = \{e_5, e_{11}\}$, $C_4 = \{e_6, e_7, e_9\}$, $C_5 = \{e_2, e_{10}, e_{16}, e_{17}, e_{18}\}$, $C_6 = \{e_{14}, e_{15}, e_{20}\}$
Vector space-based clustering method [140]	$C_1 = \{e_1, e_{12}, e_{10}\}$, $C_2 = \{e_2, e_4, e_{18}, e_{17}, e_{14}, e_6, e_{13}, e_8, e_{20}\}$, $C_3 = \{e_3, e_{19}\}$, $C_4 = \{e_5, e_{11}, e_{16}\}$, $C_5 = \{e_7, e_9\}$, $C_6 = \{e_{15}\}$
DBSCAN [57]	$C_1 = \{e_2, e_{17}, e_{18}, e_9, e_4, e_7\}$, $C_2 = \{e_{11}, e_5, e_{12}, e_{16}, e_{10}, e_1\}$, $C_3 = \{e_{15}, e_8, e_{13}\}$, $C_4 = \{e_{19}, e_3, e_6, e_{14}, e_{20}\}$
Proposed clustering method	$C_1 = \{e_1, e_7, e_9, e_{12}\}$, $C_2 = \{e_2, e_4, e_{17}\}$, $C_3 = \{e_3, e_{19}\}$, $C_4 = \{e_5, e_{10}, e_{11}, e_{16}\}$, $C_5 = \{e_6, e_{14}, e_{18}\}$, $C_6 = \{e_8, e_{13}, e_{15}, e_{20}\}$

Table 4.7 Scores of important indicators obtained by using different clustering methods

	$min\{CTS^0_{k,Intra}\}$	$min\{CCL^0_{k,Intra}\}$	$min\{CTS^0_{k,Inter}\}$	$min\{CTS^0_{k,Inter}\}$	GCL^0
K-means based clustering method [133]	0.3016	0.5822	0.4847	0.7793	0.8136
Vector space-based clustering method [140]	0.2347	0.3571	0.4464	0.7464	0.7802
DBSCAN [57]	0.4246	0.6375	0.4793	0.8212	0.8583
Proposed clustering method	0.5537	0.5862	0.4464	0.7755	0.8066

Table 4.8 presents the advantages and disadvantages of the four clustering methods. The biggest disadvantage of the proposed method is high time complexity. Although it might not perform well when dealing with large-scale data, it simultaneously accounts for multiple clustering constraints for different proposes. Hence, we set the usage boundary of the proposed method as follows: the data size is not too large, and multiple clustering purposes need to be achieved.

In summary, the biggest advantage of the proposed clustering method is that it can simultaneously achieve multiple clustering purposes by introducing multiple clustering constraints. The other three methods are based entirely on a single clustering constraint. Thus, future work can seek to improve those methods to satisfy different clustering purposes.

Table 4.8 Comparison of the main advantages and disadvantages of four clustering methods

Clustering method	Advantages/disadvantages
K-means clustering method [133]	**Advantage**: (a) The time complexity is nearly linear and suitable for mining large data sets. (b) When the difference between clusters is obvious, the clustering effect is very good. **Disadvantages**: (a) The determination of K (b) The choice of initial clustering center has a great effect on the clustering result. (c) It is sensitive to noise and isolated point samples.
Xu and Chen's method [140]	**Advantage:** It is easy to operate and requires only continuous aggregation of opinions and distance measures. **Disadvantages**: (a) The clustering result is easily affected by the initial order of DMs. (b) The determination of the clustering threshold. (c) If multiple clustering purposes are required, it needs to be improved.
DBSCAN [57]	**Advantage**: (a) There is no need to determine the value of K. (b) The clustering result is almost independent of the traversal order of points. **Disadvantages**: (a) The determination of neighborhood radius and minimum number of points in the neighborhood. (b) It is not suitable for a sample set with uneven density.
Proposed clustering method	**Advantage**: Multiple clustering constraints can be considered simultaneously. **Disadvantages**: (a) The clustering operation cannot be undone, and data samples cannot be exchanged between clusters. (b) If multiple clustering constraints are considered, the time complexity is high. (c) A clustering result in a single-chain form is easily encountered. That is, there are some clusters containing only one DM.

4.7.4   In-Depth Analysis of the Calculation of Weights Regarding Clusters

As presented in Eq. (4.10), five factors influence the calculation of the weights of clusters: the number of DMs in each cluster, intra-cluster trust score, intra-cluster consensus level, inter-cluster trust score, and inter-cluster consensus level. We divide the above factors into two categories: the number of DMs in each cluster and the

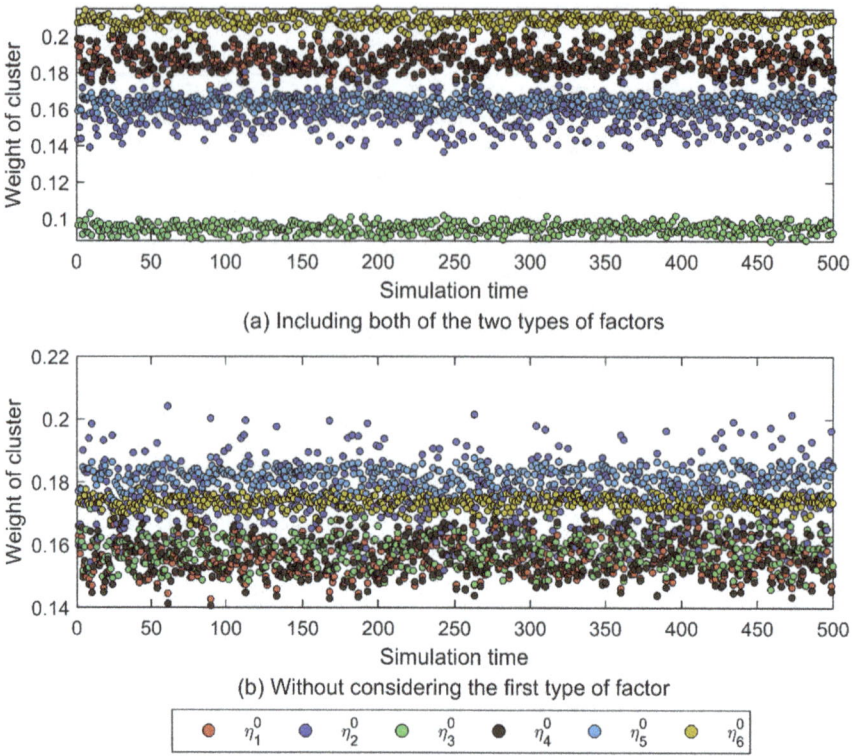

Fig. 4.5 Distribution of the weights of clusters when δ_i changes

remaining four factors. When only considering the first type of factor, the weight vector of clusters is obtained as $\eta^0 = (0.2, 0.15, 0.1, 0.2, 0.15, 0.2)^T$. Using MAT-LAB software, let the parameter δ_i in Eq. (4.10) change randomly 500 times under the conditions $\sum_{i=1}^{4} = 1, 0 \leq \delta_i \leq 1, i = 1, 2, 3, 4$. Then, two groups of simulation results are observed, in which one group includes both of the two types of factors (see Fig. 4.5a) while the other does not consider the first type (see Fig. 4.5b).

As shown in Fig. 4.5, as the value of δ_i changes, the weight of each cluster fluctuates within a fixed range. For example, in Fig. 4.5a, almost always varies around 0.1; in Fig. 4.5b, η_3^0 almost always moves around 0.16. In addition, the weight discrimination in Fig. 4.5a is high, and almost all weights are in [0.1, 0.2], while the weight distribution discrimination in Fig. 4.5b is not so high and is roughly within the range [0.14, 0.2]. This indicates that according to Eq. (4.10), the first type of factor (i.e., the number of DMs in a cluster) has a significant influence on the weight distribution. This is in line with the majority principle. If a cluster contains a large number of DMs, the weight of the cluster must not be underestimated. If a cluster contains few or even only one DM, its weight should not be very large according to Eq. (4.10). However, the possibility that the weight obtained by using the second type of factor may be very large cannot be ruled out. In practical decisions, we consider that the number of DMs in a cluster is the basic factor determining the weight allocation, but other indicators concerning the internal and external characteristics of the cluster should also be taken into account.

4.8 Conclusions

Many real-world decisions take place in the context of social networks involving large-scale DMs. In this chapter, a trust-similarity measure-based hierarchical clustering method was proposed. First, a trust-similarity function was defined that integrated trust relationship and opinion similarity. Then, a rule of undirected transformation for a directed sociomatrix was designed. Four types of clustering constraints were presented. By adding them to the hierarchical clustering method, different clustering purposes could be achieved. We proposed a novel weight-determining method for clusters that fully considered the internal and external characteristics of a cluster. Five related factors were identified, including the number of DMs in a cluster, intra-cluster consensus level, intra-cluster trust score, inter-cluster consensus level, and inter-cluster trust score.

Chapter 5
Hierarchical Punishment-Driven Consensus Model for Probabilistic Linguistic LSGDM

Abstract Large-scale group decision making (LSGDM) has attracted extensive attention and has been used to model complex decision problems. It is necessary to implement a consensus-reaching process (CRP) due to the need to obtain a decision that is acceptable to the majority. The theory of probabilistic linguistic term sets (PLTSs) is very useful in addressing uncertain information in the decision-making process. In this chapter, we develop a hierarchical punishment-driven consensus model for LSGDM problems in the context of probabilistic linguistic information. The model has three stages. In the first stage, we define probabilistic linguistic large-group decision making. To improve the performance of PLTSs in the CRP, we redefine the rules governing their normalization and operations. In the second stage, the original large group is divided into several small subgroups by hierarchical clustering. In the third stage, we propose three levels of consensus measures and two adjustment strategies to refine the scope of measure and adjustment to the matrix element level. Then, a hierarchical punishment-driven consensus model is established that can provide guidance for adjustment and soften the human supervision of the CRP. Finally, a case study on global supplier selection illustrates the utility and applicability of the model, and a comparison with other linguistic models reveals its advantages.

Keywords Probabilistic linguistic large-scale group decision making (PL-LSGDM) · Hierarchical punishment-driven consensus model (HPDCM) · Global supplier selection · Hard adjustment · Soft adjustment

5.1 Introduction

Economic globalization and fierce market competition are driving companies to seek overseas suppliers [5, 30, 52]. Global sourcing benefits companies, but it also increases the risks of supplier selection as the range of alternatives expands. Supplier selection represents a strategic managerial issue that is closely related to corporate performance and sustainability [115]. Such a complex decision is difficult for a single person or a small organization to reach. In practice, a special committee (including relevant department heads and experts) or a special board meeting will be established to conduct in-depth assessments. This configuration is a typical large-group decision-making scenario where multiple decision makers (DMs) attempt to select a common solution from a set of alternatives. Large-scale group decision-making (LSGDM) has received much attention in the field of decision analysis. Generally, a GDM problem can be called an LSGDM problem when the number of DMs is more than 20 [19, 38]. And yet in the studies of Palomares et al. [84] and Wu et al. [127], the illustrative examples included 50 experts. Situations involving large-scale DMs are considered to present new challenges for the decision process, such as scalability, constant preference supervision, different behaviors towards consensus, time cost [54, 99].

The DMs themselves play a central role in solving decision problems, but the form in which the evaluation information is expressed is also important for the decision output. Linguistic assessment information can express natural language well, and it has been one of the most commonly used forms of information expression in modeling realistic decision-making scenarios [43, 47, 63, 81, 134, 164, 189]. The characteristics of several existing linguistic models are described in Table 5.1. The traditional linguistic assessment information generally allows DMs to express their preferences with single linguistic terms. However, sometimes, it is difficult to depict complex qualitative information only by one linguistic term. For instance, a DM may evaluate an item as "very good", "good" or "somewhat good" but be unsure of how good the item is. To address such issues, Rodríguez et al. [101] proposed the concept of hesitant fuzzy linguistic term sets (HFLTSs). HFLTSs collect all possible linguistic terms provided by the DMs, and all of these terms are assigned the same importance. In reality, a DM may have different preferences for multiple linguistic terms when judging an item. Therefore, Pang et al. [87] extended the HFLTSs to a more general concept, named as probabilistic linguistic term sets (PLTSs). The PLTSs enable DMs to assign different weights to possible linguistic terms. To date, most studies on the GDM events with probabilistic linguistic information have focused on scenarios involving small-scale DMs, typically no more than 20 (e.g., [6, 178]).

A probabilistic linguistic large-scale group decision-making (PL-LSGDM) problem can be defined as a situation in which a large number of DMs seek to choose a common solution from a set of alternatives in the context of probabilistic linguistic information. We characterize its features as follows: (1) the number of DMs is large (usually no fewer than 20); (2) most or all DMs provide their evaluation information by means of PLTSs; and (3) obtaining a high-consensus output requires the implementation of a consensus reaching process (CRP). Generally, solving a PL-LSGDM problem requires the following four processes: the probabilistic linguistic representation of the evaluation information, clustering process, consensus reaching process and selection process.

The CRP is considered particularly important in LSGDM because opinions among a large number of DMs can easily be controversial. In contrast to the ideal consensus that requires unanimity, the notion of soft consensus allows differences of opinion within a reasonable range [49]. Various consensus models have been proposed to address GDM problems under different situations. However, research on consensus in the context of probabilistic linguistic information has just begun. Zhang et al.

Table 5.1 A review of the characteristics of several existing linguistic models

Linguistic formats	Number of linguistic terms	Probabilistic information	Sum of probability values
Linguistic term set [43]	single	N/A	N/A
uncertain linguistic term set [88]	A pair	N/A	N/A
Multi-granular linguistic term set [79]	Single	N/A	N/A
Hesitant fuzzy linguistic term set [101]	Several	N/A	N/A
Linguistic information based on discrete fuzzy numbers [77]	Several	N/A	N/A
Possibility distribution-based HFLTS [132]	Several	Completely known	1
Granulating linguistic information [9]	Single	N/A	N/A
Linguistic distribution assessment [160]	Several	Completely known	1
Probabilistic linguistic term set [87]	Several	Partially known	≤ 1

[178] designed a CRP with probabilistic linguistic preference relations. Wu and Liao [126] proposed a consensus-based probabilistic linguistic gained and lost dominance score method. We find that the case studies in the above literature focus on GDM problems composed of three experts and do not involve large-scale DMs.

Faced with the challenges of classical consensus models for LSGDM and the scarcity of research on consensus in PL-LSGDM, this study develops a hierarchical punishment-driven consensus model and applies it to global supplier selection. The following efforts are made to address the consensus in PL-LSGDM, which can overcome the scalability challenge and soften the human supervision of the CRP.

(1) *Problem framework construction*: We define probabilistic linguistic large-group decision making and characterize its constituent elements. We present novel operational laws to pre-process probabilistic linguistic information.

(2) *Clustering process*: A hierarchical clustering method is utilized to divide the large group into several small-scale subgroups. The cluster is regarded as the basic unit in the decision-making process.

(3) *Consensus-reaching process*: A hierarchical punishment-driven consensus model is employed to manage the differences among the opinions of clusters. According to the current group consensus index, the model can adopt different strategies to adjust the clusters' opinions.

The remainder of this chapter is organized as follows. Section 5.2 presents the problem framework configuration and the preprocessing of decision information. In Sect. 5.3, a hierarchical clustering algorithm is used to classify large-scale DMs. In Sect. 5.4, a hierarchical punishment-driven consensus-reaching model is developed. Section 5.5 applies the proposed model to a case study on global supplier selection. Section 5.6 presents the comparative analysis and managerial implications. This chapter ends with conclusions in Sect. 5.7.

5.2 Problem Framework Configuration and Preprocessing of Decision Information

As an extension of HFLTSs, the concept of PLTSs was originally proposed by Pang et al. [87], which enables DMs to express possible linguistic terms with different weights. Clearly, Pang et al. [87] defined PLTSs on the basis of an additive linguistic evaluation scale, while Zhang et al. [179] used PLTSs based on a subscript-symmetric linguistic evaluation scale.

Definition 5.1 [87] Let $S = \{s_\alpha | \alpha = -\tau, \ldots, -1, 0, 1, \ldots, \tau\}$ (τ is a positive integer) be a linguistic term set; then a PLTS is defined as

$$L(p) = \left\{ L^{(u)}(p^{(u)} | L^{(u)} \in S, p^{(u)} \geq 0, u = 1, 2, \ldots, \#L(p), \sum_{u=1}^{\#L(p)} p^{(u)} \leq 1 \right\} \quad (5.1)$$

where $L^{(u)}p^{(u)}$ is a probabilistic linguistic element that includes the linguistic term $L^{(u)}$ and the associated probability $p^{(u)}$, and $\#L(p)$ is the number of different linguistic terms in $L(p)$.

A probabilistic linguistic element consists of two parts: a linguistic term and its corresponding probability. Based on this unique construct, a PLTS can be obtained in two ways: the statistical aggregation of single linguistic terms (see [87]) and the aggregation of multiple PLTSs (see [178]). Formally, a multicriteria GDM problem with probabilistic linguistic information includes (1) a set of alternatives $X = \{x_1, x_2, \ldots, x_m\}(m \geq 2)$, which are the possible solutions to the problem; (2) a set of criteria $A = \{a_1, a_2, \ldots, a_n\}(n \geq 2)$ used to evaluate the alternatives in X; and (3) a set of DMs $E = \{e_1, e_2, \ldots, e_q\}(q \geq 2)$ who provide judgments on the alternatives. Let $V_l = (v_{l,ij})_{m \times n}$ be the individual opinion given by DM $e_l(l = 1, 2, \ldots, q)$, where $v_{l,ij}$ represents the evaluation of DM e_l on the alternative $x_i \in X$ with respect to criterion $a_j \in A$. $v_{l,ij}$ can be either a single linguistic term or a PLTS. The former expression represents a relatively precise evaluation value, while the latter reflects the DM's hesitation. To deal with the above different types of linguistic information, we attach a probability of 1 to the single linguistic term to convert it to a PLTS. For example, a given linguistic term s_3 can be changed to $\{s_3(1)\}$. In particular, if all individual opinions are expressed by means of single linguistic terms, a collective opinion can be obtained as a PLTS by aggregating linguistic terms [105]. In this chapter, we focus on a GDM in which most or all DMs provide evaluation information in the form of PLTSs. This is consistent with the fact that, due to the complexity of LSGDM problems, it is difficult for DMs to express opinions by only using single linguistic terms.

We first provide a description of the PL-LSGDM scenario studied in this study. Let $X = \{x_1, x_2, \ldots, x_m\}$ be a finite set of alternatives, $A = \{a_1, a_2, \ldots, a_n\}$ be a set of criteria, $E = \{e_1, e_2, \ldots, e_q\}(q \geq 20)$ be a set of DMs, and S be a linguistic term set as before. This study considers a group to be a large group when the number of DMs exceeds 20. Let $V_l = (v_{l,ij})_{m \times n}$ be the individual decision matrix provided by DM $e_l(l = 1, 2, \ldots, q)$, where $v_{l,ij} = \{L_{l,ij}^{(u)}(p_{l,ij}^{(u)})|L_{l,ij}^{(u)} \in S, p_{l,ij}^{(u)} \geq 0, u = 1, 2, \ldots, \#v_{i,lj}, \sum_{u=1}^{\#v_{l,ij}} p_{l,ij}^{(u)} \leq 1\}$. $\#v_{l,ij}$ is the number of different linguistic terms in $v_{l,ij}$. Generally, there are benefit types and cost types in the criteria. By using the linguistic negation operator [139], we convert the cost types to benefit types (for convenience, the converted result is still represented by $v_{l,ij}$) so that $L_{l,ij}^{(u)} = neg(L_{l,ij}^{(u)})$ when a_j is a cost criterion.

To obtain the aggregation and distance measure of a PLTS, normalization is necessary. Generally, discrete linguistic terms are used to evaluate alternatives, while virtual linguistic terms only appear in operations and rankings [137]. Intuitively, in CRPs, discrete linguistic terms enable DMs to better understand the differences between individual opinions, which is conducive to making more reasonable adjustments. Therefore, we believe that before the selection process, the normalization and aggregation of PLTSs should be expressed in terms of discrete linguistic terms associated with probability values. Here, we redefine the normalization and operational laws of PLTSs. Normalization includes two steps:

Step 1: *Granularity normalization.* All PLTSs contain the same linguistic terms;
Step 2: *Probability normalization.* The sum of the probability values of all linguistic terms in each PLTS is 1.

Definition 5.2 [87] (*Granularity normalization*) Let $L(p)_1$ and $L(p)_2$ be any two PLTSs, where $L(p)_1 = \{L_1^{(u)}(p_1^{(u)})|u = 1, 2, \ldots, \#L(p)_1\}, L(p)_2 = \{L_2^{(u)}(p_2^{(u)})|u = 1, 2, \ldots, \#L(p)_2\}$. If there is a linguistic term $L_1^{(u)}$ in $L(p)_1$ that does not appear in $L(p)_1$, then add $L_1^{(u)}$ to $L(p_2)$. By the way, a new probabilistic linguistic element is obtained as $L_2^{(u)}(p_2^{(u)})$, where $L_2^{(u)} = L_1^{(u)}$ and $p_2^{(u)} = 0$. Repeat the above steps until the two PLTSs have the same linguistic terms.

Definition 5.3 [87] (*Probability normalization*) Given any PLTS $L(p)$ satisfying that $\sum_{u=1}^{\#L(p)} p^{(u)} < 1$, the associated PLTS $\dot{L}(p)$ is obtained as

$$\dot{L}(p) = \{L^{(u)}(\dot{p}^{(u)})|L^{(u)} \in S, u = 1, 2, \ldots, \#L(p)\} \tag{5.2}$$

where $\dot{p}^{(u)} = p^{(u)}/\sum_{u=1}^{\#L(p)} p^{(u)}, u = 1, 2, \ldots, \#L(p)$. $\dot{L}(p)$ is called the normalization form of $L(p)$.

For simplicity, the normalized PLTS (NPLTS) is still written as $L(p)$. The granularity of the NPLTS $L(p)$ is denoted as $\#\#L(p)$, where $\#\#L(p) \geq \#L(p)$.

Example 5.1 Given two PLTSs $L(p)_1 = \{s_{-1}(0.1), s_1(0.4), s_1(0.4)\}$ and $L(p)_2 = \{s_0(0.2), s_1(0.3), s_2(0.5)\}$, where the linguistic terms of both are drawn from $S_1 = \{s_{-2}, s_{-1}, s_0, s_1, s_2\}$, the normalization is divided into two steps:

Step 1:   Granularity normalization: $L(p)_1 = \{s_{-1}(0.1), s_0(0), s_1(0.4), s_2(0)\}$ and $L(p)_2 = \{s_{-1}(0), s_0(0.2), s_1(0.3), s_2(0.5)\}$. Thus, we have $\#\#L(p)_1 = \#\# L(p)_2$.

Step 2:   Probability normalization: $L(p)_1 = \{s_{-1}(0.2), s_0(0), s_1(0.8), s_2(0)\}$ and $L(p)_2 = \{s_{-1}(0), s_0(0.2), s_1(0.3), s_2(0.5)\}$.

Definition 5.4 Given any two NPLTSs, $L(p)_1 = \{L_1^{(u)}(p_1^{(u)})|L_1^{(u)} \in S, u = 1, 2, \ldots,$ $\#\#L(p)_1\}$, and $L(p)_2 = \{L_2^{(u)}(p_2^{(u)})|L_2^{(u)} \in S, u = 1, 2, \ldots, \#\#L(p)_2\}, 0 \leq \lambda_1, \lambda_2 \leq 1$. Then, we have

(1) $L(p)_1 \oplus L(p)_2 = L(p)_1 = \{L_3^{(u)}(p_3^{(u)})|L_3^{(u)} \in S, u = 1, 2, \ldots, \#\#L(p)_1\}$
(2) $\lambda L(p)_1 = \{L_1^{(u)}(\lambda p_1^{(u)})|u = 1, 2, \ldots, \#\#L(p)_1\}$
(3) $\lambda_1 L(p)_1 \oplus \lambda_2 L(p)_2 = \{L_4^{(u)}(p_4^{(u)})|L_4^{(u)} \in S, u = 1, 2, \ldots, \#\#L(p)_1\}$

where $L_3^{(u)} = L_1^{(u)}, p_3^{(u)} = p_1^{(u)} + p_2^{(u)} - p_1^{(u)}p_2^{(u)}, L_4^{(u)} = L_1^{(u)}, p_4^{(u)} = \lambda_1 p_1^{(u)} + \lambda_2 p_2^{(u)} - \lambda_1 \lambda_2 p_1^{(u)}p_2^{(u)}$.

Remark 5.1 Notice that sometimes the sum of the probability values of the PLTS obtained by Definition 4 is less than 1. In this case, we need to redo the process of probability normalization.

Example 5.2 (Continued with Example 5.1) Let $\lambda_1 = 0.4$ and $\lambda_2 = 0.6$; then, we have the following results:
Pang et al.'s operational law yields [87]:

$\lambda_1 L(p)_1 \oplus \lambda_2 L(p)_2$
$= 0.4\{s_1(0.8), s_{-1}(0.2)\} \oplus 0.6\{s_2(0.5), s_1(0.3), s_0(0.2)\}$
$= \{0.4 \times 0.8s_1 \oplus 0.6 \times 0.5s_2, 0.4 \times 0s_{-1} \oplus 0.6 \times 0.3s_1, 0.4 \times 0.2s_{-1} \oplus 0.6 \times 0.2s_0\}$
$= \{0.32s_1 \oplus 0.3s_2, 0s_1 \oplus 0.18s_1, 0.08s_{-1} \oplus 0.12s_0\}$
$= \{s_{0.92}, s_{0.18}, s_{-0.08}\},$

and our operational law yields:

$\lambda_1 L(p)_1 \oplus \lambda_2 L(p)_2$
$= 0.4\{s_{-1}(0.2), s_0(0), s_1(0.8), s_2(2)\} \oplus 0.6\{s_{-1}(0), s_0(0.2), s_1(0.3), s_2(0.5)\}$
$= \{s_{-1}(0.0849), s_0(0.1273), s_1(0.4694), s_2(0.3184)\}.$

From Example 5.2, we find that the probabilities of linguistic terms are missing if Pang et al.'s operational law [87] is used. In this case, the unique feature of PLTSs compared with ordinary linguistic term sets disappears. More importantly, the virtual linguistic terms make it difficult for DMs to understand and determine the adjustments in the CRP. In our operational law, the ordinary linguistic terms remain unchanged, yet the associated probabilities always change.

To better apply PLTSs to GDM problems, the following aggregation operators are defined:

Definition 5.5 Let $L(p)_1 =$ be a set of m NPLTSs and θ_i be the weight of $L(p)$, such that $\theta_i \geq 0$, $i = 1, 2, \ldots, m$, and $\sum_{i=1}^{m} \theta_i = 1$; then, the probabilistic linguistic weighted averaging (PLWA) operator is defined as

$$L(p) = PLWA(L(p)_1, L(p)_2, \ldots, L(p)_m) = \theta_1 L(p)_1 \oplus \theta_2 L(p)_2, \cdots \oplus \theta_m L(p)_m \tag{5.3}$$

where $L(p) = \{L^{(u)}(p^{(u)}) | L^{(u)} = L_1^{(u)}, u = 1, 2, \ldots, \#\#L(p)\}$, such that

$$p^{(u)} = \sum_{i=1}^{m} \theta_i p_i^{(u)} - \sum_{1 \leq i \leq j \leq m} \theta_i p_i^{(u)} \theta_j p_j^{(u)} + \cdots + (-1)^{m-1} \prod_{i=1}^{m} \theta_i p_i^{(u)}. \tag{5.4}$$

Definition 5.6 Let $L(p)_1$ and $L(p)_2$ be any two NPLTSs; then, the distance between $L(p)_1$ and $L(p)_2$ is calculated by

$$d(L(p)_1, L(p)_2) = \frac{\left(\sum_{u=1}^{\#\#L(p)_1} \left(|I_1^{(u)}| |p_1^{(u)} - p_2^{(u)}| \right)^\lambda \right)^{(1/\lambda)}}{\#\#L(p)_1} \tag{5.5}$$

where $\lambda > 0$ and $I_1^{(u)}$ is the subscript of the linguistic term $L_1^{(u)}$. In this study, we adopt the Euclidean distance, i.e., $\lambda = 2$.

It is clear that the distance measures have the following properties:

(1) $0 \leq d(L(p)_1, L(p)_2) \leq 1$
(2) $d(L(p)_1, L(p)_2) = 0$, if $L(p)_1 = L(p)_2$
(3) $d(L(p)_1, L(p)_2) = d(L(p)_2, L(p)_1)$.

5.3   Hierarchical Clustering Algorithm

Clustering is a widely used methodology for analyzing and processing large-scales DMs, and it is considered to be effective in addressing the scalability challenge in LSGDM problems. In this study, we adopt a hierarchical clustering method to classify the large-scale DMs into $K(1 \leq K \leq q)$ subgroups. Hierarchical clustering treats each data object as a separate cluster and then finds clusters with small distances to merge in each iteration. This process repeats until a designated number of clusters is reached or there is only one cluster. The procedure for the hierarchical clustering method is described in Algorithm 5.1.

Algorithm 5.1 Hierarchical clustering method with probabilistic linguistic information

Input: Normalized individual opinions $R_l (l = 1, 2, \ldots, q)$ and the designated number of clusters K.

Output: Clusters $C_1, \ldots, C_K$.

1: Consider each DM as a cluster, denoted as $C_1, C_2, \ldots, C_q$.
2: Use Eq. (5.5) to calculate the distances among clusters, denoted as $d(R_l, R_h), l, h = 1, 2, \ldots, q$.
3: Select the minimum distance, i.e., $d(R_{l^*}, R_{h^*}) = min\{d(R - l, R_h)\}$, and merge clusters into a single cluster C_{k^*}.
4: Compute the distances between the new cluster and the old clusters, obtained by

$$d(R_{k^*}, R_l) = max\{d(R_{l^*}, R_l), d(R_{h^*}, R_h)\} \tag{5.6}$$

5: Repeat steps 3–4 until the number of clusters equals to K.
6: Output the clusters $C_1, \ldots, C_K$.

Theorem 5.1 *The time complexity of Algorithm 5.1 is $O(q^3)$.*

Proof First, it will take $O(q^2)$ time to calculate the distances between each pair of clusters. Once a new cluster is determined, the distance between the new cluster and each of the other clusters needs to be calculated. It can be seen that Algorithm 5.1 must be carried out for q iterations and that each iteration updates the distances, so the time complexity is the cube of the number of original clusters, i.e., $O(q^3)$. □

Calculating the weights of the clusters is a necessary step because it is closely related to the generation of group opinions. Inspired by Rodríguez et al. [99], this study takes into account the size and cohesion. The size refers to the number of DMs in a cluster. Based on the majority principle, the larger the size of a cluster is, the more weight it should be given. However, the representation of the size should be adjusted according to the number of DMs involved in the LSGDM problem. Based on computing with words [93], Rodríguez et al. [99] modeled the size with the fuzzy membership function μ_{size} shown in Fig. 5.1, where the universe of discourse is the number of DMs in a cluster and the membership degree reflects the cluster's influence on all the DMs in terms of the number of DMs. The points a and b of the membership function depend on the numbers of alternatives and DMs in the LSGDM scenario. The highest membership degree is for values above a, the lowest membership degree is for values below b, and varying importance is assigned between a and b.

Fig. 5.1 Membership function for the cluster size

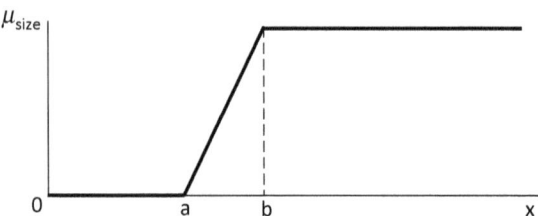

The cohesion represents the consensus index of the DMs' opinions in a cluster. The more coherent the individual opinions within a cluster are, the more weight we give the cluster.

Definition 5.7 For cluster C_k including n_k DMs, the cohesion of the cluster is defined as

$$cohesion(C_k) = 1 - \frac{1}{n_k(n_k - 1)/2} \sum_{h=1}^{n_k-1} \sum_{l=h+1}^{n_k} d(R_l, R_h) \tag{5.7}$$

where $e_l, e_h \in E$. Clearly, $0 \leq cohesion(C_k) \leq 1$.

By integrating size and cohesion, Rodríguez et al. [99] defined a function to calculate the weights of clusters, which could be flexibly adapted to a specific LSGDM problem.

Definition 5.8 Let $Y_{C_k} = \{y_1, y_2\}$ be the values obtained for cohesion and size, respectively, where $y_1, y_2 \in [0, 1]$; then, the fusion value of the cohesion and size is calculated by

$$\phi(Y_{C_k}) = (1 + y_2)^{y_1 \beta} \tag{5.8}$$

where the parameter $\beta(\beta > 0)$ is used to adjust the effect of cohesion in calculating the weight of the cluster.

The aggregated value $\phi(Y_{C_k})$ reflects the relevance of cluster C_k. Therefore, the weight vector of the clusters, $\theta = (\theta_1, \theta_2, \ldots, \theta_K)^T$, can be obtained from

$$\theta_k = \frac{\phi(Y_{C_k})}{\sum_{k=1}^{K} \phi(Y_{C_k})} \tag{5.9}$$

Clearly, $0 \leq \theta_k \leq 1 (k = 1, 2, \ldots, K)$ and $\sum_{k=1}^{K} \theta_k = 1$. By using Eq. (5.3), the cluster opinion is obtained; i.e., $G_k = (g_{k,ij})_{m \times n}$, where $g_{k,ij} = PLWA(r_{1,ij}, \ldots, r_{n_k,ij})$.

We use the case in Sect. 5.4 to illustrate the weight calculation. In this study, we consider 10% of DMs to define the point and the number of DMs divided by the number of alternatives to define the point b: $a = round(q \cdot 0.1) = 2$, $b = round(q/m) = 4$, where $round(\cdot)$ is the round function. Table 5.2 shows the values of size, membership degree, and cohesion for each cluster. Figure 5.2 shows the weights of clusters when different values of the parameter are used to solve Eq. (5.8). We find that although clusters c_2 and c_3 have the same membership degree in terms of size, they are assigned different weights due to the different values of cohesion among their members. As shown in Fig. 5.2, when the value of β increases, the weight of cluster c_2 increases more than that of cluster c_3. This means that the parameter β can adjust the degree of the influence of cohesion on the weight.

Table 5.2 The values of size, membership degree, and cohesion for each cluster

C_k	Size	Membership degree	Cohesion
C_1	4	1	0.8427
C_2	5	1	0.8446
C_3	4	1	0.8173
C_4	4	1	0.8196
C_5	2	0	0.8286
C_6	1	0	1

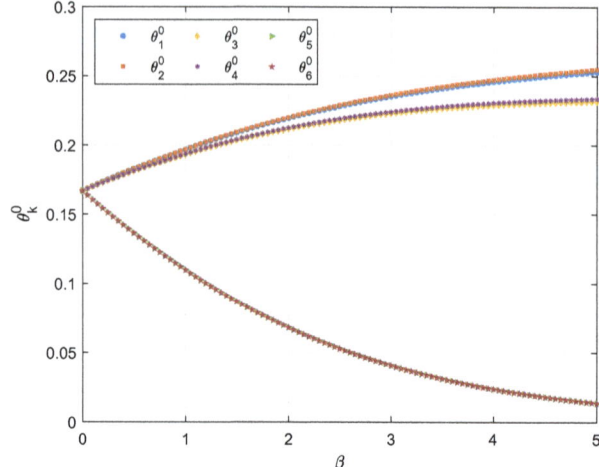

Fig. 5.2 Weights of the clusters as β varies

5.4 Hierarchical Punishment-Driven Consensus-Reaching Model in PL-LSGDM Problems

We first describe the consensus measure. Section 5.4.2 presents punishment-driven consensus iterations. In Sect. 5.4.3, a hierarchical punishment-driven consensus model is given.

5.4.1 Consensus Measure

The consensus measure is designed to compute the differences among DMs' opinions. As previously discussed, the calculation of the consensus measure can be based on the distance to the group opinion or the distances among individual opinions [54, 84]. Xu et al. [142] gave a detailed comparison of these two measures. The former measure is heavily influenced by the weights of the clusters. In this case, the CRP tends to target the opinions of low-weight clusters because their opinions contribute less to the group opinion. So that our model uses the latter measure, which is completely based on the differences among cluster's opinions, without considering the influence of the clusters' weights. We present the three-level consensus index measure below.

Level 1   Individual consensus index at the matrix element level. The consensus index of a cluster with respect to the others on alternative x_i under criterion a_j is

$$ICI_{k,ij}^t = 1 - \frac{1}{K-1} \sum_{h=1,h\neq k}^{K} d(g_{k,ij}^t, g_{h,ij}^t) \tag{5.10}$$

where $d(g_{k,ij}^t, g_{h,ij}^t)$ is the distance between $g_{k,ij}^t$ and $g_{h,ij}^t$. Clearly, $0 \leq ICI_{k,ij}^t \leq 1$. The greater the value of $ICI_{k,ij}^t$ is, the higher the consensus index of the matrix element $g_{k,ij}^t$.

Level 2   Individual consensus index at the matrix level. The consensus index of a cluster opinion with respect to the others is

$$ICI_k^t = \frac{1}{m \times n} \sum_{i=1}^{m} \sum_{j=1}^{n} ICI_{k,ij}^t. \tag{5.11}$$

Clearly, $0 \leq ICI_k^t \leq 1$. The greater the value of $ICI + k^t$ is, the higher the consensus index of cluster C_k.

Level 3   Consensus index at the group level. The group consensus index is computed by

$$GCI^t = \frac{1}{K} \sum_{k=1}^{K} ICI_k^t. \tag{5.12}$$

Clearly, $0 \leq GCI^t \leq 1$. The higher the value of GCI^t is, the higher the consensus among the clusters.

Usually, we need to define the consensus threshold (denoted as $\overline{GCL}$, where $0 \leq \overline{GCL} \leq 1$), which is used to determine whether the CRP can terminate. Calculating the threshold is an important matter, and many related studies have been published (see [54, 144, 178]).

Remark 5.2 The three-level consensus index measure provides inspiration for constructing a hierarchical consensus model. We can either adjust all elements of the opinion (based on the individual consensus indexes at the matrix level) in each iteration or adjust only some elements of the opinion (based on the individual consensus index at the matrix element level).

5.4.2 Punishment-Driven Consensus Iterations

There are usually two ways to adjust opinions: the cluster opinion that has the largest distance from the group opinion is adjusted in each iteration (e.g. [126]); or the cluster opinions that contribute less to the consensus are adjusted (e.g. [99]). The former way sorts the individual consensus indexes and adjusts the opinions of clusters accordingly until the current group consensus index meets the consensus threshold. Compared with the latter way, the former has the advantage in terms of reducing the number of adjusted opinions. This paper selects the first method. Since this study takes the cluster as the basic decision-making unit, the opinions of DMs have been merged into the opinions of clusters before the CRP begins. This means that the next step for DMs is to focus on discussing the adjustment of the clusters' opinions. Suppose cluster C_k has the lowest consensus index in the t-th iteration, i.e., $ICL_k^t = min\{ICL_k^t\}$. Cluster C_k provides the adjustment coefficient δ_k^t ($0 \le \delta_k^t \le 1$) to make its opinion closer to the others. To provide guidance to the cluster regarding the adjustment coefficient and soften the human supervision of the CRP, we propose the concept of the punishment coefficient, which is the degree to which a cluster opinion is required to move towards the collective opinion.

Definition 5.9 Given the consensus threshold $\overline{GCL}$ and identified cluster consensus index ICL_k^t in the tth iteration, the punishment coefficient is defined as

$$pc_k^t = \left(\frac{\overline{GCL} - ICL_k^t}{\overline{GCL}} \right)^\sigma. \tag{5.13}$$

where σ ($0 \le \sigma \le 1$) is the power of the punishment coefficient and is used to indicate the urgency of reaching a consensus. Clearly, $0 \le pc_k^t \le 1$.

Figure 5.3 shows the distribution of the punishment coefficient for different values of σ. We set $\sigma = 1$ as the benchmark. We find that the larger the value of σ is, the smaller the punishment coefficient pc_k^t. σ is an extreme case, indicating that the identified cluster opinion is completely replaced by the collective opinion. Another important function of the punishment coefficient is that it can be used as the lower limit of the adjustment coefficient. If the given adjustment coefficient is less than the punishment coefficient, the cluster is required to use the punishment coefficient to adjust its opinion; i.e., if $\delta_k^t = pc_k^t$, then set $\delta_k^t = pc_k^t$. This is why our model is called a punishment-driven consensus model. In this way, the model not only provides guidance for opinion adjustment, but also designs a semi-automatic mandatory adjustment mechanism, which can soften the human supervision of the CRP.

Based on the operational laws proposed in this paper, the clusters' opinions are always expressed in the form of PLTSs before the selection process begins, which include discrete linguistic terms and their corresponding probability values. We define the adjusted opinion of the CRP as follow.

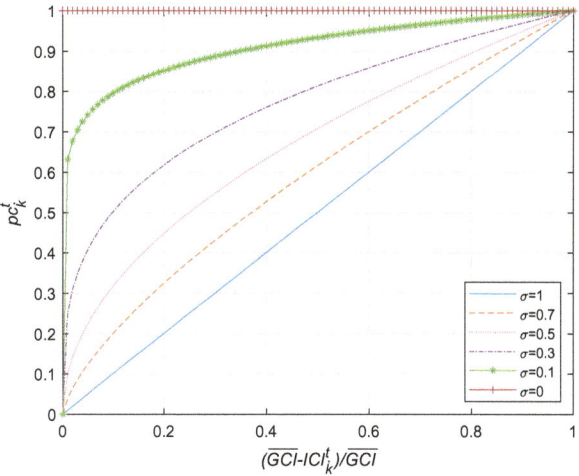

Fig. 5.3 Distribution of the punishment coefficient for different values of σ

Definition 5.10 Let G_k^t be the identified opinion with the lowest consensus index in the tth iteration, δ_k^t be the given adjustment coefficient, and pc_k^t be the punishment coefficient. If $GCL^t < \overline{GCL}$, then the opinion G_k^t should be adjusted as $G_k^{t+1} = (g_{k,ij}^{t+1})$, such that

$$g_{k,ij}^{t+1} = \begin{cases} \delta_k^t g_{c \to k,ij}^t \oplus (1 - \delta_k^t) g_{k,ij}^t & \delta_k^t \geq pc_k^t \\ pc_k^t g_{c \to k,ij}^t \oplus (1 - pc_k^t) g_{k,ij}^t & \delta_k^t < pc_k^t \end{cases} \tag{5.14}$$

where $g_{c \to k,ij}^t = \oplus_{h=1,l \neq k}^K g_{k,ij}^t \overline{\theta}_h^t$ is the collective opinion used to guide the adjustment of G_k^t and $\overline{\theta}_h^t$ is the remaining cluster C_k's weight, which satisfies $\overline{\theta}_h^t = \theta_h^t / \sum_{k=1,k \neq i}^K \theta_k^t$. The addition operation "$\oplus$" is interpreted as

$$L_{k,ij}^{(u),t+1} = \begin{cases} \delta_k^t L_{c \to k,ij}^{(u),t} \oplus (1 - \delta_k^t) L_{k,ij}^{(u),t} & \delta_k^t \geq pc_k^t \\ pc_k^t L_{c \to k,ij}^{(u),t} \oplus (1 - pc_k^t) L_{k,ij}^{(u),t} & \delta_k^t < pc_k^t \end{cases}, u = 1, \ldots, \#\#g_{k,ij}^t, \tag{5.15}$$

$$p_{k,ij}^{(u),t+1} = \begin{cases} \delta_k^t p_{c \to k,ij}^{(u),t} \oplus (1 - \delta_k^t) p_{k,ij}^{(u),t} & \delta_k^t \geq pc_k^t \\ pc_k^t p_{c \to k,ij}^{(u),t} \oplus (1 - pc_k^t) p_{k,ij}^{(u),t} & \delta_k^t < pc_k^t \end{cases}, u = 1, \ldots, \#\#g_{k,ij}^t, \tag{5.16}$$

where $p_{c \to k,ij}^{(u),t} = \sum_{h=1,h \neq k}^K p_{h,lj}^{(u),t} \overline{\theta}_h^t, L_{c \to k,ij}^{(u),t} = L_{k,ij}^{(u),t}, u = 1, \ldots, \#\#g_{k,ij}^t, i = 1, 2, \ldots, m, j = 1, 2, \ldots, n$.

5.4.3 Hierarchical Punishment-Driven Consensus Iterations

In Sect. 5.4.1, we divide the consensus measures into three levels. The group consensus index is used to determine whether the current consensus satisfies the threshold. The other consensus indexes can be used to determine which clusters' opinions or matrix elements need to be adjusted. Different matrix elements in a cluster opinion usually have different consensus indexes. Therefore, it is reasonable to use different adjustment coefficients (or punishment coefficients).

Definition 5.11 For the consensus threshold $\overline{GCL}$ and the identified cluster C_k in the t-th iteration, the punishment coefficient at the matrix element level is defined as

$$
pc_{k,ij}^{t+1} = \begin{cases} \left(\frac{\overline{GCL} - ICL_{k,ij}^t}{\overline{GCL}} \right)^\sigma & ICL_{k,ij}^t < \overline{GCL} \\ 0 & ICL_{k,ij}^t \geq \overline{GCL} \end{cases}. \tag{5.17}
$$

Let σ be the same as in Definition 5.9. Clearly, $0 \leq pc_{k,ij}^t \leq 1$, $i = 1, 2, \ldots, m$, $j = 1, 2, \ldots, n$.

Based on Eq. (5.14), we use the following formula to adjust the matrix elements in the opinion G_k^t:

$$
g_{k,ij}^{t+1} = \begin{cases} \delta_k^t g_{c \to k,ij}^t \oplus (1 - \delta_k^t) g_{k,ij}^t & \delta_k^t \geq pc_k^t \\ pc_k^t g_{c \to k,ij}^t \oplus (1 - pc_k^t) g_{k,ij}^t & \delta_k^t < pc_k^t \end{cases}, u = 1, \ldots, \#\# g_{k,ij}^t, \tag{5.18}
$$

where $\delta_{k,ij}^t (0 \leq \delta_{k,ij}^t \leq 1)$ is the adjustment coefficient given by cluster C_k that is used to modify the probability value of the matrix element of position (i, j) in G_k^t.

In general, although the identified cluster has the lowest consensus index at the individual matrix level, it does not necessarily indicate that the consensus indexes of all elements in the cluster opinion do not satisfy the threshold. Using the same coefficient to adjust all the matrix elements may result in adjusting elements that should not be adjusted, or should not be adjusted by such a large amount, which will result in opinion distortion. We consider opinion distortion to have two parts: the adjustment amount of the opinion and the proportions of the adjusted matrix elements in the opinion. The latter part reflects the number of matrix elements that were adjusted but should not have been.

Definition 5.12 Based on Eq. (5.5), the adjustment amount of the identified opinion G_k^t after the tth iteration is calculated by

$$
\overline{AA}_k^{t+1} = d(G_k^{t+1}, G_k^t) \tag{5.19}
$$

Clearly, $0 \leq \overline{AA}_k^{t+1} \leq 1$. A larger value of $\overline{AA}_k^t$ indicates a greater adjustment in going from G_k^t to G_k^{t+1}.

Definition 5.13 Let $IX(G_k^t, G_k^{t+1})$ be the number of matrix elements that have been adjusted in the tth iteration. The proportion of adjusted matrix elements is obtained by

$$\widehat{AA}_k^{t+1} = \frac{IX(G_k^t, G_k^{t+1})}{m \times n}. \tag{5.20}$$

Definition 5.14 Given the adjustment amount and the proportion of adjusted matrix elements, the distortion degree of the opinion G_k^t is defined as

$$DD_k^{t+1} = \frac{\overline{AA}_k^{t+1} + \widehat{AA}_k^{t+1}}{2} \tag{5.21}$$

Clearly, $0 \leq DD_k^{t+1} \leq 1$. A larger value of DD_k^{t+1} represents a higher distortion degree in going from G_k^t to G_k^{t+1}.

We propose the soft adjustment strategy, which allows different punishment coefficients to be used to adjust the matrix elements. Conversely, hard adjustment strategy requires that all matrix elements be adjusted with the same coefficient. Employing hard adjustment often leads to adjusting a larger number of matrix elements than employing soft adjustment in each consensus iteration. However, when the CRP begins, there are usually a large number of matrix elements in the identified opinion whose consensus indexes do not meet the requirements. Too much time will be spent reviewing the consensus index for each element and providing the adjustment coefficient if soft adjustment is used. Therefore, we consider that the hard adjustment strategy can be adopted first to improve the consensus indexes at different levels. When the group consensus index approaches the consensus threshold closely, the soft adjustment strategy is used to balance the relationship between opinion distortion and consensus improvement. To determine which adjustment strategy to adopt, we introduce a new parameter, the attainment rate of the consensus index, denoted as $ARoCI(0 \leq ARoCI \leq 1)$. This parameter elevates the punishment-driven consensus model to a hierarchical consensus model.

Definition 5.15 Given the group consensus index GCL^t and consensus threshold $\overline{GCL}$, the attainment rate of the consensus index is defined as

$$ARoCI^t = \frac{GCL^t}{\overline{GCL}} \tag{5.22}$$

Clearly, $GCL^0/\overline{GCL} \leq ARoCL^t \leq 1$. $ARoCL^t$ reflects the percentage of the current consensus index that satisfies the consensus threshold. The higher the group consensus index, the greater the value of $ARoCL^t$. DMs often set the threshold $\overline{ARoCL} \in [GCL^0/\overline{GCL}, 1]$ for $ARoCL^t$.

The essential difference between hard adjustment and soft adjustment is whether a matrix element that satisfies the consensus threshold should be adjusted when the consensus index at the matrix level does not meet the consensus threshold. We define the following rule.

Definition 5.16 Let $IX(G_k^t)$ be the number of matrix elements that contribute less to the consensus. When the conditions $AroCL^t \geq \overline{AroCI}$ and $IX(G_k^t)/m \times n \leq \overline{IX}$ are met, the soft adjustment strategy is adopted; otherwise, the hard adjustment strategy is used. $\overline{IX}\,(0 \leq \overline{IX} \leq 1)$ is the threshold of $\overline{IX}(G_k^t)/m \times n$.

If $ARoCL^t \geq \overline{ARoCL}$ and $IX(G_k^t)/m \times n \leq \overline{IX}$, this indicates that the group consensus index is high enough, and the number of elements in the identified opinion that need to be adjusted drops significantly. In this case, the soft adjustment strategy is used. Clearly, when we set $\overline{ARoCL} = 1$ or $\overline{IX} = 0$, the hard adjustment strategy will be used throughout the CRP. By combining the hard adjustment and soft adjustment, the hierarchical punishment-driven consensus model (HPDCM) is obtained. Algorithm 5.2 presents the implementation process for the model.

Algorithm 5.2 Hierarchical punishment-driven consensus model for PL-LSGDM problems

---

Input: The initial individual opinions $V_l^0(l = 1, 2, \ldots, q)$, the consensus threshold $\overline{GCL}$, the threshold of the attainment rate of the consensus index $\overline{ARoCI}$, the weight vector of the criteria ω, and parameters $\overline{IX}$, a, b, and σ.

Output: The final number of iterations, the final group opinion, and the final ranking of the alternatives.

1: Implement granularity normalization and probability normalization to obtain the standardized individual opinions $R_l^0(l = 1, 2, \ldots, q)$.
2: Adopt Algorithm 5.1 to classify the initial large group into K clusters. Use the PLWA operator to obtain the clusters' opinions $G_k^0(l = k, 2, \ldots, K)$, and compute the weight vector of the clusters with Eq. (5.9).
3: Set $t = 0$.
4: Compute the consensus measures via Eqs. (5.10)–(5.12). If $GCL^t \geq \overline{GCL}$, then proceed to Step 3.4; otherwise, proceed to the next step.
5: Calculate the attainment rate of the consensus index $ARoCI^t$ and the rate of the number of matrix elements that have small consensus indexes $IX(G_k^t)/m \times n$. If $ARoCI^t \geq \overline{ARoCI}$ and $IX(G_k^t)/m \times n \leq \overline{IX}$, then use Eq. (5.18) to perform the adjustment; otherwise, use Eq. (5.14) to adjust the identified opinion. Let $t + t + 1$, and then return to Step 3.2.
6: Let $t^* = t$. Output the final number of iterations t^* and the final opinions of the clusters $G_k^{t^*}$ ($k = 1, 2, \ldots, K$).
7: Aggregate all the clusters' opinions to obtain the group opinion R_c via Eq. (5.3).
8: Calculate the overall criterion values $Z(x_i)(i = 1, 2, \ldots, m)$ based on Eq. (5.3).
9: Use the rule in Pang et al. [87] to compare the overall criterion values and obtain the ranking of the alternatives.

5.5 Case Study

In this section, we apply the HPDCM to a PL-LSGDM problem concerning global supplier selection.

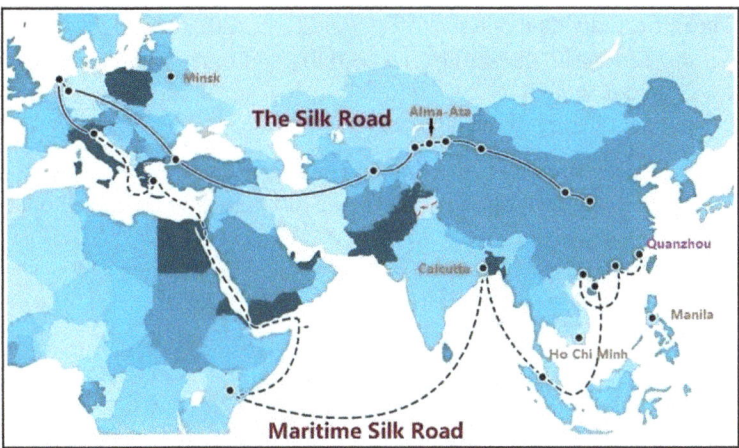

Fig. 5.4 Geographical distribution of preselected suppliers along the Belt and Road. *Source* http://www.sohu.com/a/111613685_472018

5.5.1 Problem Description

ABC, an electronics manufacturer located in Quanzhou, China, is reassessing the suppliers it currently works with. Considering the rising cost of domestic labor and the policy advantages of the Belt and Road cooperation initiative, the company has decided to select a material supplier located along this route and add it to the supplier list. Five alternatives have been preselected for further evaluation, and their geographical locations are Alma-Ata, Ho Chi Minh City, Manila, Calcutta and Minsk, as shown in Fig. 5.4. A special committee of 20 relevant department heads and experts is formed to evaluate the alternative suppliers. Drawing from the research [5, 30, 96, 115] and business practices, three comprehensive criteria are used: commercial factors (a_1), such as quality, price, quantity and delivery time; sustainability dimensions (a_2), including economic, environmental, and social bottom lines; and global risks (a_3), such as currency fluctuations, political instability, terrorism, and cultural incompatibility. The weight vector of the criteria is set as $\omega = (0.4, 0.3, 0.3)^T$. The DMs provide their evaluations by means of PLTSs, in which the linguistic evaluation scale $S = \{s_{-3} = Extrmely\ poor, s_{-2} = Poor, s_{-1} = Somewhat\ poor, s_0 = Neutral, s_1 = Somewhat\ good, s_2 = Good, s_3 = Extrmely\ good\}$.

5.5.2 Decision Process

Here, the HPDCM is used to manage the processes of consensus and selection. The following steps are involved. To save space, only the main results are listed.

Input: The initial individual opinions $V_l^0 (l = 1, 2, \ldots, 20)$, the weight vector of the criteria ω, the consensus threshold $\overline{GCL} = 0.88$, and other parameters $\overline{ARoCL} = 0.95$, $\overline{IX} = 1$, and $\sigma = 1/3$.

Output: The final ranking of the alternatives.

Process 1: Preprocessing of the decision information.

Normalize the individual opinions. Here, we just give the normalized opinion of cluster C_1:

$$
R_1^0 = \begin{pmatrix}
r_{1,11}^0 & r_{1,12}^0 & r_{1,13}^0 \\
r_{1,21}^0 & r_{1,22}^0 & r_{1,23}^0 \\
r_{1,31}^0 & r_{1,32}^0 & r_{1,33}^0 \\
r_{1,41}^0 & r_{1,42}^0 & r_{1,43}^0 \\
r_{1,51}^0 & r_{1,52}^0 & r_{1,53}^0
\end{pmatrix},
$$

where

$r_{1,11}^0 = \{s_{-3}(0), s_{-2}(0), s_{-1}(0), s_0(0.5), s_1(0), s_2(0.4), s_3(0.1)\}$,
$r_{1,12}^0 = \{s_{-3}(0), s_{-2}(1), s_{-1}(0), s_0(0), s_1(0), s_2(0), s_3(0)\}$,
$r_{1,13}^0 = \{s_{-3}(0), s_{-2}(0), s_{-1}(0.1), s_0(0), s_1(0), s_2(0.9), s_3(0)\}$,
$r_{1,21}^0 = \{s_{-3}(0), s_{-2}(0), s_{-1}(0.5), s_0(0.5), s_1(0.7), s_2(0.5), s_3(0.1)\}$,
$r_{1,22}^0 = \{s_{-3}(0), s_{-2}(0), s_{-1}(0), s_0(0.4), s_1(0.6), s_2(0), s_3(0)\}$,
$r_{1,23}^0 = \{s_{-3}(0), s_{-2}(0), s_{-1}(0.5), s_0(0), s_1(0.5), s_2(0), s_3(0)\}$,
$r_{1,31}^0 = \{s_{-3}(0), s_{-2}(0), s_{-1}(0.3), s_0(0.5), s_1(0.7), s_2(0.4), s_3(0.1)\}$,
$r_{1,32}^0 = \{s_{-3}(0), s_{-2}(0.2), s_{-1}(0.3), s_0(0), s_1(0.5), s_2(0), s_3(0)\}$,
$r_{1,33}^0 = \{s_{-3}(0), s_{-2}(0), s_{-1}(0.7), s_0(0), s_1(0.3), s_2(0), s_3(0)\}$,
$r_{1,41}^0 = \{s_{-3}(0), s_{-2}(0), s_{-1}(0.2), s_0(0.8), s_1(0), s_2(0), s_3(0.1)\}$,
$r_{1,42}^0 = \{s_{-3}(0), s_{-2}(0), s_{-1}(0.3), s_0(0), s_1(1), s_2(0), s_3(0)\}$,
$r_{1,43}^0 = \{s_{-3}(0), s_{-2}(0), s_{-1}(0.6), s_0(0), s_1(0.4), s_2(0), s_3(0)\}$,
$r_{1,51}^0 = \{s_{-3}(0), s_{-2}(0), s_{-1}(0.5), s_0(0.8), s_1(0.5), s_2(0), s_3(0.1)\}$,
$r_{1,52}^0 = \{s_{-3}(0), s_{-2}(0.2), s_{-1}(0.3), s_0(0.8), s_1(0), s_2(0), s_3(0)\}$,
$r_{1,53}^0 = \{s_{-3}(0), s_{-2}(0), s_{-1}(0), s_0(0), s_0(0.4), s_2(1), s_3(0)\}$.

Process 2: Clustering process.

Use Algorithm 5.1 to divide the large group into six clusters by setting the minimum distance to 0.23, as shown in Fig. 5.5. As previously discussed, we set $\beta = 1$, $a = round(q \cdot 0.1) = 2$, and $b = round(q/m) = 4$. Table 5.3 presents the clustering results.

Process 3: Consensus reaching process.

Use the HPDCM to manage opinion differences. Table 5.4 shows the consensus iterations.

In conclusion, after three consensus iterations (including one hard adjustment and two soft adjustments), the group consensus index satisfies the consensus threshold. Let $t^* = 3$, and the final opinions of the clusters can be obtained as $G_k^3(k = 1, 2, \ldots, 6)$.

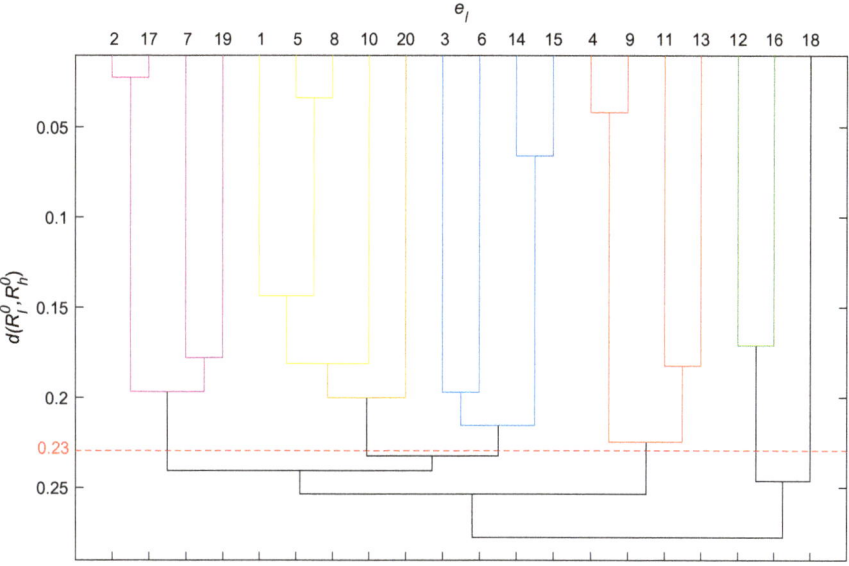

e_l

Fig. 5.5 Visual clustering processes using Algorithm 5.2

Table 5.3 Clustering results by using Algorithm 7.1

C_k	n_k	e_l	θ_k^0
C_1	4	e_2, e_{17}, e_7, e_{19}	0.1967
C_2	5	$e_1, e_5, e_8, e_{10}, e_{20}$	0.197
C_3	4	e_3, e_6, e_{14}, e_{15}	0.1933
C_4	4	e_4, e_9, e_{11}, e_{13}	0.1936
C_5	2	e_{12}, e_{16}	0.1097
C_6	1	e_{18}	0.1097

Process 4: Selection process.

Step 4.1: Aggregate all the clusters' opinions to obtain the group opinion via Eq. (5.3):

Step 4.2: Calculate the overall criterion values $Z(x_i)(i = 1, 2, \ldots, m)$ based on Eq. (5.3), as follows:

$Z(x_1) = \{s_{-3}(0.1051), s_{-2}(0.182), s_{-1}(0.1858), s_0(0.148), s_1(0.181), s_2(0.0976), s_3(0.0499)\}$,

$Z(x_2) = \{s_{-3}(0.0229), s_{-2}(0.0793), s_{-1}(0.1552), s_0(0.2322), s_1(0.1726), s_2(0.1697), s_3(0.1138)\}$,

$Z(x_3) = \{s_{-3}(0.0469), s_{-2}(0.0552), s_{-1}(0.2376), s_0(0.2046), s_1(0.1949), s_2(0.1052), s_3(0.0978)\}$,

Table 5.4 Consensus iterations using the HPDCM

t	GCL before CRP	Identified opinion	Hard/soft adjustment	Given adjustment coefficient (matrix)	Punishment coefficient (matrix)	GCL after CRP
1	0.8305	G_6^0	Hard	0.5	0.47	0.8576
2	0.8576	G_5^1	Soft	$\begin{pmatrix} 0.2 & 0.2 & 0.1 \\ 0.2 & 0 & 0.2 \\ 0.1 & 0.3 & 0.1 \\ 0.2 & 0.1 & 0.1 \\ 0.1 & 0.3 & 0.2 \end{pmatrix}$	$\begin{pmatrix} 0.3282 & 0.2036 & 0.1 \\ 0.466 & 0 & 0.5939 \\ 0.1966 & 0 & 0.1609 \\ 0.3622 & 0.4083 & 0 \\ 0.1684 & 0.7025 & 0.3788 \end{pmatrix}$	0.8741
3	0.8741	G_4^2	Soft	$\begin{pmatrix} 0.2 & 0.5 & 0 \\ 0.2 & 0.2 & 0 \\ 0.2 & 0.2 & 0.2 \\ 0 & 0 & 0.1 \\ 0.2 & 0.2 & 0.4 \end{pmatrix}$	$\begin{pmatrix} 0.2027 & 0.5443 & 0 \\ 0.3314 & 0 & 0 \\ 0.3739 & 0.0929 & 0.2729 \\ 0 & 0 & 0.4173 \\ 0.2449 & 0.222 & 0.37 \end{pmatrix}$	0.8829

$Z(x_4) = \{s_{-3}(0.0737), s_{-2}(0.0916), s_{-1}(0.2031), s_0(0.2068), s_1(0.1244),$
$s_2(0.0215), s_3(0.0499)\},$

$Z(x_5) = \{s_{-3}(0.688), s_{-2}(0.1253), s_{-1}(0.1452), s_0(0.1561), s_1(0.1651),$
$s_2(0.1871), s_3(0.1037)\}.$

Step 4.3: Based on the score function of PLTSs proposed by Pang et al. [87], we can calculate the scores of the overall criterion values: $E(Z(x_1)) = s_{-0.3392}$, $E(Z(x_2)) = s_{0.4709}$, $E(Z(x_3)) = s_{0.21}$, $E(Z(x_4)) = s_{0.035}$, $E(Z(x_5)) = s_{0.2482}$. Therefore, the ranking is $x_2 \succ x_5 \succ x_3 \succ x_4 \succ x_1$, and the best solution is x_2. That is, the DMs are more likely to include the supplier in Ho Chi Minh City on the supplier list.

5.6 Comparative Analysis and Discussion

We discuss some additional important issues about the HPDCM in Sect. 5.6.1, including a comparison of hard adjustment and soft adjustment and the determination of relevant parameters. Our proposal is compared with other linguistic models in Sect. 5.6.2. Section 5.6.3 presents the managerial implications involved in the practical application of the proposed model. Note that the data used in the comparative analysis and discussion originate from the case study in Sect. 5.5.

5.6.1 Further Discussion of the Hierarchical Punishment-Driven Consensus Model

This section analyzes two important issues regarding the HPDCM: the comparison between hard adjustment and soft adjustment and the calculation of the threshold for the attainment rate of the consensus index.

5.6.1.1 Hard Adjustment and Soft Adjustment

To eliminate DMs' subjective attitudes towards adjustment, we adopt the punishment coefficient in implementing the CRP. Figure 5.6 shows the consensus results obtained by hard adjustment and soft adjustment. First, regardless of which type of adjustment strategy is utilized, the group consensus index continues to rise as the number of consensus iterations increases. This indicates that the two adjustment strategies are effective in promoting consensus improvement. However, different adjustment strategies lead to different degrees of opinion distortion. For example, as shown in Fig. 5.6, the distortion degree is 0.5464 when using hard adjustment after the first iteration, while the soft adjustment results in only a 0.4813 distortion degree. This is because adopting a hard adjustment strategy causes some matrix elements that should not have been adjusted to be adjusted.

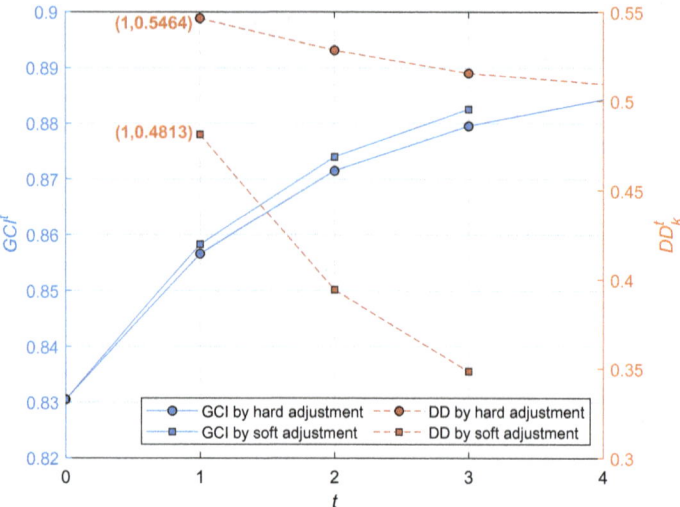

Fig. 5.6 Consensus results obtained by hard adjustment and soft adjustment

Although, as noted above, soft adjustment performs better than hard adjustment in terms of opinion distortion, this does not mean that soft adjustment can completely replace hard adjustment. Hard adjustment requires only one adjustment coefficient, which is easy to obtain, especially when no punishment coefficient is used as a reference. The hard adjustment may lead to undue distortion, because even if a certain matrix element already satisfies the consensus threshold, it will still be adjusted. Soft adjustment refines the adjustment range to the matrix element level, which helps reduce unnecessary distortion. However, for the DMs, too much time is spent providing adjustment coefficients according to the different consensus indexes of matrix elements. We conclude that hard adjustment is better suited to situations where (1) the decision process has just begun, (2) the identified matrix is low-dimensional, or (3) the decision is time-critical. When the group consensus index has increased significantly and most elements in the identified opinion have already met the consensus threshold, soft adjustment takes precedence.

5.6.1.2   Determination of the Relevant Parameters

In this section, we discuss how to assign the following two parameters: the threshold of the attainment rate of the consensus index $\overline{ARoCI}$ and the power of the punishment coefficient σ.

The attainment rate of the consensus index plays a decisive role in whether to adopt hard adjustment or soft adjustment. A high threshold can delay the use of soft adjustment strategy, which may increase opinion distortion. A low threshold will lead to premature use of soft adjustment strategy; this may make it difficult for the cluster to provide the adjustment coefficient at the matrix element level because there may be multiple elements in the identified opinion that need to be adjusted. We suggest that determining the threshold should follow two principles:

(1) Computer software is used to simulate the CRP so as to provide reference for practical operation.
(2) There are two factors to consider: the number of consensus iterations and the degree of opinion distortion.

Assume that the following requirements are met: the maximum number of iterations is 5 and the opinion distortion is no more than 0.5 in each iteration. We implement punishment-driven consensus iterations using MATLAB software. Figure 5.7 shows the simulation results of the number of iterations and the distortion degree when $\alpha = 0.5$ increases from 0 to 0.5. When , the number of iterations reaches 8 by using the hard adjustment strategy (or 6 by using the soft adjustment strategy). According to the function characteristic of punishment coefficient, the setting $\alpha > 0.5$ will lead to a greater number of iterations. Therefore, Fig. 5.7 only depicts the simulation results under the condition of $\sigma \in [0, 0.5]$. We find that as σ increases, the number of iterations and the total distortion degree increase, but from the overall trend, the average distortion degree decreases. The average distortion degree is defined as the total distortion degree divided by the number of iterations. Determining the parameter includes the following steps.

Step 1:   Observe the simulation of the number of iterations and determine the membership interval of σ. If adopting the hard adjustment strategy, then we can set $\sigma \in [0, 0.4]$; If adopting the soft adjustment strategy, then we can set $\sigma \in [0, 0.5]$. By taking the intersection of the above two intervals, the membership interval is temporarily determined as $\sigma \in [0, 0.4]$.

Step 2   Modify the temporary interval based on the simulation of opinion distortion. From Fig. 5.7, the average distortion will always be greater than 0.5 if the hard adjustment strategy is adopted, while the opposite result will be obtained if the soft adjustment strategy is adopted. Therefore, σ should be assigned a larger value so that the average distortion is as small as possible. Based on the obtained membership interval, we can set $\sigma = 0.4$. In this case, the soft adjustment strategy must be adopted at least once.

Without loss of generality, we assume that the hard adjustment strategy is allowed to be used once. In fact, this case can only happen at the beginning of the CRP. Figure 5.8 shows the changes of some parameters in the CRP when setting $\sigma = 0.4$. From Fig. 5.8, the following results can be obtained $ARoCL^0 = 0.9437$, $ARoCL^1 = 0.9698$, and $IX(G_k^t)/m \times n = 0.7333$. To ensure that the hard adjustment strategy is adopted in the first iteration, we set $\overline{ARoCL} > ARoCL^0$. In the second iteration the soft adjustment strategy can be adopted when setting $\overline{ARoCL} \leq ARoCL^1 = 0.9698$ and $\overline{IX} \geq 0.7333$. In conclusion, we have that $\overline{ARoCL} \in (0.9437, 0.9698]$ and $\overline{IX} \geq 0.7333$. Specifically, the parameters can be set as $\overline{ARoCL} = 0.95$ and $\overline{IX} = 1$.

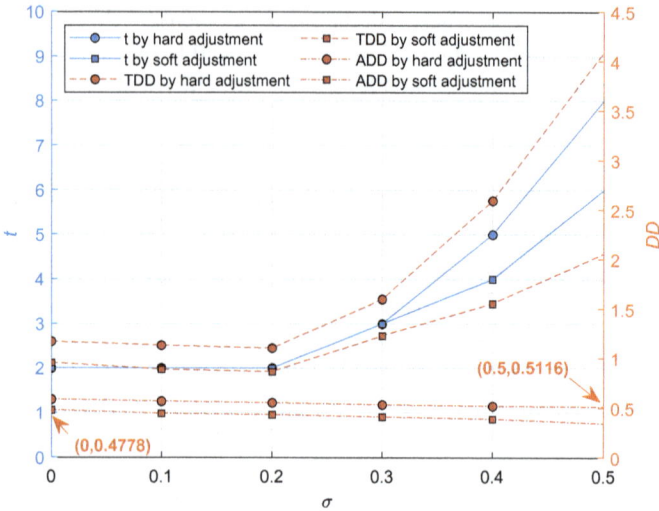

Fig. 5.7 Consensus results when σ increases from 0 to 0.5. *Note TDD* represents the total distortion degree, which is calculated by $\sum_t DD_k^t$. *ADD* is the average distortion degree, which is calculated by $\sum_t DD_k^t$

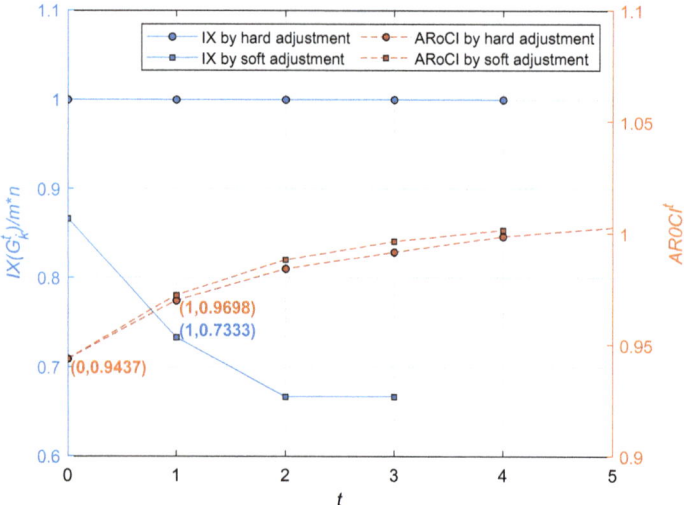

Fig. 5.8 Changes in some parameters in the CRP. *Note* Set $\sigma = 0.4$. *IX* represents the proportion of adjusted matrix elements in the identified opinion. *ARoCI* is the attainment rate of the consensus index

5.6.2   Comparison to Other Linguistic Models

This section presents a comparison of our proposal with Pang et al.'s research [87] and HFLTSs in the decision-making process.

An HFLTS represents hesitation among multiple linguistic terms but cannot reflect the importance of these linguistic terms. In the kind of case we are considering, if the decision information is expressed by HFLTSs, this can be interpreted as indicating that all possible linguistic terms in an HFLTS have the same importance degree. Accordingly, an HFLTS can be written in the form of a PLTS, in which all the linguistic terms have the same possibility. For instance, if the opinion $v^0_{1,13} = \{s_{-1}(0.1), s_2(0.9)\}$ is represented using an HFLTS, it is changed to $\{s_{-1}(0.5), s_2(0.5)\}$.

On the other hand, since the concept of PLTSs was proposed by Pang et al. [87], research on aggregation and distance measurement for PLTSs has attracted much attention. In this section, we compare our proposal with Pang et al.'s model [87] in terms of the effect that processing PLTSs has on the decision results. In general, there are two models for addressing PLTSs: (1) Probability values are incorporated into the linguistic terms in the process of information aggregation (see [87]). In this model, the probabilities of linguistic terms are not reflected in the result, and the original discrete linguistic terms are transformed into virtual ones. (2) Similar to our proposal, before entering the selection process, the information aggregation only involves operations on probability values corresponding to the same linguistic terms and does not merge probability values and linguistic terms.

To ensure comparability, we set the same number of clusters, i.e., $K = 6$. From the visual clustering processes shown in Figs. 5.5 and 5.9, the most significant differences are the order in which new clusters are formed and the distances between DMs. Table 5.5 depicts the results of the first three clusters formed by using different linguistic models. Our proposal differs from the other two models in forming the second and third clusters. This is due to the distance measure. As $d(R^0_5, R^0_8) > d(R^0_4, R^0_9)$ in our proposal, the second cluster is composed of e_4, e_9; however, in the other two models, since $d(R^0_5, R^0_8) < d(R^0_4, R^0_9)$, DMs e_5, e_8 form the second cluster. It is important to note that if HFLTSs are used, the distance between R^0_2 and R^0_{17} is 0, which is different from the result obtained by using our proposal or Pang et al.'s model [87]. This is due to the fact that HFLTSs do not reflect the weights of the linguistic terms.

Owing to different clustering results, the quantitative comparison of the CRP seems unfair. Nonetheless, we consider that it is difficult for DMs to understand the meaning of virtual linguistic terms, as opposed to the discrete linguistic terms with corresponding probabilities. Additionally, the alternative rankings prior to the CRP are depicted in Fig. 5.10. All three linguistic models yield the same optimal solution (i.e., x_2) and the same ranking (i.e., $x_2 \succ x_5 \succ x_3 \succ x_4 \succ x_1$). However, there are large differences in the scores of the alternatives, although this does not affect the selection of the best alternative.

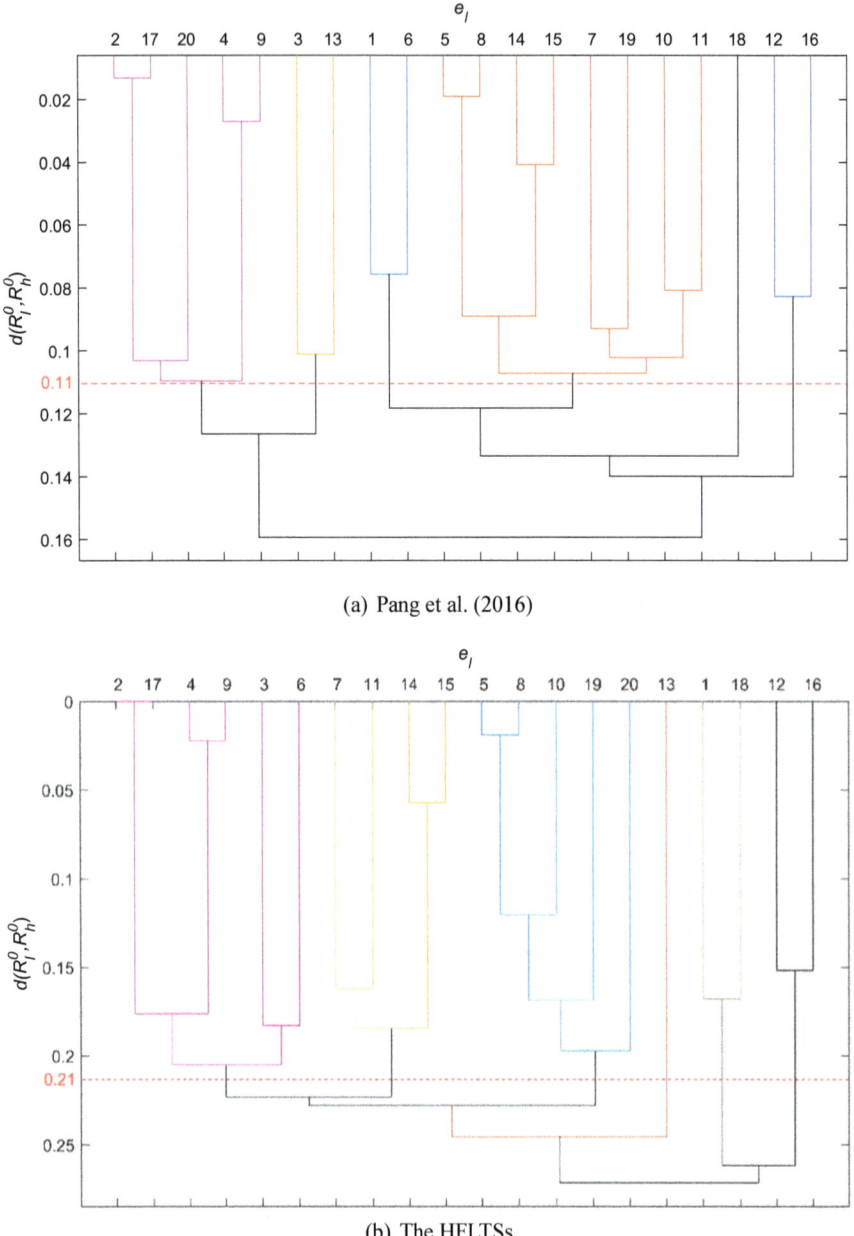

(a) Pang et al. (2016)

(b) The HFLTSs

Fig. 5.9 Simulation results of the number of clusters using trust score and similarity degree, respectively

Table 5.5 Clustering results of the first three clusters formed by using different linguistic models

Linguistic model	First three clusters formed	Distances between the DMs in each cluster
Pang et al. [87]	$\{e_2, e_{17}\}, \{e_5, e_8\}, \{e_4, e_9\}$	0.0229, 0.0341, 0.0421
The HFLTSs	$\{e_2, e_{17}\}, \{e_5, e_8\}, \{e_4, e_9\}$	0, 0.0191, 0.0222
Our proposal	$\{e_2, e_{17}\}, \{e_4, e_9\}, \{e_5, e_8\}$	0.0132, 0.0191, 0.027

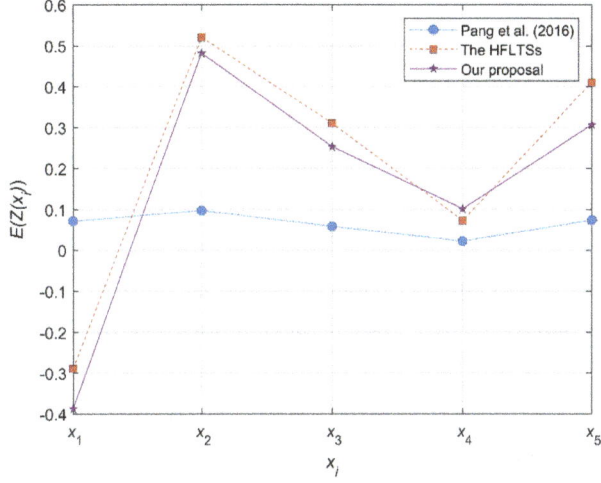

Fig. 5.10 Initial rankings of the alternatives obtained by using different linguistic models

Above all, our proposal overcomes the shortcomings of the other two models in processing linguistic information. Unlike HFLTSs, which represent hesitations regarding multiple linguistic terms, our proposal based on PLTSs considers the importance of the linguistic terms, which is more in line with actual circumstances. On the other hand, using Pang et al.'s model [87] to handle PLTSs leads to the probabilities of linguistic terms not being reflected in the result. In this way, the unique feature of PLTSs compared with ordinary linguistic term sets is lost. Furthermore, according to the statement "the ordinal discrete linguistic terms are used to evaluate alternatives, while the virtual linguistic terms can only appear in the operation and ranking" [137], virtual linguistic terms should be avoided in the CRP. Therefore, our proposal insists on preserving the original discrete linguistic term structure of PLTSs in the processes of clustering, aggregating and consensus reaching, and only after beginning the selection process are virtual linguistic terms introduced to calculate the scores of PLTSs.

5.6.3 Managerial Implications

The proposed HPDCM can be applied to the practical case of supplier selection in the manufacturing and service industries, and the following important issues are raised:

(1) Supplier selection is a strategic and complex decision with risks that is closely related to the survival and sustainable development of enterprises. It is therefore necessary to measure the group consensus index and make any useful adjustments to ensure that the result is accepted by the majority. This arrangement can reduce the risks and losses of decision-making errors, but more importantly, only when a result is approved by the majority can it obtain the maximum practical support from the majority of departments.

(2) The increase in the consensus index is due to some DMs adjusting their own views, whether voluntarily or involuntarily. In this way, the adjusted opinion may be somewhat distorted from the original opinion. Therefore, it is important to measure the degree of opinion distortion and use it as an indicator to evaluate the performance of the CRP. In business practice, some DMs insist on their opinions and are unwilling to compromise for the sake of consensus. Even if the adjustments are forced by the punishment-driven consensus model, the reasonableness of the adjusted opinion needs to be examined. The distortion degree is an important index to test rationality. If the distortion of a DM's opinion is high in an iteration (close to 1), the DM's original opinion is likely to deviate significantly from the majority opinion.

5.7 Conclusions

In this chapter, a hierarchical punishment-driven consensus model for probabilistic linguistic large-group decision-making was developed, and an application of the model to global supplier selection was presented. The obtained results show that the new model can overcome the scalability challenge and soften the human supervision of the CRP. The major contributions of this chapter are as follows:

(1) The PL-LSGDM was defined, and its characteristics were detailed. To improve the performance of PLTSs in the CRP, the rules governing their normalization and operations were redefined.

(2) A hierarchical punishment-driven consensus model for PL-LSGDM was developed, including hard adjustment and soft adjustment, which aimed to reduce the distortion of opinions with the goal of achieving a consensus within a specified number of iterations. Before the CRP begins, the large group was classified into several subgroups by hierarchical clustering, and the opinions of clusters were generated. This operation can overcome the scalability challenge when the number of DMs involved is sufficiently large. When the necessary parameters are set, the model can automatically provide guidance for the adjustment of opinions, thereby reducing the human supervision cost of the CRP.

(3) The model was applied to a case study of global supplier selection, and the application implications were discussed.

It is worth noting that there are always social relationships between DMs [19, 127]. The influence of social relationships on the CRP should be considered. As further research, we will study the theoretical framework of consensus building in LSGDM problems in the context of social networks.

Chapter 6
Confidence Consensus-Based Model for LSGDM

Abstract Because of the complexity of real-world problems, large-scale group decision-making has become a research topic of great interest in the field of decision science. Differences of opinion in a large group are highly likely. Sometimes, decision makers are unwilling to adjust their opinions to promote consensus. It is hence necessary to establish a consensus model for the effective management of opinion differences and non-cooperative behaviors. More importantly, the credibility of the adjustment information must be ensured. In this chapter, we present a confidence consensus-based model for large-scale group decision-making that provides a novel approach to addressing non-cooperative behaviors. First, some new concepts are proposed, including the collective adjustment suggestion and rationality degree. Then, we combine the rationality and non-cooperation of the adjustment information to construct the concept of a confidence level. This confidence level measures the impartiality and objectivity of the adjustment information and is the basis for managing non-cooperative behaviors. We then establish a mechanism for addressing non-cooperative behaviors. Finally, we present a case study that illustrates that the proposed model is feasible and effective. A comparative analysis reveals the features and advantages of this model for managing large-scale group decision making.

Keywords Large-scale group decision-making (LSGDM) · Non-cooperative behaviors · Confidence consensus-based model · Consensus reaching process (CRP) · Rationality degree

6.1 Introduction

Group decision-making (GDM) aims to achieve a common solution for a decision problem in which two or more decision makers (DMs) participate, and it has been paid an increasing amount of attention [3, 13, 26, 92, 129]. Traditional GDM is a type of group discussion and decision process in which the number of DMs is small (e.g., three to five people), and the complexity is often not very high (e.g., a car purchase decision for a family). In GDM for public-interest decisions, however, a large number of DMs with different interests and knowledge structures must be involved. Research into large-scale GDM (LSGDM) is a new area in the field of decision making. LSGDM problems are generally characterized by some or all the following four features [21, 25, 28, 84, 127, 167]: (a) The group usually involves a large number of DMs from different sectors and professional fields. (b) Obtaining a high-consensus solution necessitates the implementation of a consensus reaching process (CRP). (c) The social networks of the DMs and the evolution of their opinions are considered. (d) DMs often have individual concerns about alternatives, and thus they adopt heterogeneous preference representation structures to express their preferences. Note that the number of DMs in current LSGDM problems varies from dozens to thousands [131]. Xu et al. [144] and Zhang et al. [167] believe that if the number of DMs in a group exceeds 11, the group is a large group, whereas Liu et al. [65] insists that this number should be more than 20. In this study, to include all the research on consensus measures and mechanisms for managing non-cooperative behaviors in the CRP, we employ the first and second characteristics above to define LSGDM.

Clustering is an effective approach to organizing and managing a large group because it can divide a large group into small-scale subgroups. Many clustering methods have been proposed such as K-means algorithm [51, 131], fuzzy clustering algorithm [84, 110], grey clustering algorithm [66], and vector space-based [140] clustering method. Clustering in LSGDM is typically based on the similarity of DMs' opinions. If the opinions of certain DMs are sufficiently similar (i.e., over a certain threshold), these DMs are assigned to the same subgroup. This classification produces a hierarchical structure. The outer layer represents the interaction between subgroups and the inner layer represents the discussion among the members of each subgroup. The coordination among subgroups does not need to consider the internal members of the subgroup; the members in a subgroup form a unified subgroup opinion through discussion and coordination. Generally, the clustering structure does not change once it has been determined [144, 146] because this helps the members in each subgroup to establish trust feelings and form a unified opinion. In contrast, Wu and Xu [131] and Zhang et al. [167] studied consensus models in which the clusters are allowed to change. This study follows Xu et al.'s research [144] on classifying large-scale DMs and uses the cluster as a basic unit once the clustering structure has been determined.

Generally, both of the two processes are used to address LSGDM problems: the consensus process and the selection process [144]. Reaching a consensus is a dynamic and iterative group discussion process in which some DMs must make compromises. Unanimity is difficult to attain, and "soft" consensus is widely used in CRPs [49]. To date, various consensus reaching models (CRMs) have been proposed that address different decision-making problems: (1) GDM with linguistic assessments [10, 22, 44, 46, 76, 89, 130, 174, 178, 183], (2) LSGDM [54, 83, 84, 93, 131, 144, 167], (3) GDM that considers the non-cooperative behaviors [27, 28, 84, 144], and (4) GDM under a social network environment [24, 122, 123, 125]. With respect to non-cooperative behaviors in particular, Palomares et al. [84] proposed a weight penalizing method that aims to reduce the weights of non-cooperating experts' preferences, Xu et al. [144] developed a consensus model based on the level of non-cooperation to address non-cooperative behaviors, and Dong et al. [27] introduced three types of non-cooperative behaviors, in which some DMs express their opinions dishonestly or refuse to change their opinions to further their own interests. Based on the above literature, we observe the following information about the management of non-cooperative behaviors.

(1) Research on non-cooperative behaviors is still in its inceptive stage, and there are few studies in the literature, particularly those that consider the LSGDM environment.

(2) Few studies have considered the rationality of the adjustment information provided by non-cooperative DMs (or subgroups) and used it as a reference for managing non-cooperative behaviors. Hence, this is a research issue that should be addressed.

An LSGDM problem often involves multiple DMs, and they may have different attitudes toward compromise to achieve a consensus. Some DMs are in favor of adjusting their opinions, whereas others refuse to compromise or make very small compromises. Non-cooperative behaviors may seriously affect the decision process and the final decision result; hence, it is necessary to respond appropriately. In addition to the CRMs for managing non-cooperative behaviors listed above, Pelta and Yager [90] and Yager [150, 151] considered non-cooperative behaviors in the selection process of GDM problems, but not in the CRP. Managing non-cooperative behaviors in the CRP helps to better adjust the opinions of non-cooperative DMs and further influence the decision result. We prefer to manage non-cooperative behaviors and achieve agreement among the DMs' opinions before applying the selection process. Therefore, in this study, we continue the approach of [144] and propose a novel consensus model for managing non-cooperative behaviors in LSGDM that combines the non-cooperation and rationality of the adjustment information.

The CRP consists of two core elements: a consensus measure and feedback adjustment. There are usually two ways to measure consensus: the first is based on the distance to the group opinion [144, 174] and the second is based on the distances among DMs' opinions [27, 130, 178]. Different consensus measures lead to different consensus processes and decision results. Therefore, it is necessary to analyze the suitability of each measure for a particular application.

The contributions of this chapter are as follows.

(1) Different consensus measures are defined and their advantages and disadvantages are compared.

(2) A mechanism for addressing non-cooperative behaviors is proposed. First, we insert an interaction step in the management of non-cooperative behaviors that effectively enables DMs to provide better adjustment coefficients. We combine the levels of rationality and non-cooperation to construct the confidence level of a cluster's adjustment coefficient. By referring to the confidence level, non-cooperative behaviors can be better managed.

(3) An algorithm for the confidence consensus-based model for LSGDM is presented that incorporates the proposed mechanism.

(4) A detailed comparative analysis of the confidence consensus-based model with other models and a simulation that summarizes the characteristics of the CRP are presented.

6.2 Consensus Measures

Given an LSGDM problem, let $X = \{x_1, x_2, \ldots, x_m\}$ be a finite set of m alternatives, $A = \{a_1, a_2, \ldots, a_n\}$ be a set of n attributes, and $\omega = (\omega_1, \omega_2, \ldots, \omega_n)^T$ be the weight vector of the attributes, where $\sum_{j=1}^{n} \omega_j = 1$, $0 \le \omega_j \le 1$, $j = 1, 2, \ldots, n$. Let $E = \{e_1, e_2, \ldots, e_q\}(q \ge 20)$ be a set of q DMs. Each DM expresses its opinion using numerical decision matrix $V_l = (v_{l,ij})_{m \times n}$, where $v_{l,ij}$ represents the opinion of DM e_l on alternative $x_i \in X$ with respect to attribute $a_j \in A$. Before entering the CRP, individual decision matrix V_l should be normalized to standardized decision matrix $R_l = (r_{l,ij})_{m \times n}$, where

$$r_{l,ij} = \frac{v_{l,ij} - min_l\{v_{l,ij}\}}{max_l\{v_{l,ij}\} - min_l\{v_{l,ij}\}} \qquad for\ benifit\ attributes\ and$$

$$r_{l,ij} = \frac{max_l\{v_{l,ij}\} - v_{l,ij}}{max_l\{v_{l,ij}\} - min_l\{v_{l,ij}\}} \qquad for\ cost\ attributes.$$

Clustering the DMs' opinions is the basis for analyzing a large group. In this study, we adopt the clustering method in [140] to classify a large number of DMs into $K(1 \le K \le q)$ subgroups (the clustering method is described in the supplementary materials). The weight vector of the clusters $\lambda = (\lambda_1, \lambda_2, \ldots, \lambda_K)^T$ is obtained such that

$$\lambda_k = \frac{(n_k)^2}{\sum_{k=1}^{K}(n_k)^2} \tag{6.1}$$

where n_k is the number of DMs in cluster C_k. Clearly, $0 \le \lambda_k \le 1(k = 1, 2, \ldots, K)$ and $\sum_{k=1}^{K} \lambda_k = 1$. The cluster decision matrix can be obtained, i.e., $R_k = (r_{k,ij})_{m \times n}$, where $r_{k,ij} = (1/n_k) \sum_{l=1}^{n_k} r_{l,ij}$, $e_l \in C_k$. The group decision matrix is represented by $R_c = (r_{c,ij})_{m \times n}$, where $r_{c,ij} = \sum_{k=1}^{K} r_{k,ij} \lambda_k$. Two methods for calculating consensus measures exist: the first is based on the distance to the group opinion and the second is based on the distances between individual opinions. In practice, consensus measures can be classified into the following three categories.

- *Consensus measure based on the distance to the group opinion using an average operator (CM-I):*
  The individual consensus level is calculated as

$$CI_{CM-I}^{k,t} = 1 - d(R_k^t, R_c^t) = 1 - \frac{1}{m \times n} \sum_{i=1}^{m} \sum_{j=1}^{n} d(r_{k,ij}^t, r_{c,ij}^t). \tag{6.2}$$

where $d(r_{k,ij}^t, r_{c,ij}^t)$ is the distance between $r_{k,ij}^t$ and $r_{c,ij}^t$, and the group consensus level is calculated as

$$GCI_{CM-I}^t = \frac{1}{K} \sum_{k=1}^{K} CI_{CM-I}^{k,t} \tag{6.3}$$

- *Consensus measure based on the distance to the group opinion using a minimum operator (CM-II)*:
  In this rule, the individual consensus level measure is calculated using Eq. (6.2) and the group consensus level is defined as

$$GCL_{CM-II}^t = min_k\{CL_{CM-I}^t\} \tag{6.4}$$

- *Consensus measure based on the distance between DMs' opinions using a minimum operator (CM-III)*:

Here, the individual consensus level is

$$
\begin{aligned}
CL_{CM-III}^t &= 1 - \frac{1}{K-1} \sum_{g=1,g\neq k}^{K-1} d(R_k^t, R_g^t) \\
&= 1 - \frac{1}{K-1} \sum_{g=1,k\neq g}^{K-1} \frac{1}{m \times n} \sum_{i=1}^{m} \sum_{j=1}^{n} d(r_{k,ij}^t, r_{g,ij}^t)
\end{aligned} \tag{6.5}
$$

where $d(r_{k,ij}^t, r_{g,ij}^t)$ is the distance between $r_{k,ij}^t$ and $r_{g,ij}^t$, and the group consensus level is

$$GCI_{CM-III}^t = min_k\left\{CI_{CM-III}^{k,t}\right\} \tag{6.6}$$

Clearly, $0 \leq GCI_{CM-I}^t \leq 1$, $0 \leq GCI_{CM-II}^t \leq 1$, and $0 \leq GCI_{CM-III}^t \leq 1$. If the group consensus level is sufficiently high, then the selection process can be followed; otherwise, the CRP should be applied to manage the opinion differences. In Sect. 6.5, we will discuss the advantages and disadvantages of the above three consensus measures.

6.3   Mechanism for Managing Non-cooperative Behaviors

In LSGDM after clustering, it is common for some clusters to adopt a non-cooperative attitude toward opinion adjustment. Managing these non-cooperative behaviors is a challenge but also an important part of the process of consensus building. Inspired by the research in [84, 144], we employ three phases to address non-cooperative behaviors: identification, interaction, and proper modification.

6.3.1 Identification Rule for Non-cooperative Behaviors

Step 1. Detect and determine the most deviant individual opinion.

Suppose that the opinion of cluster C_k deviates most from those of the other clusters. This cluster can be determined using the following formulas:

$$CI_{CM-I}^{k^*,t} = min_k\{CI_{CM-I}^{k,t}\} \quad for \quad CM-I, \tag{6.7}$$

$$CI_{CM-II}^{k^*,t} = min_k\{CI_{CM-II}^{k,t}\} \quad for \quad CM-II, \tag{6.8}$$

$$CI_{CM-III}^{k^*,t} = min_k\{CI_{CM-III}^{k,t}\} \quad for \quad CM-III. \tag{6.9}$$

Step 2. Cluster C_k provides the adjustment coefficient and the other clusters provide the related adjustment suggestions.

Because of the complexity of decision making, the adjustment coefficient and adjustment $\overline{\eta}^{k^*,t} = [\eta^{Lk^*,t}, \eta^{Uk^*,t}]$, where $\eta^{Uk^*,t}$ and $\eta^{Lk^*,t}$ are the upper and lower limits of $\overline{\eta}^{k^*,t}$, respectively, such that $01 \leq \eta^{Lk^*,t} \leq \eta^{Uk^*,t} \leq 1$. $\overline{\eta}^{k^*,t}$ represents the degree of respect that cluster g_k has for the group opinion. The adjustment suggestion $\overline{\eta}^{k' \to k^*,t}$ ($k' = 1, 2, \ldots, K; k^* \neq k'$) is also an internal number, i.e., $\overline{\eta}^{k' \to k^*,t} = [\eta^{Lk' \to k^*,t}, \eta^{Uk' \to k^*,t}]$, where $\eta^{Uk' \to k^*,t}$ and $\eta^{Lk' \to k^*,t}$ are the upper and lower limits of $\overline{\eta}^{k' \to k^*,t}$, respectively, such that $0 \leq \eta^{k' \to k^*,t} \leq \eta^{k' \to k^*,t} \leq 1$.

Step 3. Calculate the collective adjustment suggestion.

Definition 6.1 By aggregating all adjustment suggestions, the collective adjustment suggestion, $\hat{\eta}^{k^*,t}$ can be obtained such that

$$\hat{\eta}^{k^*,t} = \sum_{k'=1,k' \neq k^*}^{K} \overline{\eta}^{k' \to k^*,t} \lambda_{k'}^t, \tag{6.10}$$

where $\lambda_{k'}^t$ is the remaining cluster's weight, $0 \leq \lambda_{k'}^t \leq 1$ and $\sum_{k'=1,k^* \neq k'}^{K} \lambda_{k'}^t = 1$.

Step 4. Measure the degree of non-cooperation and identify non-cooperative behaviors.

Use the probability degree of two interval numbers to compute the degree of non-cooperation of adjusting coefficient $\overline{\eta}^{k^*,t}$. If $p(\overline{\eta}^{k^*,t} \geq \overline{\eta}^{k' \to k^*,t}) = 1$, then this indicates that C_{k^*} is a completely cooperative subgroup; otherwise, C_{k^*} is regarded as a non-cooperative subgroup.

Note that only using the degree of non-cooperation to punish non-cooperative behaviors is likely to induce the cluster to deliberately reduce it and reduce the rationality of the adjustment coefficient. Therefore, we should further measure the rationality of the adjustment coefficient.

Based on the majority principle, an adjustment coefficient that is closer to the collective adjustment suggestion is more reasonable. Thus, using the similarity [153] to compute the proximity of the adjustment coefficient to the collective adjustment suggestion, we can measure the rationality $T^{k^*,t}$ ($0 \leq T^{k^*,t} \leq 1$) of the given adjustment coefficient. Values of $T^{k^*,t}$ closer to one indicate an adjustment coefficient that is more similar to the collective adjustment suggestion.

6.3.2 Interaction and Discussion

If cluster C_{k^*} is determined to be a non-cooperative subgroup, then more in-depth discussions can be conducted between C_{k^*} and the other clusters. Two scenarios are presented: (a) cluster C_{k^*} is urged to make its adjustment coefficient closer to the collective adjustment suggestion and (b) cluster C_{k^*} is impelled to reduce its degree of non-cooperation to obtain greater consensus. After discussion and interaction, cluster C_{k^*} changes its adjustment coefficient $\overline{\eta}^{k^*,t}$ to $^z\overline{\eta}^{k^*,t}$, where $^z\overline{\eta}^{k^*,t}$ is an interval number. Then, the non-cooperation and rationality are recalculated, denoted by $^z\tau^{k^*,t}$ and $^zT^{k^*,t}$, respectively. It is noted that cluster C_{k^*} may has the option of not changing its adjustment coefficient.

6.3.3 Proper Modification

Combining the value of rationality with that of non-cooperation, we can construct a new concept called the confidence level to measure quantitatively the extent to which cluster C_{k^*} can provide a rational adjustment coefficient. The confidence level represents three aspects: (a) other clusters' feelings that the given adjustment coefficient can be trusted; (b) the reflection of honesty and emotional expression of cluster C_{k^*} in terms of opinion adjustment; and (c) an indication of the understanding of cluster g_{k^*} of the decision problem and its impartiality in the decision-making process.

Definition 6.2 The confidence level of the given adjustment coefficient is the mapping $f :^z\tau^{k^*,t},^z T^{k^*,t} \rightarrow \zeta^{k^*,t}$ ($\zeta^{k^*,t} \in [0, 1]$).

Definition 6.3 A weighted geometric averaging operator is used to describe the mapping f and obtain $f_{WG} :^z\tau^{k^*,t},^z T^{k^*,t} \rightarrow \zeta^{k^*,t}$, such that

$$\zeta^{k^*,t} = f_{WG}(^z\tau^{k^*,t},^z T^{k^*,t}) = (1 -^z\tau^{k^*,t})^{\mu_{WG}} \times (^z T^{k^*,t})^{\nu_{WG}}, \qquad (6.11)$$

where μ_{WG} and ν_{WG} are are control coefficients that define the relative weight of the non-cooperation and rationality, respectively, such that $\mu_{WG}, \nu_{WG} \in [0, 1]$ and $\mu_{WG} + \nu_{WG} = 1$.

The following theorem can easily be determined.

Theorem 6.1 *If $\mu_{WG}, \nu_{WG} \neq 0$, then $\zeta^{k^*,t} \in [0, 1]$.*

Theorem 6.2 *If $\mu_{WG} = 0$, then Eq. (6.11) changes to $\zeta^{k^*,t} = T^{k^*,t}$. In this case, the confidence level only depends on the rationality of the adjustment coefficient.*

Theorem 6.3 *If $\nu_{WG} = 0$, then Eq. (6.11) changes to $\zeta^{k^*,t} = \tau^{k^*,t}$. In this case, the confidence level only relies on the non-cooperation of the adjustment coefficient.*

Commonly, we set $0 \leq \mu_{WG}, \nu_{WG} \leq 1$. Specifically,

(1) if $\zeta^{k^8,t} = 0$, then the confidence level of the adjustment coefficient is zero. This can result from the following:

  (a) $^z\tau^{k^*,t} = 1$: this indicates that the adjustment coefficient cannot satisfy the minimum requirement of the collective adjustment suggestion; thus, cluster g_{k^*} is regarded as a completely non-cooperative subgroup
  (b) $^zT^{k^*,t} = 1$: This indicates that the adjustment coefficient deviates far from the collective adjustment suggestion.

(2) If $\zeta^{k^*,t} \in (0, 1)$, then the confidence level can be used as the basis of the weight adjustment.

Whether cluster g_{k^*} is regarded as a completely non-cooperative subgroup or the adjustment is too deviant, the DMs in cluster g_{k^*} should be advised to exit the decision process to ensure decision quality and decision-making efficiency. In this study, we focus on the category of the non-cooperating experts; hence, the cause of non-cooperative behaviors or very deviant adjustments is a poor understanding of the decision problem or subjectively persistent with few private interest.

A DM's weights reflect its influence on the group opinion. By modifying the weights, the influence is adjusted. When confronted with non-cooperative clusters, we can reduce their weight to reduce their impact so as to promote consensus.

Definition 6.4 The weight penalty function is defined as

$$^z\lambda_{k^*}^{t+1} = \chi^t \cdot \zeta^{k^*,t} \cdot \lambda_{k^*}^t, \tag{6.12}$$

where $^z\lambda_{k^*}^{t+1}$ is the modified weight of C_{k^*} and χ^t is used to regulate the weight penalty and is calculated as

$$\chi^t = \sum_{k'=1, k' \neq k^*}^{K} \chi^{k',t} \overline{\lambda}_{k'}^t. \tag{6.13}$$

The symbol $\overline{\lambda}_{k'}^t$ is the normalized weight of the remaining clusters such that $\overline{\lambda}_{k'}^t \geq 0 (k' = 1, 2, \ldots, K; k^* \neq k')$ and $\sum_{k=1, k^* \neq k'}^{K} \overline{\lambda}_{k'} = 1$. The remaining clusters provide parameters $\chi^{k',t} (k' = 1, 2, \ldots, K; k^* \neq k')$ such that they meet the conditions $\chi^{k',t} \geq 1$ and $\chi^{k',t} \cdot \zeta^{k^*,t} < 1$. The first condition ensures that each DM's opinion can be effectively expressed, including the DMs of the non-cooperative sub-group, which is in accordance with the principle of cautious handling of and appropriate respect for non-cooperative behaviors. The second condition ensures that non-cooperative behaviors are efficiently managed. Clearly, $\chi^t \geq 1$ and $\chi^T \cdot \zeta^{k^*,t} < 1$.

Then, we use the following to adjust the decision matrix of cluster C_{k^*} as follows:

$$R^{k^*,t+1} = \frac{\eta^{Lk^*,t} + \eta^{Uk^*,t}}{2} R^{c,t} + \left(1 - \frac{\eta^{Lk^*,t} + \eta^{Uk^*,t}}{2}\right) R^{k^*,t}, \tag{6.14}$$

where the adjustment coefficient is set as the midpoint of $\overline{\eta}^{k^*,t}$. That is, $0 \leq (\eta^{LK^*,t} + \eta^{UK^*,t})/2 \leq 1$. Here, $R_{k^*}^t$ and $R_{k^*}^{t+1}$ represent the opinions of cluster C_{k^*} before and after the $t+1$-th iteration, respectively, and R_c^t represents the group opinion in the $t+1$-th iteration.

Remark 6.1 Let $\zeta^{k^*,t} = f_{WG}(^z\tau^{k^*,t}, ^z T^{k^*,t}) = (1 - ^z\tau^{k^*,t})^{\mu_{WG}} \times (^z T^{k^*,t})^{\nu_{WG}}$ be a common mathematical function that represents the mapping $^z\tau^{k^*,t}, ^z T^{k^*,t} \to \zeta^{k^*,t}$. Here, $^z\tau^{k^*,t}$ and $^z T^{k^*,t}$ are two independent variables, and $\zeta^{k^*,t}$ is a dependent variable. Let $0 \leq^z \tau^{k^*,t}, ^z T^{k^*,t} \leq 1$ and $0 \leq \mu_{WG}, \nu_{WG} \leq 1$.. We can calculate the partial derivative of this function as

$$\frac{\partial \zeta^{k^*,t}}{\partial^z \tau^{k^*,t}} = -\mu_{WG} \cdot (1 - ^z \tau^{k^*,t})^{\mu_{WG}-1} \cdot (^z T^{k^*,t})^{\nu_{WG}} \tag{6.15}$$

$$\frac{\partial \zeta^{k^*,t}}{\partial^z T^{k^*,t}} = (1 - ^z T^{k^*,t})^{\mu_{WG}-1} \cdot \nu_{WG} \cdot (^z T^{k^*,t})^{\nu_{WG}} \tag{6.16}$$

Clearly, $\frac{\partial \zeta^{k^*,t}}{\partial^z \tau^{k^*,t}} < 0$, $\frac{\partial \zeta^{k^*,t}}{\partial^z T^{k^*,t}} > 0$. Thus, $\zeta^{k^*,t}$ is a strictly monotonic decreasing function of $^z\tau^{k^*,t}$, whereas $\zeta^{k^*,t}$ is a strictly monotonic increasing function of $^z T^{k^*,t}$.

Note that in accordance with Definition 2, the values $^z\tau^{k^*,t}$ and $^z T^{k^*,t}$ depend on $^z\overline{\eta}^{k^*,t}$ and $\hat{\eta}^{k^*,t}$. Let $^z\overline{\eta}^{k^*,t}$ and $\hat{\eta}^{k^*,t}$ be two interval numbers such that $0 \leq^z \eta^{Lk^*,t} \leq^z \eta^{Uk^*,t} \leq 1$ and $0 \leq \eta^{Lk^*,t} \leq \hat{\eta}^{Uk^*,t} \leq 1$. We calculated the confidence level of these two interval numbers $1,000$ times using MATLAB software, and obtained the simulation results (see Fig. 6.1). Figure 6.1a–e show five independent sub-graphs, and Fig. 6.1f shows these five graphs overlapped as a single graph.

From the results in Fig. 6.1, we make the following observations:

(1) The simulation results presented in Fig. 6.1b–d are similar in shape.
(2) Each graph in Fig. 6.1a–e has a maximum point. This finding conforms to Theorem 6.1. Further, in Fig. 6.1b–d, the three maximum values correspond to the case in which all the values of non-cooperation are close to 0.5 and all the values of rationality are close to one (points $(0.492, 0.969, 0.798)$ in Fig. 6.1b, $(0.503, 0.989, 0.701)$ in Fig. 6.1c, and $(0.489, 0.959, 0.617)$ in Fig. 6.1d).
(3) When we set $0 \leq \mu_{WG}, \nu_{WG} \leq 1$, the relationship between the confidence level and degrees of rationality and non-cooperation can be described as one of two cases.

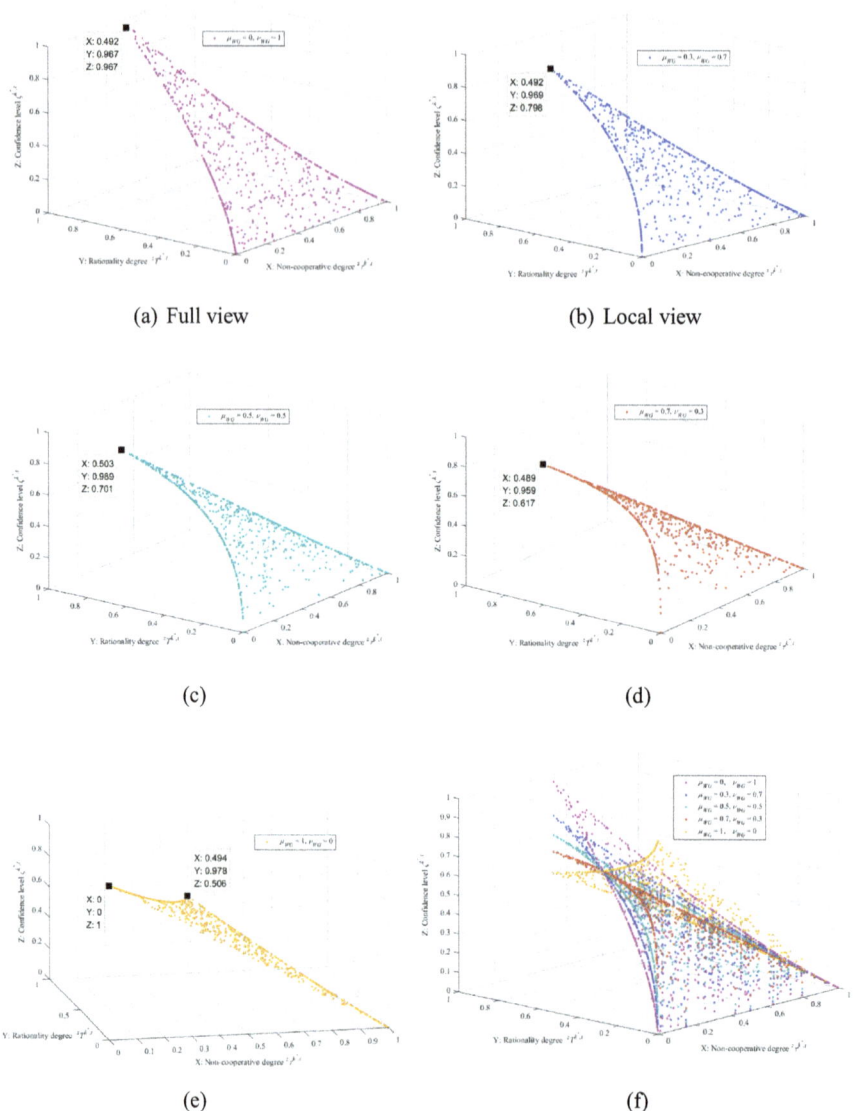

(a) Full view   (b) Local view

(c)   (d)

(e)   (f)

Fig. 6.1 Simulation results of the confidence level under different parameters μ_{WG} and ν_{WG}

(a) Partially positive relationship: The rationality is strongly positively correlated with the confidence level, whereas the non-cooperation is strongly negatively correlated with the confidence level; that is, the confidence level increases when the rationality increases and the non-cooperation decreases.

(b) Completely positive relationship: The confidence level increases with the increase in rationality and the increase in non-cooperation.

(4) Fig. 6.1a, e are two special scenarios that correspond to Theorems 6.2 and 6.3, respectively.

Note 6.1 If the adjustment coefficient and collective adjustment suggestion are expressed as interval numbers, then a completely negative relationship may emerge when different methods are used to calculate the rationality and non-cooperation. The completely negative relationship is defined as follows: the confidence level decreases when the rationality increases and non-cooperation increases. In future research, we will study the influence of different measurement formulas for rationality and non-cooperation on the relationship between the adjustment coefficient, collective adjustment suggestion, and confidence level.

6.3.4 Algorithm for the Confidence Consensus-Based Model in LSGDM

The proposed consensus model in this study aims to obtain a common decision result with a sufficiently high level of group consensus among DMs. The algorithm for this confidence consensus model is summarized as Algorithm 6.1 (also see Fig. 6.2).

6.4 Case Study

We use the case in [146] to illustrate the effectiveness of the proposed model. The decision information is summarized as follows: Emergency shelter construction is a priority task for post-earthquake recovery. Four types of materials can be selected to construct emergency shelters: tents (x_1), plastic sheeting (x_2), waste wood (x_3), and light steel (x_4). Three aspects are considered: availability (a_1), convenience (a_2), and perceived safety (a_3). These attribute values are typically given on a 0–100 scale and the weight vector of the attributes is $\omega = (0.25, 0.5, 0.25)^T$. Twenty-five experts $e_l(l = 1, 2, \ldots, 25)$ are invited to participate in the emergency decision process. Assume that the acceptable consensus threshold is $\overline{GCL} = 0.75$. The 25 experts offer their preferences over the alternatives with respect to attributes. The normalized individual decision matrices are shown in Appendix B in [146].

Algorithm 6.1 Hierarchical punishment-driven consensus model for PL-LSGDM
problems

Input: Initial normalized individual decision matrices R_l^0 ($l = 1, 2, \ldots, q$), weight vector of the
attributes ω, and acceptable threshold of the consensus level $\overline{GCI}$.

Output: Final number of iterations, final group matrix, and alternative ranking.

1: Classify the DMs into several subgroups.

   Divide the large group into K clusters and calculate the initial weight vector of the clusters
$\lambda^0 = (\lambda_1^0, \lambda_2^0, \lambda_K^0)^T$. The initial clusters' decision matrices R_k^0 ($k = 1, 2, \ldots, K$) can be obtained
using the weighted averaging operator. Let $t = 0$.

2: Compute the temporal group decision matrix.

   Aggregate the clusters' decision matrices into temporal group decision matrices $R_c^t = (r_{c,ij}^t)_{m \times n}$, where $r_{c,ij}^t = \sum_{k=1}^K r_{k,ij}^t \lambda_k^t$.

3: Consensus measure.

   Select the appropriate rule of consensus measures to calculate the clusters' consensus levels
and group consensus level. If the group consensus level is greater than the predefined consensus
threshold, then proceed to Step 5; otherwise, proceed to the next step.

4: Consensus reaching process.

   Apply the consensus model presented in Section 6.3 to manage both the CRPs and non-
cooperative behaviors. Let $t = t + 1$ and return to Step 2.

5: Output the related decision information.

   Output the final iterative time t^* and final group decision matrix R^{t^*}.

6: Select the best alternative(s).

   Using the obtained final group matrix, calculate the overall evaluation values of all alternatives and then select the best alternative(s).

Below, we apply the Algorithm 6.1 to select the best alternative. The experts
decide to use CM-I to measure the consensus levels and set $\mu_{WG} = v_{WG} = 0.5$. The
reason why CM-I is chosen will be explained in Sect. 6.5.4.

Input: normalized individual decision matrices R_k ($k = 1, 2, \ldots, 25$), weight vector
of the attributes ω, and acceptable consensus threshold $\overline{GCI} = 0.75$.

Output: final number of iterations, final group decision matrix, and alternative ranking.

Step 1. Classify the 25 DMs into several subgroups.

   Using the clustering method presented in [140], the large group is divided into five
smaller clusters (see Table 6.1). The initial weight vector of the clusters is obtained
as $\lambda^0 = (0.153, 0.055, 0.393, 0.006, 0.393)^T$. Let $t = 0$.

Step 2. Compute the temporal group decision matrix.

   Aggregate the temporal clusters' decision matrices to obtain the temporal group
matrix

$$R_c^0 = \begin{pmatrix} 0.472 \ 0.342 \ 0.401 \\ 0.737 \ 0.476 \ 0.668 \\ 0.404 \ 0.526 \ 0.466 \\ 0.274 \ 0.553 \ 0.457 \end{pmatrix}$$

Step 3. Consensus measure. Use CM-I to calculate the individual consensus levels:
$CI_{CM-I}^{1,0} = 0.702$, $\quad CI_{CM-I}^{2,0} = 0.677$, $CI_{CM-I}^{3,0} = 0.757$, $CI_{CM-I}^{4,0} = 0.668$, $\quad$ and

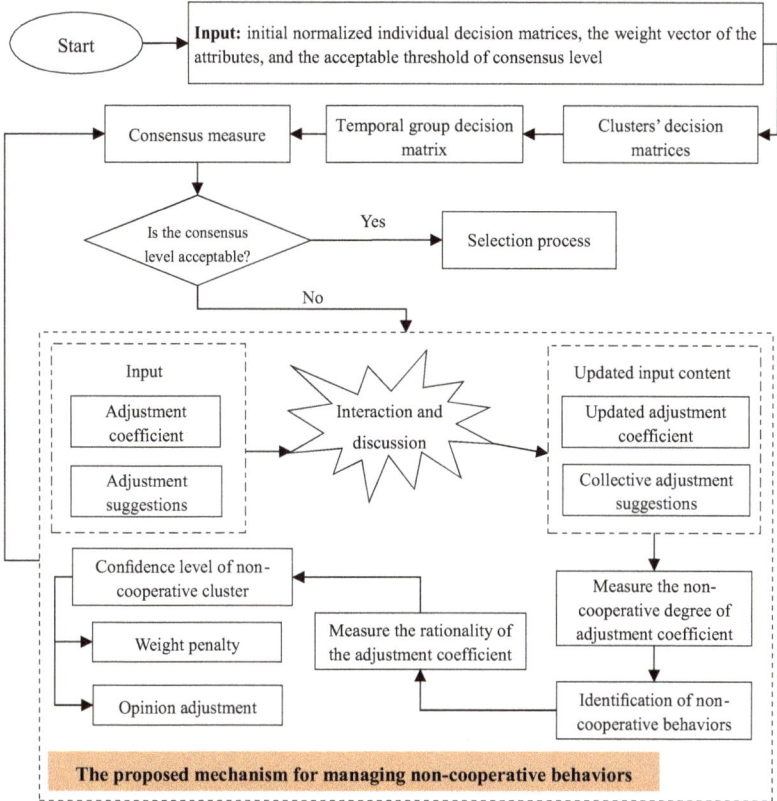

Fig. 6.2 Confidence consensus-based model for LSGDM

$CI_{CM-I}^{5,0} = 0.745$. The group consensus level is obtained as $GCI_{CM-I}^{0} = 0.71$ using Eq. (6.2). Because $GCI_{CM-I}^{0} < \overline{GCI}$, this indicates that there are large differences among the opinions of the clusters. Hence, CRP should be used.

Step 4. Consensus reaching process. *(i) First consensus iteration.*

Because $CI_{CM-I}^{4,0} = min\{CI_{CM-I}^{k,0}\}$, C_4 is furthest from the group opinion. Cluster C_4 provides the adjustment coefficient of $\overline{\eta}^{4,0} = [0.1, 0.15]$. Other clusters give their suggestions regarding the adjustment of its opinion, i.e., $\overline{\eta}^{1\rightarrow4,0} = [0.4, 0.6]$, $\overline{\eta}^{2\rightarrow4,0} = [0.5, 0.8]$, $\overline{\eta}^{3\rightarrow4,0} = [0.3, 0.4]$, and $\overline{\eta}^{5\rightarrow4,0} = [0.2, 0.4]$. The collective adjustment suggestion is $\hat{\eta}^{4,0} = [0.287, 0.453]$. The mechanism for managing non-cooperative behaviors is hence employed.

(1) Identification of non-cooperative behaviors: Because $\tau^{4,0} = 1 > 0$, cluster C_4 can be regarded as a completely non-cooperative subgroup.
(2) Interaction and discussion: Cluster C_4 changes its adjustment coefficient to $^z\overline{\eta}^{4,0} = [0.2, 0.25]$.

Table 6.1 Clustering results with threshold $\gamma = 0.73$

C_k	n_k	e_l	R_k^0
C_1	5	$e_1, e_5, e_7, e_9, e_{12}$	$\begin{pmatrix} 0.501 & 0.571 & 1.000 \\ 0.800 & 0.075 & 0.210 \\ 0.033 & 0.132 & 0.470 \\ 0.538 & 1.000 & 0.137 \end{pmatrix}$
C_2	3	e_2, e_4, e_{10}	$\begin{pmatrix} 0.000 & 0.173 & 0.430 \\ 0.868 & 1.000 & 0.767 \\ 1.000 & 0.000 & 1.000 \\ 0.331 & 0.834 & 0.000 \end{pmatrix}$
C_3	8	$e_3, e_8, e_{13}, e_{15}, e_{18}, e_{20}, e_{22}, e_{25}$	$\begin{pmatrix} 1.000 & 0.608 & 0.560 \\ 0.431 & 0.625 & 1.000 \\ 0.347 & 0.281 & 0.365 \\ 0.000 & 0.407 & 0.105 \end{pmatrix}$
C_4	1	e_6	$\begin{pmatrix} 0.460 & 1.000 & 0.640 \\ 0.745 & 0.245 & 0.000 \\ 1.000 & 0.450 & 1.000 \\ 0.000 & 0.000 & 0.320 \end{pmatrix}$
C_5	8	$e_{11}, e_{14}, e_{16}, e_{17}, e_{19}, e_{21}, e_{23}, e_{24}$	$\begin{pmatrix} 0.000 & 0.000 & 0.000 \\ 1.000 & 0.413 & 0.510 \\ 0.513 & 1.000 & 0.482 \\ 0.443 & 0.496 & 1.000 \end{pmatrix}$

Note The total adjustment amount can be calculated using Definition 3 presented in [144]

(3) Proper modification: The rationality is calculated as $^zT^{4,0} = 0$. Thus, the confidence level is $\zeta^{4,0} = 0$. To ensure the quality and efficiency of decision making, the single member that makes up cluster C_4 is advised to exit the decision process.

The weight vector of clusters is updated to $\lambda_1 = (0.154, 0.056, 0.395, 0.395)^T$. The updated consensus levels become $CI_{CM-I}^{1,1} = 0.701$, $CI_{CM-I}^{2,1} = 0.677$, $CI_{CM-I}^{3,1} = 0.757$, and $CI_{CM-I}^{5,1} = 0.744$, and the group consensus level is $GCI_{CM-I}^1 = 0.72 < \overline{GCI}$. Thus, after the first iteration, differences remain among the clusters' opinions. *(ii) Second consensus iteration.*

Because $CI_{CM-I}^{2,1} = min\{CI_{CM-I}^{k,1}\}$, this means that C_2 has an opinion with the largest difference from the group opinion. Cluster C_2 provides the adjustment coefficient $\overline{\eta}^{2,1} = [0.3, 0.5]$. Other clusters provide their suggestions regarding the adjustment of the opinion of C_2 as $\overline{\eta}^{1\rightarrow 2,1} = [0.4, 0.6]$, $\overline{\eta}^{3\rightarrow 2,1} = [0.5, 0.8]$, and $\overline{\eta}^{5\rightarrow 2,1} = [0.6, 0.9]$. The collective adjustment suggestion is hence $\hat{\eta}^{2,1} = [0.526, 0.809]$. The mechanism for managing non-cooperative behaviors proceeds as follows.

(1) Identification of non-cooperative behaviors: Because $\tau^{2,1} = 0.872 > 0$, cluster C_2 can be regarded as a non-cooperative subgroup.
(2) Interaction and discussion: Cluster C_2 changes its adjustment coefficient to $^z\overline{\eta}^{4,1} = [0.3, 0.55]$.

(3) Proper modification. The rationality degree is computed as $^zT^{2,1} = 0.048$. Thus, the confidence level is $\zeta^{2,1} = 0.047$. Suppose that $\chi^1 = 1$. The weight of cluster C_2 is modified to $^z\lambda^{2,2} = \chi^1 \cdot \zeta^{2,1} \cdot \lambda^{2,1} = 0.03$ using Eq. (6.3.1). The weight vector of the clusters is updated to $\lambda^2 = (0.163, 0.03, 0.417, 0.417)^T$. Equation (6.14) is used to modify the matrix of cluster C_2. The temporal group decision matrix becomes

$$R_c^2 = \begin{pmatrix} 0.499 & 0.347 & 0.397 \\ 0.729 & 0.447 & 0.666 \\ 0.365 & 0.557 & 0.431 \\ 0.273 & 0.54 & 0.484 \end{pmatrix}$$

After the second iteration, the cluster consensus levels are $CI_{CM-I}^{1,2} = 0.7$, $CI_{CM-I}^{2,2} = 0.807$, $CI_{CM-I}^{3,2} = 0.76$, and $CI_{CM-I}^{5,2} = 0.744$. The group consensus level is $GCI_{CM-I}^2 = 0.753 \geq \overline{GCI}$; that is, the group consensus level has reached an acceptable level (above the threshold) after two rounds of CRP.

Step 5. Output the final group decision matrix as $R_c^* = R_c^2$.
Step 6. Select the best alternative(s).

The overall evaluation value of each alternative is
$EV(x_1) = 0.398$, $EV(x_2) = 0.572$, $EV(x_3) = 0.477$, and $EV(x_4) = 0.459$.

The derived ranking of alternatives is $x_2 \succ x_3 \succ x_4 \succ x_1$, and thus x_2 is the best alternative. Hence, plastic sheeting is the most desirable material for constructing emergency shelters.

6.5 Comparative Analysis

This section comprises five parts. We analyze the effect of the proposed model on managing non-cooperative behaviors. In Sect. 6.5.2, we formulate the influence of different consensus thresholds on the CRP. In Sect. 6.5.3, we present a comparison of the proposed model with other models [144, 167]. We discuss the comparison results for different consensus measures and parameters in Sect. 6.5.4 and 6.5.5, respectively. Note that the data used in the comparative analysis come from the case study in Sect. 6.4.

6.5.1 Effect of the Confidence Consensus-Based Model on Managing Non-cooperative Behaviors

In the first iteration of the case study, cluster C_4 was regarded as a completely non-cooperative subgroup. In addition, $\tau^{4,0} = 1$ indicated that the given adjustment coefficient could not satisfy the minimum requirement of the collective adjustment suggestion. After an interaction with the other clusters, cluster g4 was still very reluctant to modify its opinion to improve consensus (i.e., $^z\tau^{4,0} = 1$). Hence, the DM in cluster C_4 was advised to exit the decision process. We can see that the group consensus level clearly increased from $GCI^0 = 0.710$ to $GCI^1 = 0.720$ after the DM in cluster C_4 exited the decision. This shows that a cluster who has very large difference of opinion from the group and is not willing to modify its opinion should be advised to exit the decision process in a timely manner. This is useful for enabling the remaining DMs to reach an agreement quickly.

In the second iteration, cluster C_2 was regarded as a partially non-cooperative subgroup. Using weight penalties and opinion adjustment, the individual consensus level was increased from $CI^{2,1}_{CM-I} = 0.677$ to $CI^{2,2}_{CM-I} = 0.807$, and eventually the group consensus level reached the consensus threshold. This suggests that to reduce the weight and modify an opinion that is substantially different from the group opinion, it is useful to reduce the differences among the DMs and reach an agreement.

6.5.2   Analysis of Different Consensus Thresholds

In the following, we analyze the effect of setting different consensus thresholds. Table 6.2 and Fig. 6.3 present the decision results for different consensus thresholds. Fig. 6.3 shows the number of iterations and group consensus levels. Table 6.2 lists the final group decision matrices, overall evaluation values of each alternative, and alternative rankings. To better reflect the impact of different consensus thresholds on the decision, in this section, we adopt the objective adjustment coefficient presented in [144] to simulate the CRP and do not consider non-cooperative behaviors.

Based on the results in Table 6.2 and Fig. 6.3, the following observations can be obtained.

(1) The number of iterations decreases as the consensus threshold decreases, and the final alternative rankings do not change. No change in alternative rankings can happen because the attribute weights are fixed.

(2) The final rankings are the same; however, the final group decision matrices and overall evaluation values of the alternatives are different.

(3) As the number of iterations increases, the group consensus level eventually meets the threshold.

(4) The closer the group consensus level to the consensus threshold, the lower the opinion adjustment amount.

(5) A higher consensus threshold requires a greater adjustment amount, which leads to a more likely distortion of opinions. Therefore, the threshold needs to be set reasonably.

(6) An available method to confirm the two important parameters (i.e., the number of iterations and acceptable consensus threshold) is to simulate the CRP using the objective adjustment coefficient presented in [144]. The simulation results demonstrate the relationship between the number of iterations and consensus threshold, which can be used as a reference to determine these two parameters.

Table 6.2 Comparison results for different consensus thresholds

Consensus threshold	Total adjustment amount	Final group decision matrix	Overall evaluation values of alternatives	Alternative ranking
0.900	0.980	$\begin{pmatrix} 0.507 & 0.347 & 0.382 \\ 0.717 & 0.488 & 0.702 \\ 0.401 & 0.544 & 0.447 \\ 0.251 & 0.523 & 0.465 \end{pmatrix}$	$EV(x_1) = 0.396,$ $EV(x_2) = 0.599,$ $EV(x_3) = 0.484,$ $EV(x_4) = 0.441$	$x_2 \succ x_3 \succ x_4 \succ x_1$
0.850	0.719	$\begin{pmatrix} 0.504 & 0.349 & 0.390 \\ 0.719 & 0.486 & 0.696 \\ 0.401 & 0.534 & 0.451 \\ 0.254 & 0.531 & 0.457 \end{pmatrix}$	$EV(x_1) = 0.398,$ $EV(x_2) = 0.597,$ $EV(x_3) = 0.480,$ $EV(x_4) = 0.443$	$x_2 \succ x_3 \succ x_4 \succ x_1$
0.800	0.465	$\begin{pmatrix} 0.504 & 0.353 & 0.397 \\ 0.717 & 0.487 & 0.695 \\ 0.400 & 0.527 & 0.453 \\ 0.254 & 0.534 & 0.450 \end{pmatrix}$	$EV(x_1) = 0.403,$ $EV(x_2) = 0.596,$ $EV(x_3) = 0.477,$ $EV(x_4) = 0.443$	$x_2 \succ x_3 \succ x_4 \succ x_1$
0.750	0.223	$\begin{pmatrix} 0.478 & 0.337 & 0.382 \\ 0.733 & 0.480 & 0.681 \\ 0.405 & 0.545 & 0.457 \\ 0.267 & 0.538 & 0.473 \end{pmatrix}$	$EV(x_1) = 0.383,$ $EV(x_2) = 0.594,$ $EV(x_3) = 0.488,$ $EV(x_4) = 0.454$	$x_2 \succ x_3 \succ x_4 \succ x_1$
0.700	0.000	$\begin{pmatrix} 0.472 & 0.342 & 0.401 \\ 0.737 & 0.476 & 0.668 \\ 0.404 & 0.526 & 0.466 \\ 0.275 & 0.553 & 0.457 \end{pmatrix}$	$EV(x_1) = 0.389,$ $EV(x_2) = 0.589,$ $EV(x_3) = 0.480,$ $EV(x_4) = 0.460$	$x_2 \succ x_3 \succ x_4 \succ x_1$

Note The total adjustment amount can be calculated using Definition 3 presented in [144]

6.5.3 Comparison with Xu et al.'s Model [144] and Zhang et al.'s Model [167]

To demonstrate the advantages of the proposed method, a comparative analysis is conducted using another technique [144]. Xu et al. [144] utilized the degree of non-cooperation to manage non-cooperative behaviors. In our study, the proposed consensus model includes not only the degree of non-cooperation but also the newly defined degree rationality. We compare these two models in the second iteration of the case study in Sect. 6.4.

The results in Table 6.3 show the following differences between our proposed model and Xu et al.'s model [144]:

(1) The updated group consensus levels obtained by the two models both exceed the consensus threshold. This finding implies that both models are effective at promoting consensus by managing non-cooperative behaviors.

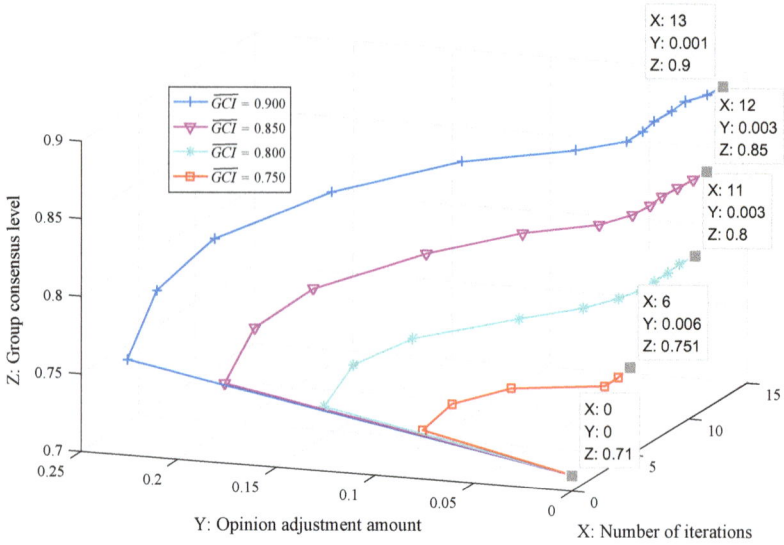

Fig. 6.3 Simulation results based on the objective adjustment coefficient for different consensus thresholds

Table 6.3 Comparison of Xu et al.'s model and our proposed model

Consensus model	Updated adjustment coefficient	Collective adjustment suggestion	Non-cooperative degree	Rationality degree	Confidence level	Modified weight	Updated group consensus level
Xu et al.'s model [144]	–	[0.225,0.900]	0.686	–	–	0.022	0.757
This study	[0.3,0.55]	[0.526,0.809]	0.954	0.048	0.047	0.003	0.753

Note To ensure the effectiveness of the comparison results, we suppose that The two models had the same adjustment coefficient (i.e., $\overline{\eta}^{2,1} = [0.3, 0.5]$) and adjustment suggestions (i.e., $\overline{\eta}^{1\to2,1} = [0.4, 0.6]$, $\overline{\eta}^{3\to2,1} = [0.5, 0.8]$, $\overline{\eta}^{5\to2,1} = [0.6, 0.9]$)

(2) The modified weights are obviously different. This is for two reasons: (a) The two models calculate the collective adjustment suggestions differently. Xu et al.'s model uses the max-min operator to combine the objective adjustment coefficient and adjustment suggestions, whereas the proposed model directly aggregates the adjustment suggestions. This causes the different results for the non-cooperation. (b) The proposed model introduces the rationality and confidence level, which not only considers the non-cooperation of the adjustment but, more importantly, the rationality of the adjustment coefficient.

(3) The proposed model adds the interaction step and a discussion that could help DMs to provide more favorable adjustment coefficients as well as reducing the distrust and emotional expression of DMs.

Table 6.4 Comparison of Zhang et al.'s model and our proposed model

Consensus model	Changeable clusters?	Expression form of satisfaction	Object of preference adjustment	Management of non-cooperative behaviors	Composition of the CRP
Zhang et al.'s model [167]	Yes	Explicit	All the preferences can be modified	No	(1) Consensus measure, (2) Satisfaction measure, (3) Feedback adjustment
This study	No	Implicit	Preference which has the lowest consensus level should be modified	Yes	(1) Consensus measure, (2) Feedback adjustment (Including addressing non-cooperative behaviors)

Note The item "Object of preference adjustment" refers to which preferences may be adjusted during each iteration of CRPs

Further considering the reasons for the existence of non-cooperative behaviors in the CRP, we recognize that the varying levels of DMs' satisfaction with respect to the consensus level can lead to non-cooperative behaviors. For example, in a CRP under a GDM environment, the DM Andy is asked to adjust his opinion to promote consensus. Suppose that Andy's consensus level is 0.7, the group consensus level is 0.75, and the consensus threshold is set as 0.8. Andy thinks his consensus level is close to the threshold; that is, he is somewhat satisfied with this level and hence is unwilling to make a noticeable adjustment to his opinion. Other DMs, however, do not agree with Andy's satisfaction regarding the consensus level, and view Andy's adjustment action as a non-cooperative behavior. Zhang et al. [167] investigated the individual satisfaction with consensus level under a heterogeneous LSGDM environment. To better demonstrate the contribution of our proposed model to managing consensus in LSGDM, we compare Zhang et al.'s model and our proposed model (Table 6.4).

A detailed explanation of each of these differences are presented below.

6.5.3.1 Explicit Satisfaction Versus Implicit Satisfaction

"Explicit satisfaction" refers to a scenario in which DMs provide their own satisfaction with the consensus level. In Zhang et al.'s research [167], the collective satisfaction index is obtained by aggregating the individual satisfactions. This collective satisfaction is compared with the established satisfaction index to determine whether a feedback mechanism is needed. An implicit expression of satisfaction is thought to be a clue to non-cooperative behaviors. Generally, non-cooperative behaviors occur for three reasons: (1) a DM (or cluster) thinks the current level of consensus is high enough (that is, he/she is satisfied with the current level of consensus), so there is no need to adjust the preference significantly; (2) a DM (or cluster) sticks to his/her own preferences and is reluctant to adjust them; and (3) a mixture of the first two reasons.

The implicit expression of satisfaction is hard to measure. An explicit expression can intuitively quantify a DM's satisfaction with the consensus level. Unlike our model, Zhang et al.'s model [167] adds a "satisfaction measure" to the CRP. However, dishonesty may exist and affect the accuracy of such expressions. For example, a non-cooperative DM can avoid being forced to adjust his/her opinion by falsely reporting a high level of satisfaction. In this sense, dishonesty and non-cooperative behaviors are two issues that must be addressed. Our model proposes a mechanism for managing non-cooperative behaviors that could be extended to consensus building where satisfaction is expressed explicitly.

6.5.3.2   The Management of Non-cooperative Behaviors

In LSGDM problems, non-cooperative behaviors always exist [28, 84, 144]. For example, some individuals may refuse to modify their preferences or move their preferences to resist consensus to further their private interests. Hence, adding the management of non-cooperative behaviors to the CRP is necessary in many decision scenarios. Compared with Zhang et al.' model [167], our proposed model presents a confidence-consensus model that contains a novel mechanism for addressing non-cooperative behaviors.

6.5.3.3   Changeable Cluster Structure Versus Unalterable Cluster Structure

Generally, the cluster structure is one of two types: (i) it does not change once it has been determined [144, 146] because a stable clustering structure prompts the members in each subgroup to establish trust feelings and form a unified opinion and (ii) it changes with the dynamic changes in similarity of DM preferences caused by preference adjustment (see [131, 167]). This study uses the cluster as a basic unit once the clustering structure has been determined.

Additionally, in Zhang et al.'s research [167], when the collective satisfaction degree is lower than the predefined threshold, all the DMs modify their own preferences. In our model, only the preference of the cluster that is the most different from the group preference should be modified. If multiple DMs adjust their preferences simultaneously, the decision-making process may quickly reach a consensus level with high satisfaction, but it could also become more complex and uncertain.

Table 6.5 Simulation results for different consensus measures ($\overline{GCL} = 0.75$)

Consensus measure rules	Total adjustment amount	Final group decision matrix	Overall evaluation values of alternatives	Alternative ranking
CM-I	0.223	$\begin{pmatrix} 0.507 & 0.347 & 0.382 \\ 0.717 & 0.488 & 0.702 \\ 0.401 & 0.544 & 0.447 \\ 0.251 & 0.523 & 0.465 \end{pmatrix}$	$EV(x_1) = 0.396,$ $EV(x_2) = 0.599,$ $EV(x_3) = 0.484,$ $EV(x_4) = 0.441$	$x_2 \succ x_3 \succ x_4 \succ x_1$
CM-II	0.227	$\begin{pmatrix} 0.504 & 0.349 & 0.390 \\ 0.719 & 0.486 & 0.696 \\ 0.401 & 0.534 & 0.451 \\ 0.254 & 0.531 & 0.457 \end{pmatrix}$	$EV(x_1) = 0.398,$ $EV(x_2) = 0.597,$ $EV(x_3) = 0.480,$ $EV(x_4) = 0.443$	$x_2 \succ x_3 \succ x_4 \succ x_1$
CM-III	0.811	$\begin{pmatrix} 0.504 & 0.353 & 0.397 \\ 0.717 & 0.487 & 0.695 \\ 0.400 & 0.527 & 0.453 \\ 0.254 & 0.534 & 0.450 \end{pmatrix}$	$EV(x_1) = 0.403,$ $EV(x_2) = 0.596,$ $EV(x_3) = 0.477,$ $EV(x_4) = 0.443$	$x_2 \succ x_3 \succ x_4 \succ x_1$

Note We use the objective adjustment coefficient presented in [144] to simulate the consensus process for different consensus measures rules in this subsection

6.5.4 Comparison with Different Consensus Measures

In terms of the consensus measure, CM-II is much stricter than CM-I. Because it uses a minimum operator, which is a more rigorous criterion, its use can avoid the situation in which some clusters' consensus levels are still lower than the consensus threshold even though the group consensus level is sufficiently high in the final decision results. In contrast to CM-I and CM-II, CM-III directly measures the difference between clusters and can avoid the deviation caused by the weighted average operation when aggregating cluster opinions. Table 6.5 and Fig. 6.4 both describe the CRP and results of using the objective adjustment coefficient to simulate the consensus process for different consensus measures.

Clearly, there are differences in the adjustment amount, final decision matrix, final alternative evaluation value, and number of iterations when different consensus measures are used. Based on the simulation results in Table 6.6 and Fig. 6.4, we conclude the following.

(1) CM-II and CM-III have more stringent requirements than CM-I. Different consensus measures may apply to different decision problems.
(2) Given the differences in consensus measures, different consensus thresholds should be set for the three measures.

In the case study presented in Sect. 6.4, the DMs believed that the construction of emergency shelters was the most important part of post-earthquake recovery and the most appropriate solution was to follow the majority of opinion. Therefore, the DMs with relatively large weights should have a significant impact on the group opinion

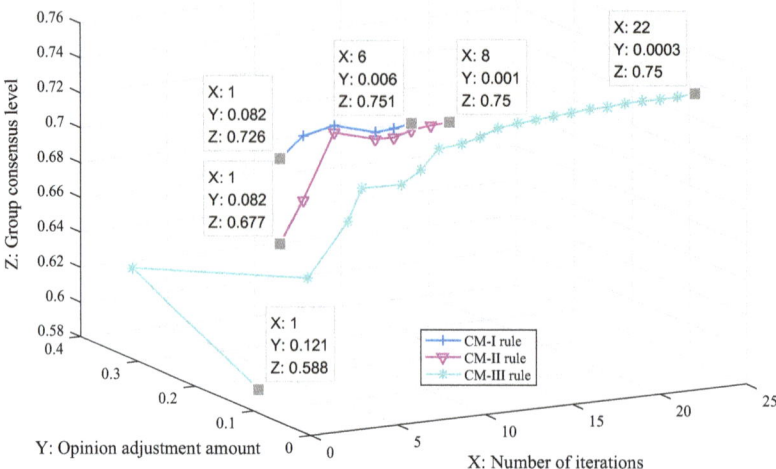

Fig. 6.4 Simulation results based on the objective adjustment coefficient for different consensus measures

and consensus measure. Moreover, just as importantly, because of the timeliness of constructing emergency shelters, it is preferable that the solution be acceptable to most DMs, rather than recognizing all opinions. Eventually, the DMs decided to use CM-I to measure the consensus levels.

6.5.5   *Comparison with Different Parameters*

In this section, we analyze the influence of parameters μ_{WG}, v_{WG}, and χ^t on the decision results. Considering the first iteration in the case study, Table 6.7 and Fig. 6.5 show the simulation results when different input parameters μ_{WG}, v_{WG}, and χ^1 are set. The simulation results in Table 6.7 use five sets of μ_{WG} and v_{WG} and three sets of χ_1 and illustrate the change in the confidence level, group consensus level, and adjusted weight. Figure 6.5 shows the results when we randomly generated input parameters μ_{WG}, v_{WG}, and χ^1 and run the simulation 1,000 times to obtain the confidence level and adjusted weight values. To compare the data more intuitively, we present four significant figures for the weights $^z\lambda^{2,2}$ and updated group consensus levels in Table 6.7 and Fig. 6.5.

The following observations are obtained.

(1) Let the auxiliary coefficient χ^1 be fixed. When setting different parameters μ_{WG} and v_{WG}, there are differences in the confidence level, adjusted weight, and updated group consensus level. For example, in Table 6.7, for $\chi^1 = 5$, when $mu_{WG} = 0$ and $v_{WG} = 1$, the updated group consensus level is 0.7511 and

Table 6.6 Comparison of the advantages and disadvantages of different measure rules

Consensus measure rules	Detailed description
CM-I	**Advantages**: (1) The DMs with relatively large weights have a significant impact on the consensus measure. The greater the weight of a DM, the greater the contribution of its opinion to the group opinion, and thus the higher its individual consensus level. (2) Only the average value of individual consensus levels needs to be higher than the predefined consensus threshold without all individual consensus levels reaching the threshold. It may not need too many iterations and the consensus process may not be difficult to implement **Disadvantages**: (1) DMs' weights need to be calculated in advance. (2) The consensus process is generally aimed at the lower-weight DMs' opinions because their opinions contribute less to the aggregated group opinion and thus are relatively far from the group opinion. (3) A compromise appears between some DMs' opinions with very high consensus levels and those with low consensus levels when the group consensus level is sufficiently high.
CM-II	**Advantages**: (1) DMs with relatively large weights have obvious advantages. (2) Using a min operator to calculate consensus allows for a more rigorous criterion that can avoid the compromise presented in CM-I rule. **Disadvantages**: A tighter measure rule leads to more iterations and a greater adjustment of opinions when the consensus threshold is fixed.
CM-III	**Advantages**: There is no need to consider the weights of DMs when measuring the consensus. All the concerns regard calculating the differences between DM's opinions. **Disadvantages**: The advantages of DMs with relatively large weights cannot be effectively embodied in a consensus measure.

Table 6.7 Comparison results based on the data in the case study for different parameters μ_{WG}, ν_{WG}, and χ^1

μ_{WG}, ν_{WG}	$\zeta^{2,1}$	$z_\lambda^{2,2}$			Updated alternative ranking	Updated group consensus level
		$\chi^1 = 5$	$\chi^1 = 2$	$\chi^1 = 1$		
0.0,1.0	0.1462	0.0405	0.0162	0.0081	2341,2341,2341	0.7511,0.7498,0.7494
0.3,0.7	0.1404	0.0388	0.0155	0.0078	2341,2341,2341	0.7511,0.7498,0.7493
0.5,0.5	0.1366	0.0378	0.0151	0.0076	2341,2341,2341	0.7510,0.7498,0.7493
0.7,0.3	0.1329	0.0368	0.0147	0.0074	2341,2341,2341	0.7509,0.7497,0.7493
1.0,0.0	0.1276	0.0353	0.0141	0.0071	2341,2341,2341	0.7509,0.7497,0.7493

Notes: (a) The data in the item "Updated alternative ranking" represent three groups of alternative rankings when parameter χ^1 is set to 5, 2 and 1, respectively. "2341" indicates that the alternative ranking is $x_2 \succ x_3 \succ x_4 \succ x_1$.

(b) The data in the item "Updated group consensus level" represent the different group consensus levels when parameter χ^1 is set to 5, 2, and 1, respectively

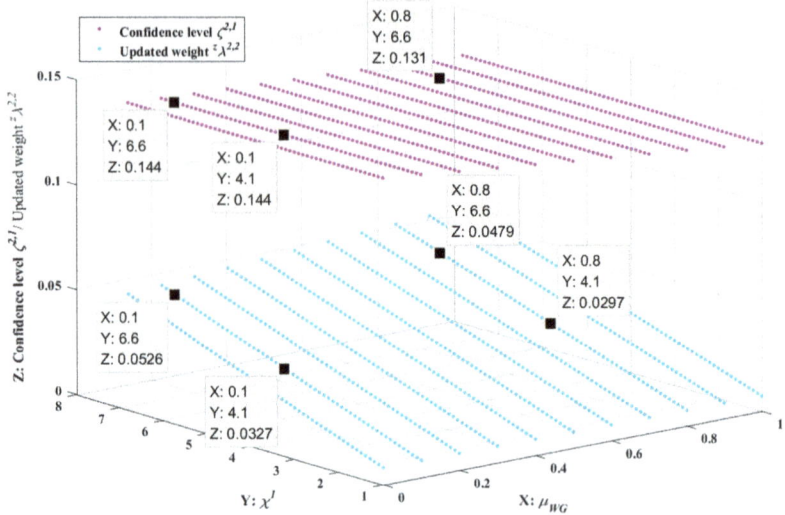

Fig. 6.5 Simulation results of confidence level $\zeta^{2,1}$ and adjusted weight $^z\lambda_2^2$ for different parameters μ_{WG}, ν_{WG}, and χ^1.

$^z\lambda^{2,2} = 0.0405$; when $\mu_{WG} = 0.7$ and $\nu_{WG} = 0.3$, the group consensus level is 0.7509 and $^z\lambda^{2,2} = 0.0368$. Furthermore, Fig. 6.5 shows our comparison of the two sets of coordinates, that is, the pair (0.1, 6.6, 0.144) and (0.8, 6.6, 0.131) and the pair (0.1, 6.6, 0.0526) and (0.8, 6.6, 0.0479). The difference in the confidence level and adjusted weight is obvious.

(2) Let μ_{WG} and ν_{WG} be fixed. When χ^1 is set to different values, then the adjusted weight of cluster C_2 may also be different. For example, in Table 6.7, when $\mu = 0.3$, $\nu = 0.7$, and χ^1 is set to 5 or 2, the corresponding adjusted weight of C_2 is 0.0388 or 0.0155. In accordance with Eq. (6.12), when the confidence level is fixed, the adjusted weight is proportional to parameter χ^1. The two coordinates shown in Fig. 6.5, i.e., (0.1, 6.6, 0.0526) and (0.1, 4.1, 0.0327), also demonstrate this proportional relation.

6.6 Conclusions

Because LSGDM can model many real-world decisions, a confidence consensus-based model that considers non-cooperative behaviors was proposed. The major contributions of this study are as follows:

(1) New concepts were proposed: the collective adjustment suggestion, degree of rationality, and confidence level.
(2) A novel mechanism for addressing non-cooperative behaviors was presented. We divide the management of non-cooperative behaviors into three phases. The interaction and discussion effectively make DMs provide more suitable adjust-

ment coefficients. In this process, we combine the degrees of rationality and non-cooperation to construct the confidence level of a cluster's adjustment coefficient. It is more accurate and objective to use the confidence level to measure the willingness of a cluster to adjust its opinion to promote agreement. Further, it ensures that the cluster has an accurate and reasonable understanding of the decision problem.

(3) An algorithm for the confidence consensus-based model in LSGDM was presented. Its aim is to better address non-cooperative behaviors and obtain a common decision result with a sufficiently high level of group consensus.

(4) We summarized different consensus measures and used simulation to compare them. The simulation results reveal the advantages and disadvantages of these different measures.

(5) A comparison with Zhang et al.'s model [167] leads to the concepts of "explicit satisfaction" and "implicit satisfaction." These concepts lead to a significant research issue: how to measure satisfaction that is implicitly expressed.

Meanwhile, there still exist some limitations:

(1) In some real-life LSGDM, trust relationships among DMs defined by a social network play a key role. As a consequence, the research on CRMs in social network-based GDM has been paid increasing attention. It could be meaningful to build an improved CRM for addressing non-cooperative behaviors within a social network environment.

(2) Zhang et al.'s research [167] indicates that in a LSGDM, DMs often have individual concerns about alternatives and satisfactions regarding the degree of consensus in CRPs. Thus, they prefer to use heterogeneous preference representation structures to express their opinions. It is important to extend the traditional CRPs to manage non-cooperative behaviors in heterogeneous LSGDM with individual concerns and satisfactions.

(3) How to more reasonably modify DMs' weights based on the confidence level is also an important issue to address. Solving this matter depends on multiple simulation analyses with real data from different sources.

Chapter 7
Integration of Independent and Supervised Consensus Models

Abstract Traditional consensus models dealing with non-cooperative behaviors focus on the situation where only one decision-maker (DM) modifies its own opinion in each consensus iteration. However, some, or even all, DMs may adjust their opinions in one iteration, especially at the beginning. In this chapter, a mixed consensus model for managing non-cooperative behaviors is proposed. We first develop a novel method to calculate the weights of DMs, which contains multiple measurement attributes. An independent consensus model is then put forward to address the situation where multiple DMs modify their opinions in each iteration. By combining this independent consensus model with traditional consensus models, a mixed consensus model is constructed. Finally, a case study is used to show the feasibility and applicability of the proposed model.

Keywords Large-scale group decision-making (LSGDM) · Non-cooperative behaviors · Mixed consensus-reaching model (MCRM) · Independent consensus-reaching model (ICRM) · Punishment approach

7.1 Introduction

Real-world decision-making is becoming increasingly complex and uncertain, and in many cases, it is difficult for small-scale decision organizations to understand and evaluate all of the relevant aspects. Large-scale group decision-making (LSGDM) has received growing attention in the field of decision science and has been applied to many practical problems, such as water-resource management [38], infrastructure construction [65, 102], emergency events [131, 144, 146], project investment [167], and other decisions [128, 170]. LSGDM is a decision scenario in which several decision-makers (DMs) try to achieve a common solution from a set of alternatives. Because the background, situation, and difficulty of real LSGDM problems are different, the number of DMs in current studies can range from dozens to thousands [93, 131]. Shi et al. [102], Xu et al. [144], and Zhang et al. [167] suggested that a large group should include more than 11 DMs. Gou et al. [38], Li et al. [56], and Liu et al. [65] argued that a group is considered large-scale when the number of group members is greater than 20. In Palomares et al. [84] and Wu et al. [127], the illustrative examples contained as many as 50 DMs. Since DMs usually come from different departments and have a variety of professional backgrounds, they may present different individual opinions and only partially share the goals of other members.

Generally, three processes are necessary for addressing LSGDM problems: the clustering process, the consensus-reaching process, and the selection process [84]. Clustering is an effective approach to organizing and managing a large group because it can divide a large group into small-scale clusters. Many clustering methods have been proposed, such as the K-means algorithm [131], density-based clustering algorithm [114], hierarchical clustering algorithm [182], and vector space-based clustering method [140]. Measuring the similarities among individual opinions is the basis of clustering. If two individual opinions are sufficiently similar, those DMs can be assigned to the same cluster. This study follows Xu et al.'s research [144] in terms of classifying large-scale DMs and uses the cluster as the basic unit once the clustering structure has been determined. This classification produces a hierarchical structure, including a top-down division of the membership structure and a bottom-up aggregation of individual opinions. It takes two steps to produce a group opinion. First, the "DM to DM" interaction forms a unified cluster opinion. Then, the "cluster to cluster" discussion eventually generates the group opinion. Such bottom-up information aggregation can guarantee orderly and efficient decision-making processes.

Reaching a consensus is a dynamic and iterative process of group discussion in which some individual opinions must be adjusted [24, 172]. Unlike the ideal consensus, which requires complete agreement, the concept of soft consensus allows for differences of opinion within a certain range and has been widely adopted [45, 91]. There will always be some DMs who are unwilling to modify their opinions to promote consensus (or are unwilling to comply with certain adjustment requirements). In an LSGDM problem, since DMs usually come from different domains and have various interests, they are more likely to adopt non-cooperative behaviors to further their individual interests. For example, some individuals will form a small group because they share similar opinions. When an adjustment signal is sent, they may refuse to make any adjustments in order to uphold the importance of their own opinions within the group opinion. Refusing to adjust is the opposite of the goal of achieving a high-consensus decision outcome, and it can bring the consensus-reaching process to a standstill. Hence, managing DMs' non-cooperative behaviors is crucial for the smooth implementation of decision-making processes and outcome quality.

Regarding the literature on solving non-cooperative behaviors in LSGDM environments, Palomares et al. [84] incorporated a fuzzy clustering-based scheme to detect and manage individual and subgroup non-cooperative behaviors. Xu et al. [144] used the comprehensive correction coefficient to implement opinion punishment and designed a non-cooperative degree-based staircase weight adjustment function. Dong et al. [28] proposed a self-management mechanism in large-scale consensus-reaching processes that allowed penalizing the weights of experts with non-cooperative behaviors. Further, Mediwaththe and Smith [80] developed a two-stage non-cooperative game to explore an electric vehicle. The non-cooperative game among DMs influences the consensus-reaching process and ultimately achieves an acceptable decision result. Li et al. [60] applied a game-theoretical model to decisions on a smart grid. Quesada et al. [93] developed a methodology based on computing with words to deal with non-cooperative behaviors and guided investment decisions. Zhang et al. [172] focused on the management of non-cooperative behaviors in a social network environment. Based on the above literature review, we conclude the following research issues that should be addressed concerning the management of non-cooperative behaviors:

(1) The main methods for managing non-cooperative behaviors are opinion punishment and weight punishment; however, few studies have investigated the differences in the effects of these two methods on consensus building.
(2) Current consensus-reaching models mainly focus on decision situations where only one DM (or cluster) is required to modify his or her (or its) opinion in each round of consensus iteration. What if multiple DMs (or clusters) adjust their opinions?

Since some DMs have not formed a complete and accurate understanding of the problem at the beginning of complex decision-making, some individual opinions may deviate greatly from the group opinion. When consensus iteration is implemented, multiple DMs' opinions will be adjusted. Until the group consensus reaches a certain level, there is no need to adjust multiple individual opinions—just those that deviate the most from the group opinion. This consensus iteration design has the following two advantages: (1) it is in line with actual decision-making situations and will not make opinion adjustments on an immature basis, and (2) it can maintain equal positions among DMs as opposed to focusing on one individual's opinion at the beginning and asking for an adjustment. Hence, we can conclude that a novel consensus-reaching model in LSGDM should be built that not only considers the processing of non-cooperative behaviors in the case of one cluster adjusting its opinion but also pays attention to the case where multiple clusters modify their opinions in each round of consensus iteration.

The contributions of this study are as follows:

(1) We summarize four punishment approaches to managing non-cooperative behaviors and elaborate on their characteristics.
(2) We propose an independent consensus-reaching model to deal with the decision scenario in which multiple clusters (rather than just one cluster) adjust opinions in each consensus iteration. Weight punishment and opinion punishment are adopted to manage non-cooperative behaviors.
(3) A mixed consensus-reaching model is built by combining a supervised consensus-reaching model that requires only one cluster per iteration to involve opinion adjustment with an independent consensus-reaching model.
(4) A novel method is developed to calculate the weights of the clusters.

7.2　Analysis of Consensus Level in LSGDM

Consider an LSGDM problem that includes a finite set of alternatives $X = \{x_1, x_2, \ldots, x_m\}$ and a set of criteria $A = \{a_1, a_2, \ldots, a_n\}$. The weight vector of the criteria is denoted as $\omega = (\omega_1, \omega_2, \ldots, \omega_n)^T$, where $\omega_j \geq 0$, $j = 1, 2, \ldots, n$ and $\sum_{j=1}^{n} \omega_j = 1$. Let $E = \{e_1, e_2, \ldots, e_q\}$ be a set of DMs. Let $V_l = (v_{l,ij})_{m \times n}$ be the individual decision matrix, where $v_{l,ij}$ is the evaluation of DM e_l on the alternative $x_i \in X$ with respect to the criterion $a_j \in A$. To ensure comparability, the individual decision matrix V_l should be normalized to standardized decision matrix $R_l = (r_{l,ij})_{m \times n}$ [144]. It is preferable that DMs should reach a relatively high-level consensus before applying the selection process [54, 73, 119].

7.2.1　Opinion Clustering

Clustering individual opinions provides the basis for analyzing a large group. This study adopts the vector space-based clustering method in [140] to divide a large group into $K (1 \leq K \leq q)$ clusters (the clustering method is described in the supplementary materials). Traditionally, according to the majority principle in which larger-scale clusters should be assigned larger weights, the weights of the clusters are determined (see [144, 167]). However, a cluster contains many attributes. The attributes related to determining the weight are the individual consensus level (marked as CL_k), the number of DMs within cluster C_k (marked as n_k), and the consensus level among the internal DMs' opinions (called internal consensus level, marked as $CL_{k,in}$. Table 7.1 shows the attributes involved in calculating the weights of clusters. We can conclude that all of the above attributes have positive effects on weight allocation. Note that DMs in the same cluster can be assigned the same weight because they have the similar individual opinions.

Definition 7.1　Given the initial individual consensus level CL_k^0, the number of DMs within cluster n_k, and the initial internal consensus level $CL_{k,in}$, the weight of cluster C_k can be obtained by

$$\theta_k^0 = \left(\frac{n_k}{q}\right)^{\alpha_1} \cdot \left(\frac{CL_k^0}{max_k\{CL_k^0\}}\right)^{\alpha_2} \cdot \left(\frac{CL_{k,in}^0}{max_k\{CL_{k,in}^0\}}\right)^{\alpha_2} \tag{7.1}$$

where $0 \leq \alpha_1, \alpha_2, \alpha_3 \leq 1$, and $\alpha_1 + \alpha_2 + \alpha_3 = 1$. Since only similar enough opinions can be assigned to the same cluster, we can set $max_k\{CL_k^0\} \neq 0$, $max_k\{CL_{k,in}^0\} \neq 0$, $k = 1, 2, \ldots, K$. Then, normalize weight θ_k^0 into λ_k^0 in order to meet $\lambda_k^0 \geq 0$, $k = 1, 2, \ldots, K$, and $\sum_{k=1}^{K} \lambda_k^0 = 1$. Since the weight calculation formula Eq. (7.1) is implemented before entering the consensus-reaching process, we call the weights calculated by Eq. (7.1) initial weights, and the symbol "0" in λ_k^0 represents the initial weight of cluster C_k. The initial cluster decision matrix can be obtained as

Table 7.1 Attributes to be considered in calculating the weights of clusters

Attributes	Direction	Description
Individual consensus level	Positive	Individual consensus level quantifies the similarities between one cluster's opinion and that of others. The higher the similarity, the closer the cluster's opinion is to the majority opinion, and the more weight the cluster should be given.
The number of DMs within one cluster	Positive	Decision-makers with significantly similar opinions are placed in the same cluster. The more DMs a cluster contains, the more weight the cluster should be given.
Internal consensus level	Positive	The higher the level of consensus within a cluster, the more the DMs' opinions within the cluster tend to be the same. The more similar the DMs' opinions, the easier it is to form a unified cluster opinion. Thus, a greater weight should be given to this cluster.

$R_k^0 = (r_{k,ij}^0)_{m \times n}$, where $r_{k,ij}^0 = (1/n_k) \sum_{l=1}^{n_k} r_{l,ij}^0$, $e_l \in C_k$. The initial group decision matrix is represented by $R_c^0 = (r_{c,ij}^0)_{m \times n}$, where $r_{c,ij}^0 = \sum_{k=1}^{K} r_{k,ij}^0 \lambda_k^0$.

7.2.2 Consensus Measure

There are two methods for calculating consensus measures: the first is based on distance to the group opinion [125, 146], and the second is based on the distances between individual opinions [61, 178]. This study follows the latter definition because it can directly measure the difference between clusters without considering the weights of clusters.

Definition 7.2 Given cluster C_k's decision matrix $R_k^t = (r_{k,ij}^t)_{m \times n}$ in the t-th iteration, the individual consensus level is defined as

$$CL_k^t = 1 - \frac{1}{K-1} \sum_{h=1, k \neq h}^{K} d(R_k^t, R_h^t) \qquad (7.2)$$

where $d(r_{k,ij}^t, r_{h,ij}^t)$ is the distance between $r_{k,ij}^t$ and $r_{h,ij}^t$.

The group consensus level is

$$GCL^t = \frac{1}{K} \sum_{k=1}^{K} CL_k^t \tag{7.3}$$

Clearly, $0 \leq GCL^t \leq 1$. If the group consensus level is adequately high, the selection process is followed; otherwise, the consensus-reaching process should be applied to reduce differences of opinion. Similar to the consensus measure in Definition 7.2, the internal consensus level is set as the average of the individual consensus levels of DMs contained in a cluster. Thus, when a cluster contains only one DM, the internal consensus level of the cluster is set to 1.

7.3 Proposed Consensus-Reaching Models for Managing Non-cooperative Behaviors

There are often two consensus principles for group decision-making problems.

Consensus Principle I: Multiple DMs (not just one) move their opinions to the group opinion in each round of consensus iteration. Although reluctance to adjust opinions may be punished, DMs can independently provide their individual adjustment information.

Consensus Principle II: In each consensus iteration, the first step is to identify the DM whose opinion differs the most from that of the group. The identified DM is then asked to adjust his or her individual opinion. Only one DM per iteration is involved in the decision regarding opinion adjustment. Unlike Consensus Principle I, this principle only requires the identified DM to adjust his or her own opinion, and the adjustment is supervised and guided by other DMs.

By combining these two principles, a new consensus principle is developed, called Consensus Principle III. Since the consensus level may be relatively low at the beginning of the consensus iteration, most DMs need to modify their opinions. When the consensus level grows to a certain degree, there will be less need for so many DMs to adjust their opinions, and only the individual opinion that deviates the most from the group will need to make a corresponding adjustment.

Through the permutation and combination of the above three consensus principles and the four presented punishment approaches to addressing non-cooperative behaviors, 12 consensus-reaching models can be obtained (see Fig. 7.1). We define three models obtained by adopting the approach of no punishment as the basic consensus model. When full punishment is adopted, the following three consensus-reaching models can be developed: independent consensus-reaching model (ICRM), supervised consensus-reaching model (SCRM), and mixed consensus-reaching model (MCRM).

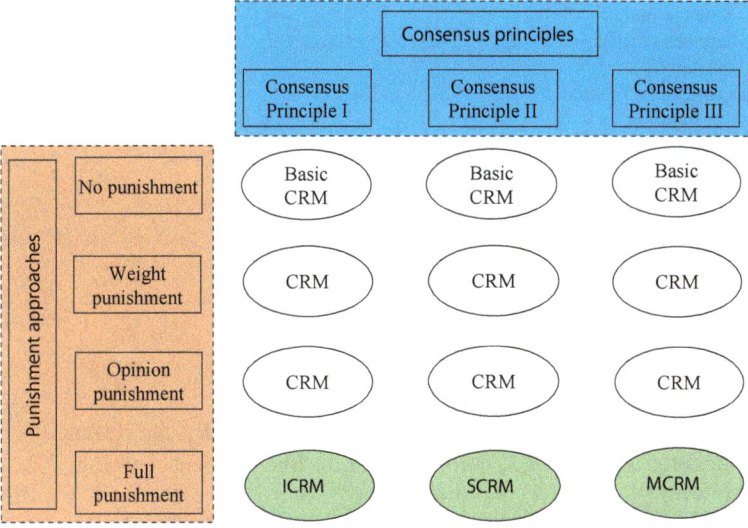

Fig. 7.1 List of consensus-reaching models obtained through the permutation and combination of consensus principles and punishment approaches

7.3.1 Independent Consensus-Reaching Model

ICRM is based on Consensus Principle I. Before the consensus threshold requirement is met, there are situations where multiple clusters can move their opinions toward the group opinion. Clusters adjust their own opinions independently and freely according to the current consensus level without any supervision or coercion from other clusters. Although clusters have different weights, they have the same right to adjust their opinions. Hence, the consensus model used in this stage is called an independent consensus-reaching model. Usually, Eq. (7.4) is used to modify the clusters' decision matrices, such that [144]:

$$R_k^{t+1} = \eta_k^t R_c^t + (1 - \eta_k^t) R_k^t \tag{7.4}$$

where $\eta_k^t (0 \le \eta_k^t \le 1)$ is the given adjustment coefficient, R_k^t and R_k^{t+1} present the opinions of cluster C_k before and after the t-th iteration, respectively, and R_c^t is the group opinion.

Theorem 7.1 *When adopting Eq. (7.4) to adjust the cluster's decision matrix, the individual consensus level will increase.*

Proof Namely, we need to prove that $CL_k^{t+1} \ge CL_k^t, k = 1, 2, \ldots, K$.

The clusters' decision matrices can be abstracted as points in a two-dimensional space. Measuring the distance between any two clusters' decision matrices can be regarded as calculating the straight-line distance between the corresponding points

Fig. 7.2 Change in the
distance between cluster
C_k's and cluster C_h's
decision matrices before and
after the t-th iteration.

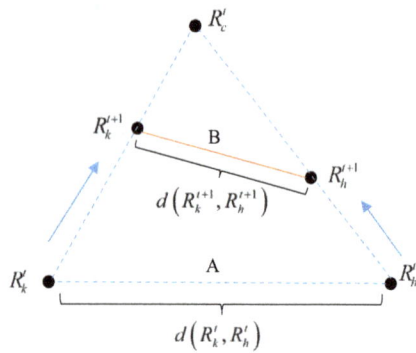

(see Fig. 7.2). Given any two clusters' opinions R_k^t and R_h^t, the distance between them is denoted as $d(R_k^t, R_h^t)$, corresponding to line segment A in Fig. 7.2 . After moving toward R_c^t, R_k^t and R_h^t are adjusted to R_k^{t+1} and R_h^{t+1}, respectively. The distance between R_k^{t+1} and R_h^{t+1} is denoted as $d(R_k^{t+1}, R_h^{t+1})$, corresponding to line segment B in Fig. 7.2. According to the formula for calculating the side length of a triangle, we can conclude that the length of line segment A is greater than or at least equal to B; that is, $d(R_k^{t+1}, R_h^{t+1}) \leq d(R_k^t, R_h^t)$. On the basis of Eq. (7.2), we can determine that $CL_k^{t+1} \geq CL_k^t$.

This completes the proof of Theorem 7.1.   □

After the adjustments, all individual consensus levels will be changed. Below, we define the change rate of the individual consensus level.

Definition 7.3 Suppose the individual consensus levels in the t-th and $t+1$-th iterations are CL_k^t and CL_k^{t+1}, respectively. The change rate of these two sequential consensus levels can be obtained as:

$$\delta_k^{t+1} = \frac{CL_k^{t+1} - CL_k^t}{CL_k^t} \tag{7.5}$$

δ_k^t is is used to measure the change in the scale and direction of the individual consensus level.

Remark 7.1 It is necessary to explain why, instead of the change of adjustment coefficient, we use the change rate of the individual consensus level to represent the degree to which one cluster is willing to adjust its opinion. The purpose of the consensus-reaching process is to improve the level of individual consensus and then make the level of group consensus meet the threshold requirements. The adjustment coefficient is only a means of raising the level of individual consensus. Increases and decreases in the adjustment coefficient do not necessarily lead to increases or decreases in the individual consensus level to the same degree since other factors are included, such as the choice of the distance-measure formula. In terms of results-oriented problem solving, we tend to use variations in individual consensus levels to characterize the degree to which a cluster is unwilling to adjust its opinion. For example, when an adjustment coefficient increases from 0.3 to 0.5 (rate of change: 0.6667), the individual consensus level increases from 0.7 to 0.8 (rate of change is only 0.1429). The two results are markedly different.

Remark 7.2 Usually, we require the condition $0.5 \leq CL_k^t \leq 1$ to be true. If an individual consensus level is less than 0.5, it indicates that the individual opinion deviates greatly from the group, and the reliability of the opinion is in question. The consensus-reaching process is meaningful only when differences among individual opinions exist to a certain extent, which is not enough to meet the requirements, but no extreme opinions should appear. Otherwise, it is more reasonable and easier to remove extreme individual opinions rather than try to make drastic adjustments. Based on the above analysis, we can obtain $0 \leq \delta_k^{t+1} \leq 1, k = 1, 2, \ldots, K$.

Consider two different variations on the individual consensus level.

Case 1. *The individual consensus level of a cluster increases significantly.*

After one consensus iteration, if a cluster's consensus level increases greatly, it indicates that the cluster is willing to adjust its own opinion, and the adjustment amount is significantly large. A cooperative attitude toward adjustment contributes to the achievement of a high-consensus decision result. Thus, there is reason to believe that the corresponding cluster's weight should be increased as a reward for significant adjustment.

Case 2. *The individual consensus level of a cluster increases by only a small fraction.*

In this case, the cluster will be identified as a non-cooperative subgroup. A negative and non-cooperative attitude toward adjustment contributes less to a high-consensus decision outcome. The cluster is supposed to be punished. Noncooperation refers to the extent to which adjustment fails to meet certain requirements.

By comparing the change rates of individual consensus levels, the change rate interval of the individual consensus level is obtained as $[min\{\delta_k^{t+1}\}, max\{\delta_k^{t+1}\}]$. We divide the interval into two areas, where $[0, \overline{\delta}^{t+1})$ is called the punishment area, $[\overline{\delta}^{t+1}, 1]$ is called the reward area (see Fig. 7.3). $\overline{\delta}^{t+1}$ is the critical point used to identify the above two areas, satisfying $\overline{\delta}^{t+1} \in [min\{\delta_k^{t+1}\}, max\{\delta_k^{t+1}\}]$.

Intuitively, if the change rate of individual consensus level belongs to the punishment area, the related cluster's weight should be punished and reduced since the cluster is subjectively unwilling to significantly adjust its opinion. By contrast, if the change rate of the individual consensus level falls into the reward area, the cluster's weight needs to be rewarded and increased. However, the above processing ignores an important piece of decision information—group consensus level. By adding this information to the division of the change rate of the individual consensus level, Fig. 7.3 is improved, as shown in Fig. 7.4.

In Fig. 7.4, the change rate of the individual consensus level is classified into four areas

(1) *Area I (reward area)*: $CL_k^{t+1} \geq GCL^{t+1}, \delta_k^{t+1} \geq \overline{\delta}_k^{t+1}$. Not only is the individual consensus level higher than the group consensus level, but the change rate of the

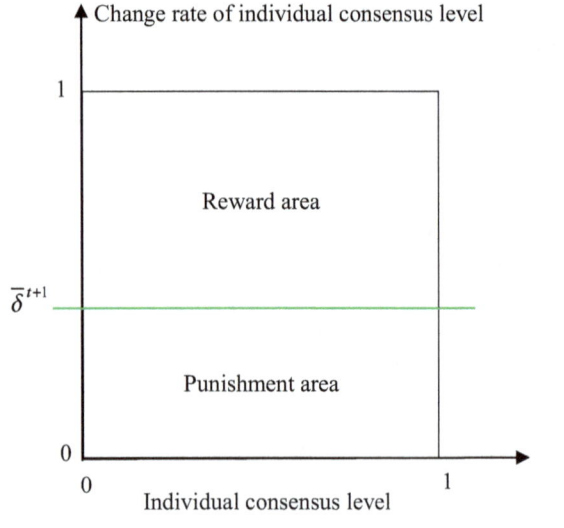

Fig. 7.3 Division of the change rates of individual consensus levels

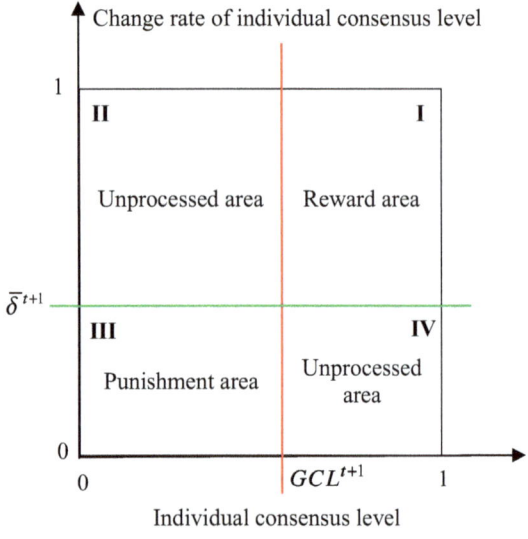

Fig. 7.4 Improved division of the change rates of individual consensus levels

individual consensus level is also higher than the critical point. This indicates that cluster C_k adjusted its opinion, even though it did not have to do so to such an extent. Thus, its weight should be increased, not the least because its adjustment behavior promotes consensus. Moreover, the high level of initial consensus indicates that the cluster's opinion is close to the majority opinion, and improving the expression degree of its opinion in the group opinion contributes to the expression of the majority opinion.

(2) *Area II (unprocessed area)*: $CL_k^{t+1} < GCL^{t+1}$, $\delta_k^{t+1} \geq \overline{\delta}_k^{t+1}$. The individual consensus level is lower than the group consensus level, but the change rate of the individual consensus level is higher than the critical point. Although the individual consensus level has not exceeded the threshold requirement, cluster C_k has made a significant adjustment. Thus, its weight should not be reduced.

(3) *Area III (punishment area)*: $CL_k^{t+1} < GCL^{t+1}$, $\delta_k^{t+1} < \overline{\delta}_k^{t+1}$. The individual consensus level is less than the group consensus, and the change rate of the individual consensus level belongs to the punishment area. Intuitively, if a cluster's consensus level is lower than the group consensus level, then its opinion should be significantly adjusted to increase the consensus level. The result is that the change rate of the individual consensus level is likely to fall within the reward area. Conversely, if the change rate falls within the punishment area, it means the cluster's opinion should have been adjusted more than it was. Such non-cooperative action is not conducive to consensus building. Therefore, its weight needs to be punished and reduced.

(4) *Area IV (unprocessed area)*: $CL_k^{t+1} \geq GCL^{t+1}$, $\delta_k^{t+1} < \overline{\delta}_k^{t+1}$. When the individual consensus level exceeds the group consensus level, even if the change rate of the individual consensus level is very small, the cluster will not fall into the punishment area. This is because after the consensus iterations, the cluster's consensus level still exceeds the group consensus level. This indicates that its opinion and given adjustment coefficient still play a positive role in consensus building. Therefore, there is no need to punish its weight.

Definition 7.4 In line with the division in Fig. 7.4, the modification function for the cluster's weight can be defined as two piecewise functions, as shown in Eqs. (7.6) and (7.7) :

$$\lambda_k^{t+1,l} = \begin{cases} \lambda_k^t & \delta_k^{t+1} \in [0, \overline{\delta}^{t+1}) \\ f(\delta_k^{t+1}, \overline{\delta}^{t+1}, \lambda_k^t) & \delta_k^{t+1} \in [\overline{\delta}^{t+1}, 1] \end{cases}, for CL_k^{t+1} \geq GCL^{t+1} \qquad (7.6)$$

$$\lambda_k^{t+1,l} = \begin{cases} g(\delta_k^{t+1}, \overline{\delta}^{t+1}, \lambda_k^t) & \delta_k^{t+1} \in [0, \overline{\delta}^{t+1}) \\ \lambda_k^t & \delta_k^{t+1} \in [\overline{\delta}^{t+1}, 1] \end{cases}, for CL_k^{t+1} < GCL^{t+1} \qquad (7.7)$$

where $f(\delta_k^{t+1}, \overline{\delta}^{t+1}, \lambda_k^t)$ and $g(\delta_k^{t+1}, \overline{\delta}^{t+1}, \lambda_k^t)$ are called the punishment function and reward function, respectively, and $\lambda_k^{t+1,l}$ represents the modified weight of cluster C_k using ICRM.

Here, we use the punishment coefficient to construct the calculation formula of $\overline{\delta}^{t+1}$:

$$\overline{\delta}^{t+1} = min\{\delta_k^{t+1}\} + \beta^{t+1}(max\{\delta_k^{t+1}\} - min\{\delta_k^{t+1}\}) \tag{7.8}$$

where β^{t+1} is the punishment coefficient used to determine how much less than the rate of the change in individual consensus level would fall into the punishment area, meeting $0 \le \beta^{t+1} \le 1$. It should be emphasized that this value is not necessarily a constant throughout all of the consensus iterations.

We sort the clusters' weights in strictly ascending order and obtain the ordered weight vector of the clusters, i.e., $\vartheta^t = (\vartheta_1^t, \vartheta_2^t, \ldots, \vartheta_{K'}^t)$, $1 \le K' \le K$, where ϑ_q^t is the q-th smallest weight. For example, given the weight vector of the clusters $\lambda^t = (0.2, 0.4, 0.1, 0.2, 0.1)$, the ordered weight vector can be calculated as $\vartheta^t = (0.1, 0.2, 0.4)$.

If $\delta_k^{t+1} < \overline{\delta}^{t+1}$ and $CL_k^{t+1} < GCL^{t+1}$, the change rate of the individual consensus level falls into the punishment area. After the t+1-th iteration, the difference between the opinion of cluster ck and the others' opinions is still not significantly shortened. This implies that the adjustment coefficient proposed by cluster ck contributes less to consensus. The punishment operation is implemented to manage this non-cooperative behavior. An effective method is to modify the weight of cluster ck to reduce its importance in the group. The weight punishment function is defined as $\lambda_k^{t+1,l} = f(\delta_k^{t+1}, \overline{\delta}^{t+1}, \lambda_k^t)$, where

$$f(\delta_k^{t+1}, \overline{\delta}^{t+1}, \lambda_k^t) = \begin{pmatrix} \lambda_k^t - \frac{\overline{\delta}^{t+1} - \delta_k^{t+1}}{\overline{\delta}^{t+1}} \cdot (\vartheta_q^t - \vartheta_{q-1}^t) & q > 1 \\ \frac{\delta_k^{t+1}}{\overline{\delta}^{t+1}} \cdot \lambda_k^t & q = 1 \end{pmatrix} \tag{7.9}$$

If $\delta_k^{t+1} \ge \overline{\delta}^{t+1}$ and $CL_k^{t+1} \ge GCL^{t+1}$, the change rate of the individual consensus level falls into the reward interval. The individual consensus level of cluster ck has been significantly increased after the t+1-th iteration. Thus, cluster ck can be regarded as being cooperative with consensus building. Thus, its weight should be improved. The reward function is defined as $\lambda_k^{t+1,l} = g(\delta_k^{t+1}, \overline{\delta}^{t+1}, \lambda_k^t)$, where

$$g(\delta_k^{t+1}, \overline{\delta}^{t+1}, \lambda_k^t) = \begin{pmatrix} \lambda_k^t + \frac{\delta_k^{t+1} - \overline{\delta}^{t+1}}{1 - \overline{\delta}^{t+1}} \cdot (\vartheta_{q+1}^t - \vartheta_q^t) & \vartheta_{q+1}^t > \vartheta_q^t \\ \lambda_k^t + \frac{\delta_k^{t+1} - \overline{\delta}^{t+1}}{1 - \overline{\delta}^{t+1}} \cdot \lambda_k^t & \vartheta_q^t = max\{\vartheta_q^t\} \end{pmatrix} \tag{7.10}$$

Clearly, $0 \le \lambda_k^{t+1,l} \le 1$.

Since the full punishment approach is used to manage noncooperative behavior, after processing the weight punishment, we need to take punitive measures for individual opinions that have fallen into the punishment area.

Definition 7.5 Supposing the change rate of the individual consensus level δ_k^{t+1} falls into the punishment area, the punished opinion of cluster C_k can be obtained as:

$$R_k^{t+1,I} = (1 + \delta_k^{t+1})\eta_k^t R_c^t + (1 - (1 + \delta_k^{t+1})\eta_k^t)R_k^t, \tag{7.11}$$

where $R_k^{t+1,I}$ represents the adjusted opinion obtained using the full punishment approach.

Note that if $(1 + \delta_k^{t+1})\eta_k^t \geq 1$, then let $(1 + \delta_k^{t+1})\eta_k^t = 1$. Based on Theorem 7.1, we can see that by adopting Eq. (7.11) to adjust the cluster decision matrix, the individual consensus level will increase.

Algorithm 7.1 presents the implementation process using ICRM to manage the consensus-reaching process in consideration of non-cooperative behavior.

Algorithm 7.1 Independent consensus-reaching model (ICRM)

Input: Initial clusters' decision matrices $R_k^0 (k = 1, 2, \ldots, K)$, initial weight vector of the clusters λ^0, and the acceptable consensus threshold $\overline{GCL}$.

Output: Final number of iterations and the final group matrix.

1: Set $t = 0$.
2: Consensus measure. Compute the individual consensus levels using Eq. (7.2); i.e., $CL_k^t, k = 1, 2, \ldots, K$. The group consensus level GCL^t can then be obtained via Eq. (7.3). If $GCL^t \geq \overline{GCL}$, then proceed to Step 3; otherwise, proceed to Step 2.2 I .
3: If $t = 0$, proceed to Step 2.2 I .a; if $t > 0$, proceed to Step 2.2 I .b.
4: Use Eq. (7.4) to modify the clusters' decision matrices. Let $t = t + 1$, and then return to Step 2.1.
5: Calculate the change rates of individual consensus levels using Eq. (7.5).
6: Determine which area each change rate of consensus level belongs to, and implement the punishment operation. Let $t = t + 1$, and then return to Step 2.1.
7: Output the related decision information.
   Let $t^* = t$. The final group decision matrix is obtained as $R_c^{t^*} = (r_{c,ij}^{t^*})_{m \times n}$ final group decision matrix $r_{c,ij}^{t^*} = \sum_{k=1}^K r_{k,ij}^{t^*} \lambda_k^{t^*}$. Output the final iterative time t^* and final group decision matrix $R_c^{t^*}$.

7.3.2 Supervised Consensus-Reaching Model

The SCRM is based on Consensus Principle II, whose core idea is to detect and manage the cluster opinion that is the farthest distance from the group in each round of iteration. Compared to the ICRM, it will not be effective for determining whether a cluster belongs to the opinionated group according to change rate of the individual consensus level when only one cluster opinion needs to be adjusted in each iteration. Since the decision situation here is the same as in [144], we can use Xu et al.'s model [144] to manage non-cooperative behaviors. By replacing Step 2.2^I with Step 2.2^S, a novel model, the **supervised consensus-reaching model (SCRM)**, is obtained.

Step 2.2^S: Consensus iteration process.

Use Xu et al.'s model [144] to manage the consensus-reaching process and non-cooperative behaviors.

Note that it is called "supervised" because only one cluster needs to adjust its opinion, and the rest of the clusters will not only monitor the whole adjustment process but also provide adjustment suggestions used to determine whether a non-cooperative behavior exists.

7.3.3 Mixed Consensus-Reaching Model

ICRM and SCRM are applicable to two different decision-making situations and adopt different measures to deal with non-cooperative behaviors. These two decision scenarios are sequential. In general, ICRM is used when the group consensus level is very low at the start, and multiple clusters need to adjust their opinions. When the group consensus level rises to a certain level, it may require only one cluster to make a compromise. Hence, by integrating ICRM and SCRM, we further propose a mixed consensus-reaching model (MCRM). To achieve this combination, we introduce a control coefficient, ρ^t, to determine whether ICRM or SCRM should be selected in each consensus iteration, where

$$\rho^t = \frac{\overline{GCL} - GCL^t}{\overline{GCL}}. \tag{7.12}$$

Obviously, $0 \leq \rho^t \leq 1$. The symbol ρ^t reflects the gap between the group consensus level and the consensus threshold. The smaller the value of ρ^t, the higher the group consensus level.

Decision-makers often set a threshold $\overline{\rho} \in [0, 1]$ for ρ^t. If $\rho^t > \overline{\rho}$, it indicates that the group consensus level is not high enough, and multiple clusters' opinions may need to be adjusted. In this stage, ICRM is used to manage the consensus-reaching process. As the group consensus level increases, the number of clusters that need to adjust will continue to decrease. If $\rho^t \leq \overline{\rho}$, SCRM is used to modify the opinion that is the farthest distance from the group opinion. Obviously, when $\overline{\rho} = 0$, MCRM will reduce to ICRM; when $\overline{\rho} = 1$, MCRM will reduce to SCRM.

MCRM is the combination of ICRM and SCRM; thus, the threshold $\overline{\rho}$ will play a very important role. By adding $\overline{\rho}$ as the input parameter and replacing Step 2.2^I with Step 2.2^M, a novel model, the **mixed consensus-reaching model**, is established. **Step 2.2^M**: Consensus iteration process.

If $\rho^t > \overline{\rho}$, ICRM is used to manage the consensus iteration; otherwise, SCRM is utilized.

Fig. 7.5 shows the different consensus-reaching models mentioned above that involve the management of non-cooperative behaviors in LSGDM.

This study aimed to obtain a high-consensus decision result by dealing with non-cooperative behaviors. Using the proposed consensus-reaching models, the algorithm for solving an LSGDM problem is summarized as Algorithm 7.2.

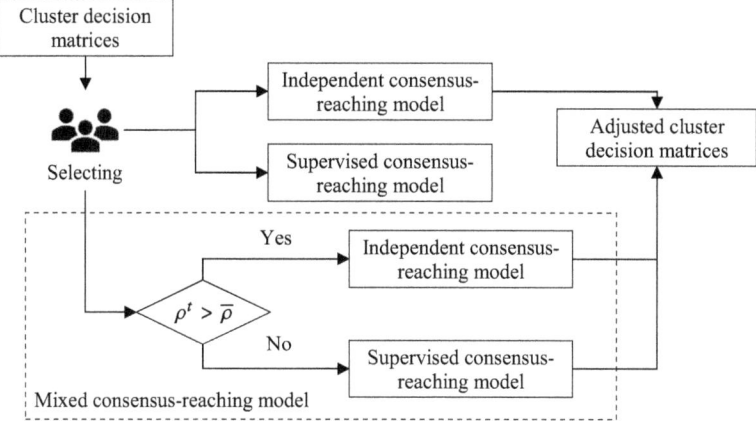

Fig. 7.5 Different consensus models used to manage the consensus-reaching process in LSGDM

Algorithm 7.2 Decision process for dealing with non-cooperative behaviors in an LSGDM problem using the proposed consensus models.

Input: Initial normalized individual decision matrices $R_l^0 (l = 1, 2, \ldots, q)$, the weight vector of the criteria ω, consensus threshold $\overline{GCL}$, and the parameter $\overline{\rho}$ (if necessary).
Output: The final number of iterations t^*, final group decision matrix $R_c^{t^*}$, and the ranking of alternatives.
1: Apply the clustering method [140] to classify the DMs with similar opinions into K clusters, denoted as $C_k (k = 1, 2, \ldots, K)$.
2: Use Eq. (7.1) to calculate the initial weight vector of the clusters, i.e., $\lambda^0 = (\lambda_1^0, \lambda_2^0, \ldots, \lambda_K^0)$.
3: Determine which consensus-reaching model is selected, and then apply it to manage the consensus iterations as well as the non-cooperative behaviors.
4: Use the WA operator to compute the overall evaluation value of each alternative, and select the best alternative(s).
5: Output the related decision information. Let $t^* = t$. By utilizing the WA operator, the final group decision matrix is obtained as $R_c^{t^*} = (r_{c,ij}^{t^*})_{m \times n}$. Output the final iterative time t^* and final group decision matrix $R_c^{t^*}$.
6: End.

7.4 Case Study

Here, a case study is presented to explain how the proposed consensus-reaching models work in practice. Fierce domestic competition, continuously improving global logistics, and increasingly advanced communication technologies have pushed the growth of enterprises' offshore outsourcing activities. A growing number of manufacturing enterprises are considering or have decided to set up production bases overseas. ABC is a leading manufacturer and designer of athletic casual footwear, apparel, and accessories, headquartered in Quanzhou, China. Considering rising domestic labor costs and the policy advantages of the Belt and Road Initiative, the company decides to establish a new production base in one of the countries or regions along the Belt and

Road. Preliminary selections for further evaluation include Ho Chi Minh City, Aktau, Minsk, Selangor, and West Java (denoted as $X = \{x_1, x_2, x_3, x_4, x_5\}$). The heads of the company's business divisions were selected to form a 20-member expert committee to conduct a comprehensive and effective evaluation of the five areas. Drawing from existing research [1, 4, 5, 52, 95, 96] and business practices, the following three comprehensive criteria are considered: commercial factors (a_1, benefit criterion), such as quality, price, quantity, and delivery time; sustainability dimensions (a_2, benefit criterion), including economic, environmental, and social bottom lines; and global risks (a_3, cost criterion), such as currency risks, disruption risks from political instability, terrorism, and cultural compatibility. The weight vector of the criteria is set as $\omega = (0.5, 0.3, 0.2)$. It is noted that in addition to the weights given subjectively by DMs, the weights of the criteria can also be obtained based on the decision information itself through certain calculation rules [161]. In the following, the DMs use MCRM to manage the consensus-reaching process. To get the best alternative(s), the following steps are involved (Algorithm 7.2).

Input: The initial normalized individual decision matrices $R_l^0 (l = 1, 2, \ldots, 20)$, the weight vector of criteria ω, the acceptable threshold of consensus level $\overline{GCL} = 0.75$, and the threshold of control coefficient $\overline{\rho} = 0.05$.

Stage 1: Clustering process.

Step 1: Apply the clustering method [140] to classify the DMs into six clusters (see Table 7.2).

Step 2: Use Eq. (7.1) to calculate the initial weight vector of clusters, i.e., $\lambda^0 = (0.2189, 0.2159, 0.1527, 0.1399, 0.1401, 0.1325)^T$.

Stage 2: Consensus-reaching process.

Step 3: Use MCRM to manage the consensus-reaching process.

Tables 7.3 and 7.4 show the consensus-reaching results. The detailed consensus-reaching process is listed in the supplementary materials

Step 4: Output the final number of iterations $t^* = 3$ and the final group decision matrix

$$R_c^{3^8} = R_c^3 = \begin{pmatrix} 0.5293 & 0.4329 & 0.6566 \\ 0.5182 & 0.3881 & 0.623 \\ 0.6036 & 0.3852 & 0.3767 \\ 0.4416 & 0.3443 & 0.4894 \\ 0.5436 & 0.5898 & 0.4655 \end{pmatrix}$$

Stage 3: Selection process.

Step 5: Select the best alternative(s).

Aggregate the overall evaluation value of every alternative:

$EV_1 = 0.5258$, $EV_2 = 0.5002$, $EV_3 = 0.4927$, $EV_4 = 0.422$, $EV_5 = 0.5418$. Then, rank the alternatives, such as $x_5 \succ x_1 \succ x_2 \succ x_3 \succ x_4$. Thus, West Java is determined to the best candidate for building a production base.

Step 6: End.

Table 7.2 Clustering results with threshold $\gamma = 0.73$

C_k	n_k	e_l	R_k^0
C_1	8	$e_1, e_{10}, e_{13}, e_{15}, e_{16}, e_{17}, e_{18}, e_{20}$	$\begin{pmatrix} 0.256 & 0.496 & 0.658 \\ 0.406 & 0.504 & 0.578 \\ 0.565 & 0.476 & 0.519 \\ 0.325 & 0.391 & 0.149 \\ 0.485 & 0.485 & 0.534 \end{pmatrix}$
C_2	7	$e_2, e_8, e_9, e_{11}, e_{12}, e_{14}, e_{19}$	$\begin{pmatrix} 0.642 & 0.487 & 0.657 \\ 0.659 & 0.404 & 0.714 \\ 0.417 & 0.614 & 0.334 \\ 0.456 & 0.459 & 0.55 \\ 0.531 & 0.593 & 0.526 \end{pmatrix}$
C_3	2	e_3, e_6	$\begin{pmatrix} 0.79 & 0.13 & 0.24 \\ 0.38 & 0.895 & 0.15 \\ 0.41 & 0.77 & 0.61 \\ 0.485 & 0.855 & 0.12 \\ 0.085 & 0.51 & 0.35 \end{pmatrix}$
C_4	1	e_4	$\begin{pmatrix} 0.79 & 0.42 & 0.32 \\ 0.42 & 0.66 & 0.3 \\ 0.95 & 0.43 & 0.18 \\ 0 & 0.71 & 0.65 \\ 0.99 & 0.86 & 0.75 \end{pmatrix}$
C_5	1	e_5	$\begin{pmatrix} 0.35 & 0.38 & 0.94 \\ 0.33 & 0.21 & 0.78 \\ 0.93 & 0.13 & 0.1 \\ 0.76 & 0.07 & 0.58 \\ 0.29 & 0.39 & 0.32 \end{pmatrix}$
C_6	1	e_7	$\begin{pmatrix} 0.91 & 0.35 & 0.55 \\ 0.98 & 0.02 & 0.67 \\ 0.12 & 0.02 & 0.87 \\ 0.52 & 0 & 0.87 \\ 0.83 & 0.95 & 0.17 \end{pmatrix}$

7.5 Comparative Analysis and Discussion

Section 7.5.1 presents a sensitivity analysis to illustrate the influence of some important parameters on the decision-making process. Section 7.5.2 provides a detailed comparative analysis of ICRM, SCRM, and MCRM. In Sect. 7.5.3, we compare the four punishment approaches to non-cooperative behaviors and expound on their characteristics and advantages/disadvantages. Section 6.4 presents a comparison of the proposed models with Xu et al.'s model [144]. Note that the data used in the comparative analysis come from the case study in Sect. 7.4.

Table 7.3 Consensus-reaching process using MCRM

Number of iterations	Consensus model	GCL before iteration	Number of clusters to be adjusted	Identified clusters	Adjustment coefficient	Objective adjustment coefficient	GCL after iteration
1	ICRM	0.6785	6	–	$\eta_1^0 = 0.1,$ $\eta_2^0 = 0.1,$ $\eta_3^0 = 0.2,$ $\eta_4^0 = 0.1,$ $\eta_5^0 = 0.02,$ $\eta_6^0 = 0.4$	–	0.7401
2	SCRM	0.7401	1	R_5^1	$\eta_5^1 = 0.13$	0.1332	0.749
3	SCRM	0.749	1	R_4^2	$\eta_4^2 = 0.1$	0.102	0.7545

Table 7.4 Changes in the weights of clusters in the consensus-reaching process

Number of iterations	Consensus model	Weights of clusters before iteration	Trajectory of weight changes	Weights of clusters after iteration
1	ICRM	(0.2189, 0.2159, 0.1527, 0.1399, 0.1401, 0.1325)	$\lambda_4^0 = 0.1399 \rightarrow$ $\lambda_4^{1,I} = 0.1381,$ $\lambda_5^0 = 0.1401 \rightarrow$ $\lambda_5^{1,I} = 0.14$	(0.2193, 0.2163, 0.153, 0.1383, 0.1403 ,0.1328)
2	SCRM	(0.2193, 0.2163, 0.153, 0.1383, 0.1403, 0.1328)	$\lambda_5^1 = 0.1403 \rightarrow$ $\lambda_5^{2,I} = 0.0561$	(0.2395, 0.2362, 0.1617, 0.151, 0.0613, 0.145)
3	SCRM	(0.2395, 0.2362, 0.1617, 0.151, 0.0613, 0.145)	$\lambda_4^2 = 0.151 \rightarrow$ $\lambda_4^{3,I} = 0.1208$	(0.2469, 0.2436, 0.1723, 0.1246, 0.0632, 0.1495)

Note we set $\beta^1 = 1/3$

7.5.1 Sensitivity Analysis

7.5.1.1 Comparative Results with Different Consensus Thresholds

The consensus threshold plays an important role in the process of consensus building. To provide guidance for determining a reasonable threshold, we need to investigate the influence of threshold change on the consensus-reaching process. To facilitate the simulation analysis, we simplify the proposed consensus-reaching models into an automatic iteration process by introducing the objective adjustment coefficient presented in [144]. The adjustment coefficient in each iteration can always be set as 0.7 times the objective adjustment coefficient to indicate certain noncooperation. Table 7.5 shows the results for the number of iterations obtained using different consensus-reaching models.

Table 7.5 Number of iterations obtained by using different consensus-reaching models

$\overline{GCL}$	ICRM	SCRM	MCRM				
			$\overline{\rho} = 0.25$	$\overline{\rho} = 0.2$	$\overline{\rho} = 0.15$	$\overline{\rho} = 0.1$	$\overline{\rho} = 0.05$
0.7	1	2	ICRM: 0	ICRM: 0	ICRM: 0	ICRM: 0	ICRM: 0
			SCRM: 2	SCRM: 2	SCRM: 2	SCRM: 2	SCRM: 2
0.75	2	6	ICRM: 0	ICRM: 0	ICRM: 0	ICRM: 0	ICRM: 1
			SCRM: 6	SCRM: 6	SCRM: 6	SCRM: 6	SCRM: 2
0.8	3	10	ICRM: 0	ICRM: 0	ICRM: 1	ICRM: 1	ICRM: 1
			SCRM: 10	SCRM: 10	SCRM: 5	SCRM: 5	SCRM: 5
0.85	3	15	ICRM: 0	ICRM: 1	ICRM: 1	ICRM: 1	ICRM: 2
			SCRM: 15	SCRM: 8	SCRM: 8	SCRM: 8	SCRM: 5

Note ICRM Independent consensus-reaching model, *SCRM* Supervised consensus-reaching model, *MCRM* Mixed consensus-reaching model

We can make the following observations:

(1) Regardless of which consensus-reaching model is adopted, the higher the consensus threshold, the more the required iterations. Suppose SCRM is used. If $\overline{GCL} = 0.7$, the number of iterations is 2; however, if $\overline{GCL} = 0.85$, the number rises to 15. Hence, if only SCRM is used in the whole consensus process, and the number of iterations is required to be no more than six, the consensus threshold can belong to the interval $[0.7, 0.75]$.

(2) When the control coefficient $\overline{\rho}$ is set to different values, the number of consensus iterations using different consensus models may be different. Suppose MCRM is used, and $\overline{GCL} = 0.85$. When we set $\overline{\rho} = 0.05$, the group consensus level can satisfy the threshold by using ICRM twice and SCRM five times. However, when $\overline{\rho} = 0.1$, we need to use ICRM once and SCRM eight times. This shows that the setting of the control coefficient is important for the number of iterations.

The determination of $\overline{GCL}$ and $\overline{\rho}$ depends on the maximum number of iterations allowed by the DMs and the selected consensus-reaching model. The following three steps are involved:

(1) The DMs conclude the maximum number of consensus iterations according to the specific decision scenario.
(2) It should be determined in advance which of the three consensus-reaching models will be used.
(3) The DMs' attitudes toward adjusting opinions to promote consensus need to be clarified.

Suppose the DMs are somewhat unwilling to substantially adjust their opinions, the maximum consensus iteration is no more than four, and MCRM is adopted (where ICRM and SCRM are used at least once). The adjustment coefficient in each consensus iteration can be set to 0.7 times the objective adjustment coefficient to indicate the adjustment intention. Based on the simulation results for the number of iterations in Table 7.5, we can set $\overline{GCL} = 0.75$ and $\overline{\rho} = 0.05$. After using ICRM once and SCRM twice in succession, the group consensus level is considered to be up to the threshold.

7.5.1.2   Discussion of the Determination of Critical Point $\overline{\delta}^{t+1}$

In the independent consensus-reaching model, critical point $\overline{\delta}^{t+1}$ plays a core role in the weight punishment because it is used to divide the reward area and punishment area. Table 7.6 lists three ways to calculate the critical point: average, median, and adjustable average.

Different approaches will produce different results for the division of the reward area and punishment area. There are two suggestions for the selection:

(1) Usually, we set $\overline{\delta}^{t+1} \in [min_k\{\delta_k^{t+1}\}, max_k\{\delta_k^{t+1}\}]$, as opposed to belonging to the interval $[0, 1]$. Clearly, we know that $[min_k\{\delta_k^{t+1}\}, max_k\{\delta_k^{t+1}\}] \subset [0, 1]$ This narrows the range of critical points for more accurate assignment.
(2) The critical point should be calculated dynamically. Not only should the change of group consensus level be noticed, but the distribution of the change rate of the individual consensus level should also be considered in each consensus iteration. If the level of group consensus is low, DMs can be urged to adopt a more cooperative attitude toward consensus by punishing multiple clusters' weights. When the consensus level is significantly improved (close to the threshold), the range of weight punishment should be narrowed.

7.5.2   Comparative Analysis of ICRM, SCRM, and MCRM

Comparing the mechanisms and results of different consensus models in the consensus-reaching process can be examined in terms of changes in the following indicators: group consensus level, the number of clusters to be adjusted in each iteration, the weights of clusters, and opinion adjustment amount. The first two indicators are involved in all of the consensus-reaching models, while the latter two are caused by weight punishment and opinion punishment, respectively. To ensure comparability and eliminate the effects of artificial adjustment, we use the objective adjustment coefficient (proposed in [144]) to guide the consensus-reaching process and set the adjustment coefficient in each iteration as 0.7 times the objective adjustment coefficient. Figures 7.6 and 7.7 show the consensus-reaching processes using different consensus models.

We can make the following observations:

(1) Compared to a consensus-reaching process without punishing non-cooperative behaviors, these three consensus-reaching models can use fewer iterations to reach the consensus threshold. In Fig. 7.6a, the consensus process terminates

Table 7.6 Classification of the critical point $\overrightarrow{\delta}^{t+1}$

Classification	Specific form	$\delta^{t=1}$	Division of two areas
Average	$\dfrac{\sum_{k=1}^{K} \delta_k^{t+1}}{K}$	0.0927	Punishment area: c_4, c_5 Reward area: none
Median	$\begin{cases} \delta_{k/2}^{\prime t+1} & k \text{ is an odd number} \\ (\delta_{k/2}^{\prime t+1} + \delta_{k/2+1}^{\prime t+1})/2 & k \text{ is an even number} \end{cases}$	0.0694	Punishment area: c_5 Reward area: none
Adjustable average	$min_k\{\beta_k^{t+1}\} + \beta^{t+1} \cdot (min_k\{\beta_k^{t+1}\} - max_k\{\beta_k^{t+1}\}), \beta^{t+1} \in [0, 1]$	$0.1005(\beta^1 = 1/3)$	Punishment area: c_4, c_5 Reward area: none

Note The data come from the case study in Sect. 7.4. $\delta_k^{\prime t+1}$ is the ordered change rage in ascending order

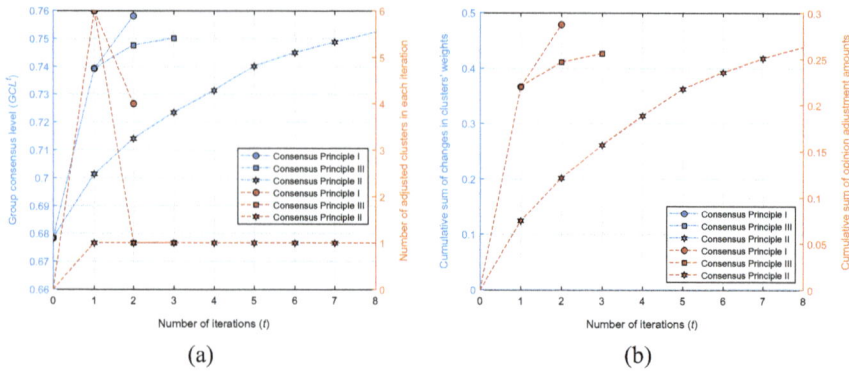

Fig. 7.6 Consensus process using different consensus principles when the first punishment approach is adopted (i.e., no punishment). *Note* We set $\overline{GCL} = 0.75$ and $\overline{\rho} = 0.05$

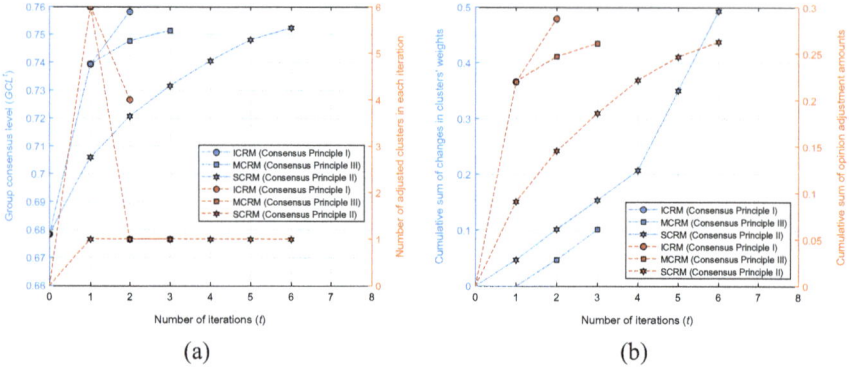

Fig. 7.7 Consensus process using different consensus models when the fourth punishment approach is adopted (i.e., full punishment). *Note* We set $\overline{GCL} = 0.75$ and $\overline{\rho} = 0.05$

after eight iterations when Consensus Principle II is adopted, while SCRM only takes six iterations (see Fig. 7.7a).

(2) No matter which model is adopted, the level of group consensus will improve as the number of iterations increases. This indicates that these three consensus-reaching models can effectively manage the consensus process and reduce differences. In Fig. 7.7a, when the number of iterations increases from zero to two and ICRM is used, the group consensus level increases from 0.6785 to 0.7582 and finally satisfies the threshold requirement. When SCRM is adopted, the group consensus level increases to 0.7524, as the number of iterations is up to six.

(3) The independent consensus-reaching model requires the lowest number of iterations but the largest number of adjusted cluster opinions in each iteration. In Fig. 7.7a, when using ICRM only twice, the group consensus level exceeds the threshold, but all six clusters' opinions are adjusted in the first iteration. If only SCRM is used, the group consensus level has to undergo six iterations to meet

the threshold, but only one cluster's opinion is adjusted in each iteration, and the cumulative sum of the number of adjusted opinions is only six

(4) The independent consensus-reaching model often produces the lowest cumulative sum of changes in clusters' weights. Figure 7.7b shows that when adopting ICRM, the cumulative sum of changes in clusters' weights is always equal to 0 while SCRM results in a cumulative weight change of 0.4932. This is because in ICRM, weight punishment can be initiated unless both conditions (individual consensus level and the change rate of the individual consensus level) are satisfied.

(5) As an integration of ICRM and SCRM, the ideal operation of MCRM is that ICRM is first used, and then SCRM is activated when a certain condition is reached. In Fig. 7.7a, after implementing MCRM three times (including using ICRM once and SCRM twice), the group consensus can be raised to the required level.

Based on Figs. 7.6 and 7.7, we can see that there are significant differences between these three models. The following conclusions can be drawn:

(1) ICRM allows one or more clusters' opinions to move toward the group opinion, which can accelerate the convergence of opinions better than SCRM.
(2) ICRM and SCRM use different references to identify non-cooperative behaviors. ICRM depends on the change rate of the individual consensus level while SCRM examines two aspects—the remaining clusters' adjustment suggestions and the objective adjustment suggestion (see [144]).
(3) There is also a great difference between ICRM and SCRM with regard to punishing non-cooperative behaviors. ICRM utilizes the change rate interval of individual consensus level to guide weight punishment while SCRM adopts the non-cooperative degree.
(4) As a fusion of ICRM and SCRM, MCRM has all of the advantages of both models. However, an important issue concerns how to calculate the control coefficient to determine which model (ICRM or SCRM) to adopt (as discussed in Sect. 7.5.1.

7.5.3 Comparative Analysis of Four Punishment Approaches to Non-cooperative Behaviors

Weight punishment and opinion punishment are two basic ways to punish non-cooperative behavior. Weight punishment aims to reduce the importance of DMs who hold non-cooperative behaviors while opinion punishment is designed to force non-cooperative DMs to move toward the group opinion. Through the combination of weight punishment and opinion punishment, four punishment approaches can be obtained. This section will compare and discuss the effects of these four approaches on non-cooperative behavior and the consensus-reaching process. To ensure comparability, suppose the objective adjustment coefficient [144] is used to implement the consensus-reaching process, and the adjustment coefficient is set to 0.7 times the objective adjustment coefficient. Setting such a non-cooperative degree aims to ensure the prominent existence of non-cooperative behavior to better observe the process and results of handling non-cooperative behaviors with different approaches.

Figures 7.8 and 7.9 present the consensus-reaching processes when using different punishment approaches to address non-cooperative behaviors. We use the number of consensus iterations to represent the time required to reach consensus.

(1) Consistent with intuition, the time required to satisfy the consensus threshold with full punishment is the shortest while no punishment takes the longest. Figure 7.9a shows that the full punishment approach needs six iterations to increase the consensus level from 0 to above the consensus threshold while the no punishment approach needs eight iterations. This indicates that punishing non-cooperative behaviors is conducive to rapidly forming a consensus level that reaches the threshold.

(2) The opinion punishment approach requires a smaller number of iterations than the weight punishment approach. In Fig. 7.9a, when the opinion punishment approach is adopted, it takes six iterations to raise the consensus level to above the threshold while the weight punishment approach needs as many as eight iterations. This is because weight punishment only reduces the importance of non-cooperative members in the group opinion whereas opinion adjustment is entirely based on the individual adjustment coefficient (which is sometimes very small). We can conclude that opinion punishment can effectively increase the originally low adjustment range to quickly and significantly achieve consensus growth.

(3) When fewer iterations are used to improve the consensus level, it does not mean a larger amount of opinion adjustment is required. As shown in Fig. 7.9b, although the number of iterations using full punishment is smaller than when using no punishment, the corresponding two amounts of opinion adjustment are almost equal. Using the full punishment approach, the cumulative sum of the adjustment amount finally reaches 0.2627. When using no punishment, the adjustment amount is 0.2634.

(4) Fig. 7.9b shows that when adopting weight punishment or full punishment, the weights of the clusters will change as the consensus iteration increases.

(5) We find that when adopting Consensus Principle I, the consensus-reaching processes using different punishment approaches are the same. This is because the independent consensus model only punishes individual opinions and weights within the punishment area.

In Table 7.7, we summarize the advantages and disadvantages of different punishment approaches to non-cooperative behaviors.

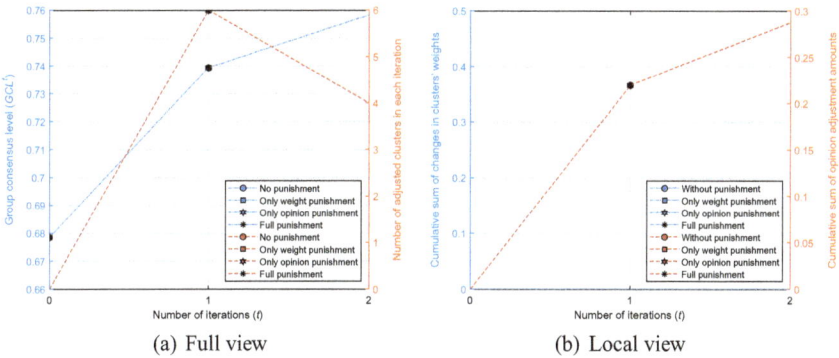

(a) Full view   (b) Local view

Fig. 7.8 Consensus-reaching processes using different punishment approaches when Consensus Principle I is adopted. *Note* We set $\overline{GCL} = 0.75$

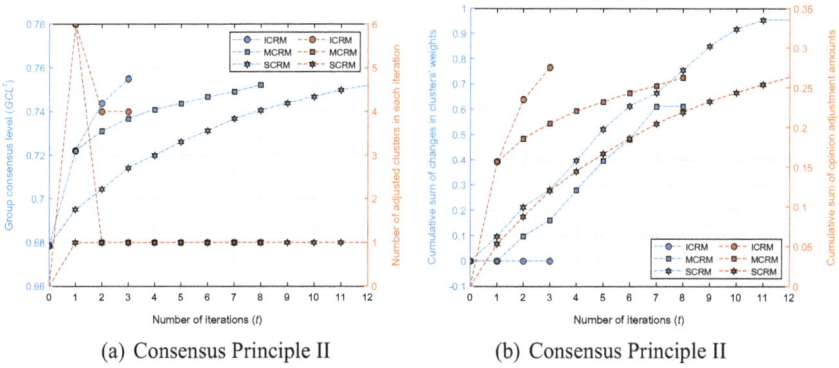

(a) Consensus Principle II   (b) Consensus Principle II

Fig. 7.9 Consensus-reaching processes using different punishment approaches when Consensus Principle II is adopted

7.5.4 Comparison with Xu et al.' Model [144]

Xu et al. [144] developed a consensus-reaching model for large-scale emergency group decision-making problems that focused on managing minority opinions and non-cooperative behaviors. Our study developed a mixed consensus-reaching model that integrated an independent consensus model and a supervised consensus model via a control coefficient to deal with non-cooperative behaviors. Table 7.8 details the comparison of Xu et al.'s model [144] and our proposed models. In fact, the supervised consensus model is Xu et al.'s model—that is, Xu et al.'s model for non-cooperative behavior is part of the mixed consensus model.

Suppose the objective adjustment coefficient is used to manage the consensus-reaching process. By removing the redundant abscissa scale in Fig. 7.7, a clearer comparison of consensus results using Xu et al.'s model [144] and the proposed models can be shown (see Fig. 7.10). The main differences between Xu et al.'s

Table 7.7 Comparison of the advantages and disadvantages of different punishment approaches to non-cooperative behaviors

Punishment approach	Detailed description
No punishment	**Advantage**: No cluster is diminished in importance No mandatory opinion adjustment **Disadvantage**: Longest time to gain consensus
Only weight punishment	**Advantage**: Reduces the weight of non-cooperative opinion Independent opinion adjustment **Disadvantage**: Cannot contribute much to consensus building
Only opinion punishment	**Advantage**: Mandatory opinion adjustment significantly increases the consensus level **Disadvantage**: Forces a larger opinion adjustment than subjective willingness Risk of opinion distortion
Full punishment	**Advantage**: Has the advantages of both opinion punishment and weight punishment **Disadvantage**: Has the disadvantages of both opinion punishment and weight punishment

Note We set $\overline{GCL} = 0.75$

Table 7.8 Comparison of Xu et al.'s model [144] and our proposed models

Consensus model	Minority opinion	Adjustment suggestion	Adjustment rule in each iteration	Basis for weighting punishment function
ICRM	No	–	Can be more than one cluster	Change rate of the individual consensus level
SCRM	No	· Other clusters' suggestions · Objective adjustment suggestion	Only one cluster	Non-cooperative degree
Xu et al.'s model [144]	Yes	· Other clusters' suggestions · Objective adjustment suggestion	Only one cluster	Non-cooperative degree

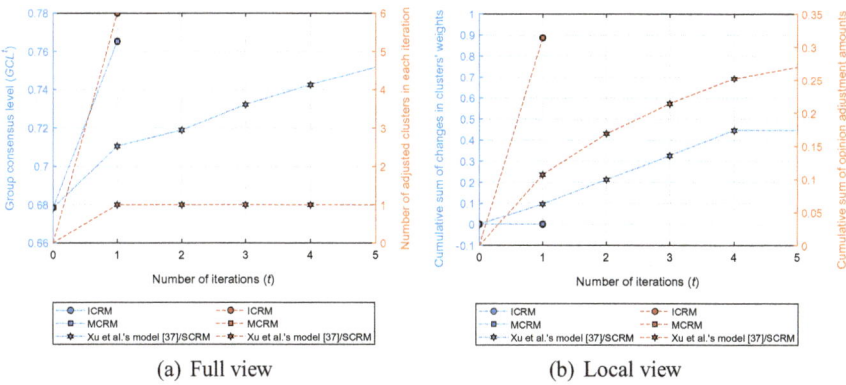

(a) Full view   (b) Local view

Fig. 7.10 Consensus-reaching process using different models. *Note* We set $\overline{GCL} = 0.75$ and $\overline{\rho} = 0.05$

model [144] and our proposed models for dealing with non-cooperative behaviors, as well as the advantages of our models, are as follows:

(1) Usually, the mixed consensus-reaching model requires fewer iterations than Xu et al.'s model for the consensus level to exceed the threshold. In Fig. 7.10a, under the condition that the consensus threshold is set to $\overline{GCL} = 0.75$, the mixed consensus model requires three iterations (i.e., using ICRM once and SCRM twice) to get the consensus level above the threshold, while Xu et al.'s model requires six iterations.

(2) Our proposed mixed consensus-reaching model is more flexible than Xu et al.'s model for dealing with non-cooperative behaviors and can be applied to more decision-making scenarios. The former model can handle a situation where six clusters adjust their opinions as well as a situation where only one cluster adjusts its opinion (see Fig. 7.10a). However, the latter model is used to manage the decision situation where only one cluster adjusts its opinion in each iteration

(3) The mixed consensus model combines all the advantages of the independent consensus model and Xu et al.'s model (namely, the supervised consensus model) but is also the most complex. Its complexity is mainly reflected in the need to calculate the threshold of the control coefficient to determine whether ICRM or SCRM should be used.

Furthermore, this study summarized four approaches to non-cooperative behavior (i.e., no punishment, weight punishment, opinion punishment, and full punishment). However, Xu et al.'s model [144] only adopted full punishment. In fact, through the permutation and combination of the three consensus principles and these four approaches, 12 consensus reaching models can be obtained.

7.6 Conclusions

Based on the analysis of the characteristics of LSGDM environments and non-cooperative behaviors, novel consensus reaching models were proposed. The major contributions of this chapter are as follow.

(1) Four punishment approaches to addressing non-cooperative behaviors were summarized. The characteristics of these approaches and their effects on consensus building were presented.

(2) We reviewed three consensus principles for group decision-making problems and developed an independent consensus reaching model considering the management of non-cooperative behaviors in LSGDM. This model was applied to a situation where multiple clusters (not just one cluster) could move their opinions toward the group opinion in each consensus iteration.

(3) A mixed consensus-reaching model was built by combining a supervised consensus-reaching model, which required only one cluster per iteration to be involved in the decision about opinion adjustment, with an independent consensus reaching model.

(4) We analyzed certain attributes related to weight assignment and developed a novel weighting method to calculate the weights of clusters.

Meanwhile, this chapter's limitations are as follows.

(1) In many decision scenarios, social-network relationships exist among DMs [17, 122, 124]. It is important, therefore, to build an improved consensus-reaching model to deal with non-cooperative behaviors in a social network environment.

(2) Some studies have noted that in an LSGDM environment, DMs often have individual concerns about alternatives and use heterogeneous representation structures to express their opinions [23, 167, 175]. Thus, there is a need to extend the proposed consensus-reaching models to heterogeneous LSGDM.

In addition to being applied to decisions about production base selection, the proposed consensus-reaching models can also provide new solutions for other practical applications by constructing a group decision-making scenario and focusing on consensus building, such as vehicular platoon coordination [40, 41], supplier selection [5, 95], and supply chain risk modeling [4]. Further, the proposed consensus-reaching models can be combined with other decision-making techniques, such as Markov chain [42, 121], analytic hierarchy process [5], and multi-attribute auction [95], to provide better solutions.

Chapter 8
Consensus Building: Coordination Between Trust Relationships and Opinion Similarity

Abstract Individual opinions in group decision-making under the large-group social network environment tend to be controversial and conflicting. Implementing a consensus-reaching process (CRP) is deemed necessary, but some decision-makers are non-cooperative with regard to adjusting their opinions to promote consensus due to the differences in self-interest and perception. This may delay consensus convergence and consequently affect decision quality. This chapter proposes a two-dimensional consensus model considering non-cooperative behaviors. The model explores the effects of trust loss on the management of non-cooperative behaviors and the CRP.

Keywords Group decision-making (GDM) · Large-group social network environment (LGSNE) · Two-dimensional consensus-reaching model · Non-cooperative behaviors · Trust loss

8.1 Introduction

The group decision-making (GDM) in large-group social network environment (LGSNE) is a particular and common decision-making scenario that combines social networks with large-scale group decision-making (LSGDM). It characteristics have been presented in Chap. 4. The consensus-reaching process (CRP), usually an iterative process of group discussion and consensus improvement, is considered a key step in GDM problems involving large-scale decision-makers (DMs) [154, 166, 173]. In Chapters 3 and 4, we presented a conclusion that trust relationships among DMs is an important measurement attribute of clustering operation. This chapter will explore the mechanism of trust relationship on the CRP.

Most trust-based consensus models use trust relationships to perform two functions for the decision-making process: the calculation of the weights of DMs [122, 125] and the generation of adjustment recommendations [64, 124]. Few studies have investigated the role of trust relationships in coping with non-cooperative behaviors. There is a situation that a DM with high trust holds the opinion that deviates the most from that of the group. Then, the DM will be asked to implement the opinion adjustment to promote consensus. However, the DM might hold a non-cooperative attitude toward opinion adjustment. In that case, the DM will be punished through, including opinion punishment or weight punishment [28, 33]. Since the DM has a high trust score, it is meaningful to explore whether he/she can reduce the amount of opinion punishment by lowering the trust score. This is because a high trust score indicates that other DMs have sufficient trust in the DM's opinion.Therefore, we raise the following issue that need to be further addressed:

- Research on the different roles played by trust relationship and opinion similarity in the CRP is still in its infancy. Consensus level based on opinion similarity is used to measure the current difference between individual opinions, while the trust score derived from the trust relationship can guide opinion adjustment. We hold that a DM with a high trust score but a low consensus level can reduce the opinion adjustment by losing some trust. In this way, the DM's original opinion can be largely preserved.

To this end, this chapter develops a two-dimensional consensus model for GDM problems in LGSNE. The model mainly discusses the effects of trust relationship and opinion similarity on consensus building and especially on the management of non-cooperative behaviors.

8.2   Consensus Measure

A CRP is usually carried out through consensus measure and consensus iteration. The former is used to determine whether the CRP ends by measuring the current consensus level. As the core of consensus convergence, the latter seeks to improve the group consensus level.

Suppose after adopting the hierarchical clustering method proposed in Chap. 4, the clusters' opinions and group opinion have been obtained as $R_k = (r_{k,ij})_{m \times n}$ ($k = 1, 2, \ldots, K$) and $R_c = (r_{c,ij})_{m \times n}$, respectively. We use the inter-cluster consensus level previously defined as the consensus level at the cluster level. The group consensus level is calculated by aggregating the inter-cluster consensus levels.

Definition 8.1 Given the inter-cluster consensus levels in the tth iteration $CCL_{k,Inter}$, $k = 1, 2, \ldots, K$, the group consensus level is defined as

$$GCL^t = \frac{1}{K} \sum_{k=1}^{K} CCL_{k,Inter}^t. \tag{8.1}$$

Clearly, $0 \leq GCL^t \leq 1$. The greater the value of GCL^t, the higher the consensus among clusters.

In general, the consensus threshold (denoted by $\overline{GCL}(0 \leq \overline{GCL} \leq 1)$ should be defined in advance to determine whether the CRP can be terminated. If $GCL^t \geq \overline{GCL}$, then the selection process is followed; otherwise, the CRP is implemented.

8.3 Consensus-Reaching Process Considering Trust Loss

For a GDM problem in LGSNE, it is common to encounter clusters/DMs with a non-cooperative attitude toward opinion adjustment. The definition of non-cooperative behaviors and the common corresponding treatment methods have been described in Chap. 2. Non-cooperative behaviors are mainly manifested as some clusters/DMs refuse to adjust their opinions, or the adjustment amount is too small to meet certain requirements. In this chapter, we use clusters as the basic decision-making unit. The treatment of non-cooperative behaviors begins with identification.

8.3.1 Identification of Non-cooperative Behaviors

CRP is an iterative process in which clusters' opinions move toward the group opinion. Suppose clusters' opinion have been obtained by the trust-similarity measure-based hierarchical clustering method, denoted as $R_k = (r_{ij})_{m \times n} (k = 1, 2, \ldots, K)$. The group opinion $R_c = (r_c)_{m \times n}$ is calculated by aggregating the clusters' opinions.

Definition 8.2 Given cluster opinion R_k^t and group opinion R_c^t in the tth iteration, the following equation is used for opinion adjustment

$$R_k^{t+1} = AC_k^t R_c^t + (1 - AC_k^t)R_k^t, \tag{8.2}$$

where $AC_k^t (0 \leq AC_k^t \leq 1)$ is the adjustment coefficient provided by cluster C_k and R_k^{t+1} is the adjusted opinion of cluster C_k.

We define the punishment coefficient as a baseline to identify the non-cooperative behavior. The punishment coefficient is also an adjustment coefficient in nature, but it is based on the mathematical relationship between the inter-cluster consensus level and the consensus threshold, rather than given by the identified cluster.

Definition 8.3 Given inter-cluster consensus level $CCL_{k,Inter}^t$ and consensus threshold $\overline{GCL}$, the punishment coefficient is defined as

$$PC_k^t = \frac{\overline{GCL} - CCL_{k,Inter}^t}{1 - CCL_{k,Inter}^t}. \tag{8.3}$$

Clearly, $0 \leq PC_k^t \leq 1$. If the given adjustment coefficient is less than the corresponding punishment coefficient (i.e., $AC_k^t < PC_k^t$), cluster C_k is considered to hold a non-cooperative behavior toward opinion adjustment.

8.3.2 Management of Non-cooperative Behaviors

As mentioned in Chap. 2, there are usually two ways to deal with non-cooperative behaviors, including opinion punishment and weight punishment [28, 110, 144, 155]. Opinion punishment forces the non-cooperative cluster to adjust its own opinion with a larger adjustment coefficient. Weight punishment is used to reduce the weight of the non-cooperative cluster to lower its importance in the group.

To deal with non-cooperative behaviors in the social network environment, we set two thresholds, namely consensus threshold and trust threshold. Consensus threshold $\overline{GCL}$ is used to determine whether the current consensus level meets the threshold requirements so as to enter the selection process. We consider that if a cluster is highly trusted, its opinion is shared by the majority. Therefore, the trust threshold $\overline{CTS}\,(0 \leq \overline{CTS} \leq 1)$ is defined, which specifies the minimum trust score for modifying the punishment coefficient to reduce the adjustment amount. Suppose cluster C_k is regarded as a non-cooperative cluster in the tth iteration. From the viewpoint of trust score, there are two cases of non-cooperative behaviors:

Case A. $CTS^t_{k,Inter} < \overline{CTS}$.
Case B. $CTS^t_{k,Inter} \geq \overline{CTS}$.

$CTS^t_{k,Inter}$ represents the inter-cluster trust score of cluster C_k in the tth iteration, which has been defined in Definition 4.7. Case A indicates that cluster C_k did not get enough trust scores from other clusters. The following punishment operations are used to deal with this type of non-cooperative behaviors, including

- *Opinion punishment*: Let $AC^t_k = PC^t_k$, and then use Eq. (8.2) to adjust the opinion R^t_k.
- *Weight punishment*: Reduce the weight η^t_k in the following way.

Definition 8.4 If the trust score of cluster C_k in the tth iteration belongs to Case A, the punished weight is calculated by

$$\eta^{t+1}_k = \eta^t_k - \eta^t_k \cdot \left(\frac{PC^t_k - AC^t_k}{PC^t_k} \right)^{\beta^t_k}, \tag{8.4}$$

where β^t_k indicates the number of times C_k is identified as a non-cooperative cluster since entering the CRP. The greater the value of β^t_k, the less the punished weight. We define $(PC^t_k - AC^t_k)/(PC^t_k)$ as the non-cooperative degree of cluster C_k in the tth iteration, denoted as NCD^t_k for simplicity. Clearly, $0 \leq NCD^t_k \leq 1$.

To better understand the weight punishment, we analyze the properties of Eq. (8.4). First, change Eq. (8.4) to $\eta^{t+1}_k = \eta^t_k(1 - (NCD^t_k)^{\beta^t_k})$. Pick out function $1 - (NCD^t_k)^{\beta^t_k}$ and abstract it as function $g(v, z) = 1 - v^z$, where $v(0 \leq v \leq 1)$ corresponds to NCD^t_k, and z is a positive integer number corresponding to β^t_k. The following properties can be obtained: (1) When z is fixed, the greater the value of v, the lower the value of $g(v, z)$. (2) When v is fixed, the greater the value of z, the greater the value of $g(v, z)$. The first property conforms to the actual decision logic, that is, the greater the non-cooperative degree, the more weight punishment should be. The second property indicates that if a cluster is first judged to be non-cooperative, its weight will be heavily penalized.

In Case B, although the given adjustment coefficient is lower than the punishment coefficient obtained by Eq. (5.3), the inter-cluster trust score of cluster C_k is larger than the trust threshold. Therefore, its adjustment coefficient need not be equal to the original punishment coefficient, which can be implemented by trust score.

Definition 8.5 Given the punishment coefficient PC_k^t, the original punishment coefficient can be modified as

$$UPC_k^t = CTS_{k,Inter}^t \cdot PC_k^t, \tag{8.5}$$

where UPC_k^t is the updated punishment coefficient of cluster C_k guided by the inter-cluster trust score.

While cluster C_k can lower the punishment coefficient with a high trust score, there is a cost to doing so. The cost is that the cluster has to lose some trust. The definition of trust loss is given below.

Definition 8.6 Given the inter-cluster trust score $CTS_{k,Inter}^t$ and the non-cooperative degree NCD_k^t in the tth iteration, the trust loss of cluster C_k is defined as

$$TL_k^{t+1} = CTS_{k,Inter}^t \cdot (NCD_k^t)^{\gamma_k^t}, \tag{8.6}$$

where γ_k^t indicates the number of times cluster C_k was determined to implement the trust loss by the tth iteration. Clearly, $0 \leq TL_k^{t+1} \leq 1$. We can see that the formula for trust loss is similar to Eq. (8.4), whose properties have been presented. This setup serves two purposes: (i) If a cluster is first judged to be non-cooperative (i.e., $\gamma_k^t = 1$), its trust loss is large. However, the magnitude of trust loss may be reduced if the cluster is again identified as holding a non-cooperative behavior. (ii) The greater the non-cooperative degree, the greater trust loss needed.

For the non-cooperative behavior belongs to Case B, the punishment operations are implemented as follows:

- Conditional opinion punishment: Let $AC_k^t = UPC_k^t$, and use Eq. (8.2) to adjust the opinion R_k^t.
- Weight punishment: Reduce the weight η_k^t in the following way.

Definition 8.7 Suppose cluster C_k belongs to Case B in the tth iteration, the weight punishment is defined as:

$$\eta_k^{t+1} = \begin{cases} \eta_k^t \cdot (NCD_k^t)^{\beta_k^t - \gamma_k^t} & \beta_k^t = \gamma_k^t \\ \eta_k^t - \eta_k^t \cdot (NCD_k^t)^{\beta_k^t - \gamma_k^t} & \beta_k^t > \gamma_k^t \end{cases} \tag{8.7}$$

Clearly, $\beta_k^t \geq \gamma_k^t$ and $\eta_k^{t+1} \leq \eta_k^t$. If $\beta_k^t = \gamma_k^t$, , it indicates that cluster C_k replaces partial weight punishment with trust loss.

Based on the above analysis, Algorithm 8.1 describes the mechanism for dealing with non-cooperative behaviors for GDM problems in LGSNE.

Algorithm 8.1 Mechanism for dealing with non-cooperative behaviors for GDM problems in LGSNE

Input: Initial clusters' opinions $R_k^0 (k = 1, 2, \ldots, K)$, initial weight vector of clusters η^0, inter-cluster trust score $CTS_{k,Inter}^0$, inter-cluster consensus level $CCL_{k,Inter}^0$, consensus threshold $\overline{GCL}$, and trust threshold $\overline{CTS}$.

Output: Final number of consensus iterations t^*, final clusters' opinions, and final group opinion.

1: Set $t = 0$.

2: Use Eq. (8.1) to calculate group consensus level, denoted as GCL^t.

3: Use Definition 8.3 to identify non-cooperative behaviors.

4: Determine the case that the identified non-cooperative behavior belongs to.

5: If the identified non-cooperative behavior belongs to Case A, then use Eqs. (8.4) and (8.2) to implement weight punishment and opinion punishment, respectively. If the non-cooperative behavior belongs to Case B, then use Eq. (8.7) for weight punishment, and use Eqs. (8.7) and (8.7) for opinion punishment. Then, let $t = t + 1$, and return to Step 2.

6: Output the relevant decision information.

8.3.3   Decision-Making Algorithm Based on Two-Dimensional Consensus Model

The proposed consensus model in this chapter aims to obtain a high-consensus decision result for GDM problems in LGSNE. The decision-making algorithm by combining the trust-similarity measure-based hierarchical clustering method is summarized as Algorithm 8.2.

8.4   Numerical Experiment

The numerical experiment in Sect. 4.6 continues here. The following decision-making steps are implemented.

Input: Initial normalized individual opinions $R_l^0 (l = 1, 2, \ldots, 20)$, sociomatrix TM, the weight vector of the attributes ω, and consensus threshold $\overline{GCL} = 0.85$.

Stage 1: Decision information preprocessing.

Step 1.1: Use Eq. (4.1) to calculate the similarity matrix SM and use Eq. (4.3) to obtain the adjusted sociomatrix ATM.

Step 1.2: Compute the undirected trust-similarity matrix $UTSM$ via Eq. (4.4).

Algorithm 8.2 Two-dimensional consensus-reaching model for GDM problems in LGSNE

Input: Initial normalized individual opinions $R_i^0 (l = 1, 2, \ldots, q)$, sociomatrix TM, the weight vector of the attributes ω, consensus threshold $\overline{GCL}$, and trust threshold $\overline{CTS}$.

Output: Final number of iterations, final group opinion, and alternative ranking.

1: Use Eq. (4.1) to calculate the similarity matrix AM, and use Eq. (4.3) to obtain the adjusted sociomatrix ATM.

2: Compute the undirected trust-similarity matrix $UTSM$ via Eq. (4.4).

3: Set the case of the clustering constraint.

4: Use the selected clustering algorithm to classify the large group into K clusters.

5: Calculate the initial weight vector of the clusters via Eq. (4.11), denoted as η^0.

6: Obtain the initial clusters' opinions $R_k^0 (k = 1, 2, \ldots, K)$ and group opinion R_c^0.

7: Use Algorithm 8.1 to deal with non-cooperative behaviors and manage the consensus iterations.

8: Output the final number of iterations t^* and final group opinion R_c^*.

9: Use the weighted averaging operator [136] to calculate the overall evaluation score of each alternative and obtain the final ranking.

Stage 2: Clustering process.

Set the clustering constraints $\overline{TS} = 0.2$, $\overline{SD} = 0.7$, and $\overline{TSS} = 0.45$. Table 4.4 presents the clustering results based on Algorithm 4.1.

Stage 3: Consensus-reaching process.

Step 3.1: Let $t = 0$. Set the trust threshold as $\overline{CTS} = min\{CTS_{k,Intra}^0 + 0.25 \times (max\{CTS_{k,Inter}^0\} - min\{CTS_{k,Inter}^0\})\} = 0.4689$.

Step 3.2: Calculate the group consensus level as $GCL^0 = 0.8066$. As $GCL^0 = \overline{GCL}$, proceed to CRP. Table 8.1 presents the consensus iterations.

Step 3.3: Output the final number of iterations $t^* = 5$ and final group opinion

$$R_c^* = \begin{pmatrix} 0.3585 & 0.4367 & 0.4922 \\ 0.4439 & 0.4128 & 0.6559 \\ 0.5341 & 0.5898 & 0.5199 \\ 0.5462 & 0.5076 & 0.4035 \\ 0.6216 & 0.3738 & 0.4697 \end{pmatrix}.$$

Table 8.1 Results of the consensus-reaching process

t	GCL before CRP	Identified opinion	Weight before CRP	Given adjustment coefficient	Punishment coefficient	Updated adjustment coefficient	Trust loss	Weight after CRP	GCL after CRP
1	0.8066	R_3^0	0.0953	0.2	0.3318	0.3318	–	0.0378	0.8193
2	0.8193	R_2^1	0.1631	0.2	0.2271	0.1251	0.0719	0.1631	0.8237
3	0.8327	R_3^2	0.0597	0.5	0.1822	–	–	0.0597	0.8395
4	0.8395	R_1^3	0.1975	0.1	0.1426	0.0755	0.2255	0.1975	0.8498
5	0.8438	R_1^4	0.1975	0.2	0.1009	–	–	0.1925	0.8501

Note Identified opinion refers to the cluster's opinion with the lowest consensus level in a consensus iteration

Stage 4: Selection process.

Use the weighted averaging operator to calculate the overall evaluation score of each alternative: $ES(x_1) = 0.4193$, $ES(x_2) = 0.486$, $ES(x_3) = 0.55$, $ES(x_4) = 0.4971$, $ES(x_5) = 0.4969$. Rank all alternatives $x_i (i = 1, 2, \ldots, 5)$ according to the overall evaluation scores: $x_3 \succ x_4 \succ x_5 \succ x_2 \succ x_1$. Therefore, x_3 is the optimal alternative.

8.5 Further Discussion of Two-Dimensional Consensus Model

Different from traditional consensus models, the proposed CRP considers the role of trust score in consensus by defining two thresholds (i.e., consensus threshold and trust threshold). The consensus threshold is used to measure whether the current consensus is sufficiently high, while the trust threshold moderates the punishment through the trust score.

We set the non-cooperative degree of the identified cluster in each iteration to be constant 0.1 for each iteration (i.e., $NCD_k^t = 0.1$). Table 8.2 shows the comparison results of the first round of CRP with/without the trust threshold. A significant difference is seen in the updated adjustment coefficient. If the trust threshold is used, then $AC_2^1 = UPC_2^1 = 0.1169$; if not, the updated adjustment coefficient does not change. This leads to the differences in weight punishment and group consensus level.

Further, we simulate CRPs with/without the trust threshold with setting $NCD_k^t = 0.1$. As shown in Fig. 8.1, using the trust threshold leads to more consensus iterations. This is because the opinion punishment is reduced by losing the trust score.

Fig. 8.2 shows the trade-off between weight punishment and trust loss caused by the trust threshold. As long as the inter-cluster trust score of the identified cluster is greater than the trust threshold, the weight punishment can be reduced. As a result, however, its inter-cluster trust score will be lowered. As shown in Fig. 8.2a, in the fifth iteration, if using the trust threshold, the change rate of the weight of cluster C_4 is -0.01, while the change rate drops to -0.08 without considering the trust threshold. Figure 8.2b shows that the inter-cluster trust score of cluster C_4 drops from 0.52 to 0.465.

Table 8.2 Comparison of CRPs with/without the trust threshold

t	Using trust threshold	GCL before CRP	Identified opinion	Weight before CRP	Given adjustment coefficient	Punishment coefficient	Updated adjustment coefficient	Trust loss	Weight after CRP	GCL after CRP
1	Yes	0.8223	R_2^1	0.1584	0.1983	0.2203	0.1169	0.059	0.1584	0.8266
1	No	0.8223	R_2^1	0.1584	0.1983	0.2203	0.2203	–	0.079	0.8296

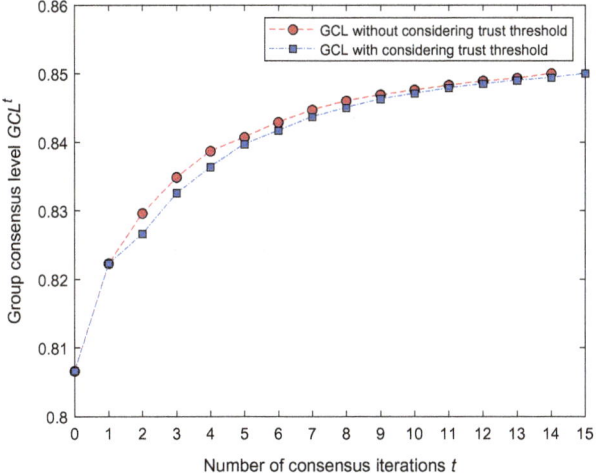

Fig. 8.1 Comparison of group consensus level with/without the trust threshold

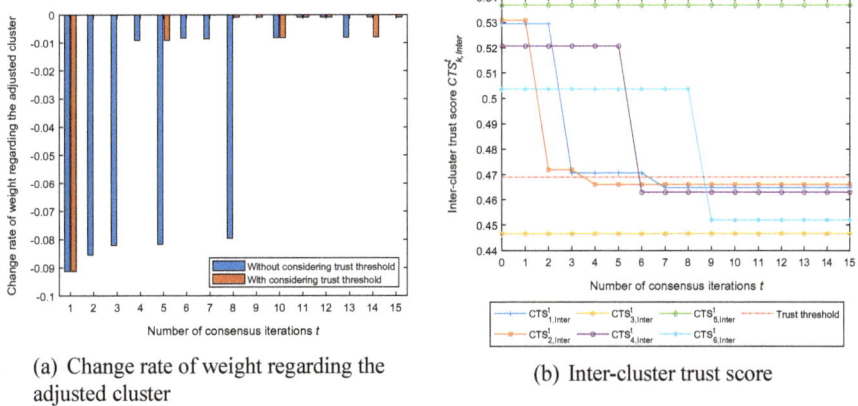

(a) Change rate of weight regarding the
adjusted cluster

(b) Inter-cluster trust score

Fig. 8.2 Comparison of weights and intra-cluster trust scores with/without the trust threshold

Opinion punishment and trust loss can be regarded as pursuing different directions, which act together in the CRP. Trust loss makes sense in terms of reducing opinion distortion. It is important to emphasize that trust loss can reduce opinion punishment, but the lost trust score will not be recovered in the later decision-making process.

8.6   Conclusions

This chapter developed a two-dimensional consensus model for GDM problems in LGSNE. The model defined two thresholds, namely consensus threshold and trust threshold. A mechanism for managing non-cooperative behaviors was designed. The mechanism used punishment coefficients to identify non-cooperative clusters and took into account the moderating effect of trust score on punishment operation.

Future research will focus on the following two points:

(1) The trust loss leads to the weight punishment, but reduces opinion punishment. So for the identified cluster, how to balance the weight punishment and opinion punishment?
(2) Dong et al. [21] and Ding et al. [19] pointed out that leadership plays an important role in opinion dynamics and guiding consensus. Therefore, it is meaningful to improve the two-dimensional consensus model based on leaderships.

Chapter 9
Conclusions and Future Research Directions

Abstract This chapter summarizes the main conclusions, shortcomings and challenges in the latest research progress of LSGDM presented by the authors. Finally, the future research direction of this topic is put forward.

Keywords Large-scale group decision-making (LSGDM) · Consensus cost · Limitations · Application scope

9.1 Conclusions

LSGDM techniques are widely used to model real-world decisions, ranging from small group decisions of a dozen people to decisions made in hundreds of social networks. This book focuses on the study of two key processes in LSGDM problems, namely clustering process and consensus-reaching process. Clustering is an effective tool to reduce the dimensions of large-scale DMs and to address the scalability challenges of LSGDM. We provide two novel clustering methods, all of which emphasize the influence of trust relationship on clustering.

(1) *A trust-similarity analysis-based clustering method,* which holds that opinion similarity and trust relationship are both important for clustering in LSGDM under a social network environment.
(2) *A trust-similarity measure-based hierarchical clustering method*, aimed at using the undirected trust score as the trust constraint to guide clustering.

In addition, by introducing different factors related to the DMs and decision-making process, multiple weight-determining methods for clusters and DMs are proposed.

This book proposes the corresponding consensus-reaching models for two different types of LSGDM situations, namely, in the social network context and considering non-cooperative behaviors. In view of the consensus issues for LSGDM in the context of social networks, this book proposes a two-dimensional consensus-reaching model. The model uses punishment coefficients to identify non-cooperative clusters and fully considered the moderating effect of trust score on punishment operation.

To deal with non-cooperative behaviors, this book proposes four consensus-reaching models, elaborated as follows.

(1) A *hierarchical punishment-driven consensus model* for LSGDM problems in the context of probabilistic linguistic information is developed. The model presents three levels of consensus measures and two adjustment strategies to refine the scope of measure and adjustment to the matrix element level.

(2) A *confidence consensus-based model* for LSGDM that provides a novel approach to addressing non-cooperative behaviors. By combining the rationality and non-cooperation of the adjustment information, the concept of a confidence level is constructed. This confidence level measures the impartiality and objectivity of the adjustment information and is the basis for managing non-cooperative behaviors.

(3) A *mixed consensus-reaching model* for managing non-cooperative behaviors is proposed, which is the integration of independent and supervised consensus-reaching models. The model aims at the situation where some, or even all, DMs adjust their opinions in one consensus iteration.

(4) A *two-dimensional consensus model* for GDM problems in LGSNE. The model considers the moderating effect of trust on the opinion adjustment.

9.2   Future Research Directions

Although LSGDM is an increasingly hot research topic, it is still in its early stage of development. Unlike most studies, this book argues that trust relationships and similarity of opinion are both important for clustering and consensus building in LSGDM and cannot be separated. Therefore, if we continue this research idea, the following future research directions on LSGDM can be obtained.

- *Comparing which is more important for clustering between trust relationship and similarity of opinion.* In other words, we need to discuss when trust relationship takes precedence for clustering, and when similarity of opinion takes precedence for clustering.
- *The balance between individual consensus cost, group consensus cost and group consensus level.* If the moderating effect of trust loss on consensus-reaching process is considered, the following problems will arise: the reduction of individual trust leads to the reduction of individual consensus cost, which may increase the overall consensus cost based on the least-cost consensus model, and may also be detrimental to the improvement of group consensus level. Therefore, the game between consensus cost and consensus level between individuals and groups should be further discussed in the future.
- *Limitations of sample size.* The number of decision makers involved in the arithmetic experiments or case studies in this book is mostly 20. So are the clustering methods and consensus models proposed in the book still applicable to decision-making problems involving 50 or even hundreds of people? This is a significant research problem, and it is also necessary to test and improve the adaptability and robustness of the proposed methods and models.

Clustering methods and consensus models proposed in this book have been applied to emergency decisions, supplier selection and other practical decision-making problems. In the future, we hope to expand the application scope of the proposed methods and models, such as route selection in tourism management, bilateral/multilateral matching of supply and demand on investment platforms, and site selection for infrastructure construction.

References

1. Acquaye, A., Ibn-Mohammed, T., Genovese, A., Afrifa, G. A., Yamoah, F. A., & Oppon, E. (2018). A quantitative model for environmentally sustainable supply chain performance measurement. *European Journal of Operational Research, 269*(1), 188–205.
2. Akram, M., Kahraman, C., & Zahid, K. (2021). Group decision-making based on complex spherical fuzzy VIKOR approach. *Knowledge-Based Systems, 216*, 106793.
3. Alonso, S., Herrera-Viedma, E., Chiclana, F., & Herrera, F. (2010). A web based consensus support system for group decision making problems and incomplete preferences. *Information Sciences, 180*(23), 4477–4495.
4. Aqlan, F., & Lam, S. S. (2015). Supply chain risk modeling and mitigation. *International Journal of Production Research, 53*(17–18), 1–17.
5. Awasthi, A., Govindan, K., & Gold, S. (2018). Multi-tier sustainable global supplier selection using a fuzzy AHP-VIKOR based approach. *International Journal of Production Economics, 195*, 106–117.
6. Bai, C., Zhang, R., Shen, S., Huang, C., & Fan, X. (2018). Interval-valued probabilistic linguistic term sets in multi-criteria group decision making. *International Journal of Intelligent Systems, 33*, 1301–1321.
7. Ben-Arieh, D., & Easton, T. (2007). Multi-criteria group consensus under linear cost opinion elasticity. *Decision support systems, 43*(3), 713–721.
8. Ben-Arieh, D., Easton, T., & Evans, B. (2008). Minimum cost consensus with quadratic cost functions. *IEEE Transactions on Systems, Man, and Cybernetics-Part A: Systems and Humans, 39*(1), 210–217.
9. Cabrerizo, F. J., Morente-Molinera, J. A., Pedrycz, W., Taghavi, A., & Herrera-Viedma, E. (2018). Granulating linguistic information in decision making under consensus and consistency. *Expert Systems with Applications, 99*, 83–92.
10. Cabrerizo, F. J., Pérez, I. J., & Herrera-Viedma, E. (2010). Managing the consensus in group decision making in an unbalanced fuzzy linguistic context with incomplete information. *Knowledge-Based Systems, 23*(2), 169–181.
11. Cai, C. G., Luo, Y., Zhu, G., & j., Zou, H. (2021). A Public-Participation-Based Mixed Multiattribute Decision-Making Approach for Major Public Affairs. *Mathematical Problems in Engineering.* https://doi.org/10.1155/2021/7550055
12. Chao, X., Kou, G., Peng, Y., Herrera-Viedma, E., & Herrera, F. (2021). An efficient consensus reaching framework for large-scale social network group decision making and its application in urban resettlement. *Information Sciences, 575*, 499–527.

13. Chen, X., Zhang, H., & Dong, Y. (2015). The fusion process with heterogeneous preference structures in group decision making: A survey. *Information Fusion, 24*, 72–83.

14. Chen, X. H., Zhang, W. W., Xu, X. H., & Cao, W. Z. (2022). A public and large-scale expert information fusion method and its application: Mining public opinion via sentiment analysis and measuring public dynamic reliability. *Information Fusion, 78*, 71–85.

15. Chu, J., Liu, X., Wang, Y., & Chin, K. S. (2016). A group decision making model considering both the additive consistency and group consensus of intuitionistic fuzzy preference relations. *Computers & Industrial Engineering, 101*, 227–242.

16. Chu, J., Wang, Y., Liu, X., & Liu, Y. (2020). Social network community analysis based large-scale group decision making approach with incomplete fuzzy preference relations. *Information Fusion, 60*, 98–120.

17. Ding, Z., Chen, X., Dong, Y., & Herrera, F. (2019). Consensus reaching in social network DeGroot model: The roles of the self-confidence and node degree. *Information Sciences, 486*, 62–72.

18. Ding, R. X., Palomares, I., Wang, X., Yang, G. R., Liu, B., Dong, Y., Herrera-Viedma, E., & Herrera, F. (2020). Large-scale decision-making: Characterization, taxonomy, challenges and future directions from an artificial intelligence and applications perspective. *Information Fusion, 59*, 84–102.

19. Ding, R. X., Wang, X., Shang, K., & Herrera, F. (2019). Social network analysis-based conflict relationship investigation and conflict degree-based consensus reaching process for large scale decision making using sparse representation. *Information Fusion, 50*, 251–272.

20. Ding, R. X., Wang, X. Q., Shang, K., Liu, B. S., & Herrera, F. (2019). Sparse representation-based intuitionistic fuzzy clustering approach to find the group intra-relations and group leaders for large-scale decision making. *IEEE Transactions on Fuzzy Systems, 27*(3), 559–573.

21. Dong, Y., Ding, Z., Martínez, L., & Herrera, F. (2017). Managing consensus based on leadership in opinion dynamics. *Information Sciences, 397*, 187–205.

22. Dong, Y., Li, C. C., Xu, Y., & Gu, X. (2015). Consensus-based group decision making under multi-granular unbalanced 2-tuple linguistic preference relations. *Group Decision and Negotiation, 24*(2), 217–242.

23. Dong, Y., Luo, N., & Liang, H. (2015). Consensus building in multiperson decision making with heterogeneous preference representation structures: A perspective based on prospect theory. *Applied Soft Computing, 35*, 898–910.

24. Dong, Y., Zha, Q., Zhang, H., Gang, K., Fujita, H., Chiclana, F., & Herrera-Viedma, E. (2018). Consensus reaching in social network group decision making: Research paradigms and challenges. *Knowledge-Based Systems, 162*(15), 3–13.

25. Dong, Y., Zhan, M., Kou, G., Ding, Z., & Liang, H. (2018). A survey on the fusion process in opinion dynamics. *Information Fusion, 43*, 57–65.

26. Dong, Y., Zhang, H., & Herrera-Viedma, E. (2016). Consensus reaching model in the complex and dynamic MAGDM problem. *Knowledge-Based Systems, 106*, 206–219.

27. Dong, Y., Zhang, H., & Herrera-Viedma, E. (2016). Integrating experts' weights generated dynamically into the consensus reaching process and its applications in managing non-cooperative behaviors. *Decision Support Systems, 84*, 1–15.

28. Dong, Y.C., Zhao, S., Zhang, H., Chiclana, F., Herrera-Viedma, E.(2018). A self-management mechanism for noncooperative behaviors in large-scale group consensus reaching processes, *IEEE Transactions on Fuzzy Systems*, 26, 3276–3288.

29. Du, Y. W., Chen, Q., Sun, Y. L., & Li, C. H. (2021). Knowledge structure-based consensus-reaching method for large-scale multiattribute group decision-making. *Knowledge-Based Systems, 219*(1), 106885.

30. Du, Z. J., Chen, Z. X., & Yu, S. M. (2021). Improved failure mode and effect analysis: Implementing risk assessment and conflict risk mitigation with probabilistic linguistic information. *Mathematics, 9*, 1266.

31. Du, Z. J., Luo, H. Y., Lin, X. D., & Yu, S. M. (2020). A trust-similarity analysis-based clustering method for large-scale group decision-making under a social network. *Information Fusion, 63*, 13–29.

32. Du, Z. J., Yu, S. M., Luo, H. Y., & Lin, X. D. (2021). Consensus convergence in large-group social network environment: Coordination between trust relationship and opinion similarity. *Knowledge-Based Systems, 217*, 106828.

33. Du, Z. J., Yu, S. M., & Xu, X. H. (2020). Managing noncooperative behaviors in large-scale group decision-making: Integration of independent and supervised consensus-reaching models. *Information Sciences, 531*, 119–138.

34. Gai, T., Cao, M., Cao, Q., Wu, J., Yu, G., & Zhou, M. (2020). A joint feedback strategy for consensus in large-scale group decision making under social network. *Computers & Industrial Engineering, 147*, 106626.

35. Gao, P., Hung, J., & Xu, Y. (2020). A k-core decomposition-based opinion leaders identifying method and clustering-based consensus model for large-scale group decision making. *Computers & Industrial Engineering, 150*, 106842.

36. Gong, Z., Zhang, H., Forrest, J., Li, L., & Xu, X. (2015). Two consensus models based on the minimum cost and maximum return regarding either all individuals or one individual. *European Journal of Operational Research, 240*(1), 183–192.

37. Gonzalez, T. F. (1985). Clustering to minimize the maximum intercluster distance. *Theoretical Computer Science, 38*, 293–306.

38. Gou, X., Xu, Z., & Herrera, F. (2018). Consensus reaching process for large-scale group decision making with double hierarchy hesitant fuzzy linguistic preference relations. *Knowledge-Based Systems, 157*, 20–33.

39. Gou, X., Xu, Z., Liao, H., & Herrera, F. (2021). Consensus model handling minority opinions and noncooperative behaviors in large-scale group decision-making under double hierarchy linguistic preference relations. *IEEE Transactions on Cybernetics, 51*(1), 283–296.

40. Guo, G., & Li, D. (2019). Adaptive sliding mode control of vehicular platoons with prescribed tracking performance. *IEEE Transactions on Vehicular Technology, 68*(8), 7511–7520.

41. Guo, G., & Wang, Q. (2019). Fuel-efficient en route speed planning and tracking control of truck platoons. *IEEE Transactions on Intelligent Transportation Systems, 20*(8), 3091–3103.

42. Guo, G., & Wang, L. (2015). Control over medium-constrained vehicular networks with fading channels and random access protocol: A networked systems approach. *IEEE Transactions on Vehicular Technology, 64*(8), 3347–3358.

43. Herrera, F., Herrera-Viedma, E., & Verdegay, J. L. (1996). A linguistic decision process in group decision making. *Group Decision and Negotiation, 5*(2), 165–176.

44. Herrera, F., & Herrera-Viedma, E. (1996). A model of consensus in group decision making under linguistic assessments. *Fuzzy Sets and Systems, 78*(1), 73–87.

45. Herrera-Viedma, E., Cabrerizo, F. J., Kacprzyk, J., & Pedrycz, W. (2014). A review of soft consensus models in a fuzzy environment. *Information Fusion, 17*, 4–13.

46. Herrera-Viedma, E., Martínez, L., Mata, F., & Chiclana, F. (2005). A consensus support system model for group decision-making problems with multigranular linguistic preference relations. *IEEE Transactions on Fuzzy Systems, 13*(5), 644–658.

47. Herrera, F., Alonso, S., Chiclana, F., & Herrera-Viedma, E. (2009). Computing with words in decision making: Foundations, trends and prospects. *Fuzzy Optimization Decision Making, 8*(4), 337–364.

48. Hong, Y., & Kwong, S. (2009). Learning assignment order of instances for the constrained k-means clustering algorithm. *IEEE Transactions on Systems Man & Cybernetics Part B, 39*(2), 568–574.

49. Kacprzyk, J., & Fedrizzi, M. (1988). A 'soft' measure of consensus in the setting of partial (fuzzy) preferences. *European Journal of Operational Research, 34*(3), 316–325.

50. Kamis, N. H., Chiclana, F., & Levesley, J. (2019). An influence-driven feedback system for preference similarity network clustering based consensus group decision making model. *Information Fusion, 52*, 257–267.

51. Kanungo, T., Mount, D. M., Netanyahu, N. S., Piatko, C. D., Silverman, R., & Wu, A. Y. (2002). An efficient k-means clustering algorithm: Analysis and implementation. *IEEE transactions on pattern analysis and machine intelligence, 24*(7), 881–892.

52. Kim, B., Park, K. S., Jung, S. Y., & Park, S. H. (2018). Offshoring and outsourcing in a global supply chain: Impact of the arm's length regulation on transfer pricing. *European Journal of Operational Research, 266*(1), 88–98.

53. Labella, Á, Liu, H., Rodríguez, R. M., & Martínez, L. (2020). A cost consensus metric for consensus reaching processes based on a comprehensive minimum cost model. *European Journal of Operational Research, 281*(2), 316–331.

54. Labella, Á., Liu, Y., Rodríguez, R. M., & Martínez, l. (2018). Analyzing the performance of classical consensus models in large scale group decision making: A comparative study. *Applied Soft Computing, 67*, 677–690.

55. Lesser, O., Naamani-Dery, L., Kalech, M., & Elovici, Y. (2017). Group decision support for leisure activities using voting and social networks. *Group Decision and Negotiation, 26*(3), 473–494.

56. Li, C. C., Dong, Y., & Herrera, F. (2018). A consensus model for large-scale linguistic group decision making with a feedback recommendation based on clustered personalized individual semantics and opposing consensus groups. *IEEE Transactions on Fuzzy Systems, 27*(2), 221–233.

57. Li, S., Qin, N., Huang, D., Huang, D., & Ke, L. (2019). Damage localization of stacker's track based on EEMD-EMD and DBSCAN cluster algorithms. *IEEE Transactions on Instrumentation and Measurement, 69*(5), 1981–1992.

58. Li, S., Rodríguez, R. M., & Wei, C. (2021). Two-stage consensus model based on opinion dynamics and evolution of social power in large-scale group decision making. *Applied Soft Computing, 111*, 107615.

59. Li, S., & Wei, C. (2020). A two-stage dynamic influence model-achieving decision-making consensus within large scale groups operating with incomplete information. *Knowledge-Based Systems, 189*, 105132.

60. Li, C., Xu, Y., Yu, X., Ryan, C., & Huang, T. (2017). Risk-averse energy trading in multi-energy microgrids: A two-stage stochastic game approach. *IEEE Transactions on Industrial Informatics, 13*(5), 2620–2630.

61. Liao, H., Xu, Z., Zeng, X. J., & Xu, D. L. (2016). An enhanced consensus reaching process in group decision making with intuitionistic fuzzy preference relations. *Information Sciences, 329*, 274–286.

62. Liu, Y., Fan, Z. P., & Zhang, X. (2016). A method for large group decision-making based on evaluation information provided by participators from multiple groups. *Information Fusion, 29*, 132–141.

63. Liu, P., He, L., & Yu, X. (2016). Generalized hybrid aggregation operators based on the 2-dimension uncertain linguistic information for multiple attribute group decision making. *Group Decision and Negotiation, 25*(1), 103–126.

64. Liu, Y., Liang, C., Chiclana, F., & Wu, J. (2017). A trust induced recommendation mechanism for reaching consensus in group decision making. *Knowledge-Based Systems, 119*, 221–231.

65. Liu, B., Shen, Y., Chen, X., Chen, Y., & Wang, X. (2014). A partial binary tree DEA-DA cyclic classification model for decision makers in complex multi-attribute large-group interval-valued intuitionistic fuzzy decision-making problems. *Information Fusion, 18*, 119–130.

66. Lin, C. H., Wu, C. H., & Huang, P. Z. (2009). Grey clustering analysis for incipient fault diagnosis in oil-immersed transformers. *Expert Systems with Applications, 36*(2), 1371–1379.

67. Liu, Q., Wu, H., & Xu, Z. (2021). Consensus model based on probability K-means clustering algorithm for large scale group decision making. *International Journal of Machine Learning and Cybernetics, 12*(6), 1609–1626.

68. Liu, P., & Wang, Y. (2014). Multiple attribute group decision making methods based on intuitionistic linguistic power generalized aggregation operators. *Applied Soft Computing, 17*, 90–104.

69. Liu, X., Xu, Y., & Herrera, F. (2019). Consensus model for large-scale group decision making based on fuzzy preference relation with self-confidence: Detecting and managing overconfidence behaviors. *Information Fusion, 52*, 245–256.

70. Liu, X., Xu, Y., Montes, R., & Herrera, F. (2019). Social network group decision making: Managing self-confidence-based consensus model with the dynamic importance degree of experts and trust-based feedback mechanism. *Information Sciences, 505,* 215–232.

71. Liu, X., Xu, Y., Montes, R., Ding, R. X., & Herrera, F. (2018). Alternative ranking-based clustering and reliability index-based consensus reaching process for hesitant fuzzy large scale group decision making. *IEEE Transactions on Fuzzy Systems, 27*(1), 159–171.

72. Liu, F., Zhang, J., & Liu, T. (2020). A PSO-algorithm-based consensus model with the application to large-scale group decision-making. *Complex & Intelligent Systems, 6,* 287–298.

73. Liu, B., Zhou, Q., Ding, R. X., Palomares, I., & Herrera, F. (2018). Large-scale group decision making model based on social network analysis: Trust relationship-based conflict detection and elimination. *European Journal of Operational Research, 275,* 737–754.

74. Lu, Y., Xu, Y., Herrera-Viedma, E., & Han, Y. (2021). Consensus of large-scale group decision making in social network: The minimum cost model based on robust optimization. *Information Sciences, 547,* 910–930.

75. Ma, Z., Zhu, J., Ponnambalam, K., & Zhang, S. (2019). A clustering method for large-scale group decision-making with multi-stage hesitant fuzzy linguistic terms. *Information Fusion, 50,* 231–250.

76. Mata, F., Martínez, L., & Herrera-Viedma, E. (2009). An adaptive consensus support model for group decision-making problems in a multigranular fuzzy linguistic context. *IEEE Transactions on fuzzy Systems, 17*(2), 279–290.

77. Massanet, S., Riera, J. V., Torrens, J., & Herrera-Viedma, E. (2014). A new linguistic computational model based on discrete fuzzy numbers for computing with words. *Information Sciences, 258,* 277–290.

78. Moradi, P., & Ahmadian, S. (2015). A reliability-based recommendation method to improve trust-aware recommender systems. *Expert Systems with Applications, 42*(21), 7386–7398.

79. Morente-Molinera, J. A., Kou, G., Pang, C., Cabrerizo, F. J., & Herrera-Viedma, E. (2019). An automatic procedure to create fuzzy ontologies from users' opinions using sentiment analysis procedures and multi-granular fuzzy linguistic modeling methods. *Information Sciences, 476,* 222–238.

80. Mediwaththe, C. P., & Smith, D. B. (2018). Game-theoretic electric vehicle charging management resilient to non-ideal user behavior. *IEEE Transactions on Intelligent Transportation Systems, 19*(11), 3486–3495.

81. Merigò, J. M., & Gil-Lafuente, A. M. (2013). Induced 2-tuple linguistic generalized aggregation operators and their application in decision-making. *Information Sciences, 236,* 1–16.

82. Oliveira, R. M., & d., Chaves, A. A., Lorena, L. A. N. (2017). A comparison of two hybrid methods for constrained clustering problems. *Applied Soft Computing, 54,* 256–266.

83. Palomares, I. (2014). Consensus model for large-scale group decision support in IT services management. *Intelligent Decision Technologies, 8*(2), 81–94.

84. Palomares, I., Martínez, L., & Herrera, F. (2014). A consensus model to detect and manage noncooperative behaviors in large-scale group decision making. *IEEE Transactions on Fuzzy Systems, 22*(3), 516–530.

85. Palomares, I., Martínez, L., & Herrera, F. (2014). MENTOR: A graphical monitoring tool of preferences evolution in large-scale group decision making. *Knowledge-Based Systems, 58,* 66–74.

86. Pan, X., Wang, Y., & Chin, K. S. (2021). Dynamic programming algorithm-based picture fuzzy clustering approach and its application to the large-scale group decision-making problem. *Computers & Industrial Engineering, 157,* 107330.

87. Pang, Q., Wang, H., & Xu, Z. (2016). Probabilistic linguistic term sets in multi-attribute group decision making. *Information Sciences, 369,* 128–143.

88. Park, J. H., Gwak, M. G., & Kwun, Y. C. (2011). Uncertain linguistic harmonic mean operators and their applications to multiple attribute group decision making. *Computing, 93*(1), 47–64.

89. Parreiras, R. O., Ekel, P. Y., Martini, J. S. C., & Palhares, R. M. (2010). A flexible consensus scheme for multicriteria group decision making under linguistic assessments. *Information Sciences, 180*(7), 1075–1089.

90. Pelta, D. A., & Yager, R. R. (2009). Decision strategies in mediated multiagent negotiations: An optimization approach. *IEEE Transactions on Systems, Man, and Cybernetics-Part A: Systems and Humans, 40*(3), 635–640.

91. Pérez, I. J., Cabrerizo, F. J., Alonso, S., Dong, Y. C., Chiclana, F., & Herrera-Viedma, E. (2018). On dynamic consensus processes in group decision making problems. *Information Sciences, 459*, 20–35.

92. Pérez, L. G., Mata, F., & Chiclana, F. (2014). Social network decision making with linguistic trustworthiness-based induced OWA operators. *International Journal of Intelligent Systems, 29*(12), 1117–1137.

93. Quesada, F. J., Palomares, I., & Martínez, L. (2015). Managing experts behavior in large-scale consensus reaching processes with uninorm aggregation operators. *Applied Soft Computing, 35*, 873–887.

94. Rabiee, M., Aslani, B., & Rezaei, J. (2021). A decision support system for detecting and handling biased decision-makers in multi criteria group decision-making problems. *Expert Systems with Applications, 171*(3), 114597.

95. Rao, C., Xiao, X., Goh, M., Zheng, J., & Wen, J. (2017). Compound mechanism design of supplier selection based on multi-attribute auction and risk management of supply chain. *Computers & Industrial Engineering, 105*, 63–75.

96. Reefke, H., & Sundaram, D. (2018). Sustainable supply chain management: Decision models for transformation and maturity. *Decision Support Systems, 113*, 56–72.

97. Ren, R., Tang, M., & Liao, H. (2020). Managing minority opinions in micro-grid planning by a social network analysis-based large scale group decision making method with hesitant fuzzy linguistic information. *Knowledge-Based Systems, 189*, 105060.

98. Ren, P., Xu, Z., Wang, X., & Zeng, X. J. (2021). Group decision making with hesitant fuzzy linguistic preference relations based on modified extent measurement. *Expert Systems with Applications, 171*(1), 114235.

99. Rodríguez, R. M., Labella, Á, De Tré, G., & Martínez, L. (2018). A large scale consensus reaching process managing group hesitation. *Knowledge-Based Systems, 159*, 86–97.

100. Rodríguez, R. M., Labella, Á., Sesma-Sara, M., Bustince, H., & Martínez, L. (2021). A cohesion-driven consensus reaching process for large scale group decision making under a hesitant fuzzy linguistic term sets environment. *Computers & Industrial Engineering, 155*, 107158.

101. Rodríguez, R. M., Martínez, L., & Herrera, F. (2012). Hesitant fuzzy linguistic term sets for decision making. *IEEE Transactions on Fuzzy Systems, 20*(1), 109–119.

102. Shi, Z., Wang, X., Palomares, I., Guo, S., & Ding, R. X. (2018). A novel consensus model for multi-attribute large-scale group decision making based on comprehensive behavior classification and adaptive weight updating. *Knowledge-Based Systems, 158*, 196–208.

103. Shih, H. S., Shyur, H. J., & Lee, E. S. (2007). An extension of TOPSIS for group decision making. *Mathematical & Computer Modelling, 45*(7–8), 801–813.

104. Sparks, B. A., & Browning, V. (2011). The impact of online reviews on hotel booking intentions and perception of trust. *Tourism Management, 32*(6), 1310–1323.

105. Song, Y., & Li, G. (2019). A large-scale group decision-making with incomplete multigranular probabilistic linguistic term sets and its application in sustainable supplier selection. *Journal of the Operational Research Society, 70*(5), 827–841.

106. Song, G. X., & Yang, H. (2000). The decision-making behavior of group decision analysis. *Academy Research, 3*, 48–49.

107. Sparks, B. A., & Browning, V. (2011). The impact of online reviews on hotel booking intentions and perception of trust. *Tourism Management, 32*(6), 1310–1323.

108. Sung, K. H., & Lee, M. J. (2015). Do online comments influence the public's attitudes toward an organization? Effects of online comments based on individuals' prior attitudes. *The Journal of Psychology, 149*(4), 325–338.

109. Tan, X., Zhu, J., Cabrerizo, F. J., & Herrera-Viedma, E. (2021). A cyclic dynamic trust-based consensus model for large-scale group decision making with probabilistic linguistic information. *Applied Soft Computing, 100*, 106937.

110. Tang, M., Liao, H., Xu, J., Streimikiene, D., & Zheng, X. (2020). Adaptive consensus reaching process with hybrid strategies for large-scale group decision making. *European Journal of Operational Research, 282*(3), 957–971.

111. Tian, Z. P., Nie, R. X., & Wang, J. Q. (2019). Social network analysis-based consensus-supporting framework for large-scale group decision-making with incomplete interval type-2 fuzzy information. *Information Sciences, 502*, 446–471.

112. Ureña, R., Kou, G., Dong, Y., Chiclana, F., & Herrera-Viedma, E. (2019). A review on trust propagation and opinion dynamics in social networks and group decision making frameworks. *Information Sciences, 478*, 461–475.

113. Victor, P., Cornelis, C., De Cock, M., & da Silva, P. P. (2009). Gradual trust and distrust in recommender systems. *Fuzzy Sets & Systems, 160*, 1367–1382.

114. Viswanath, P., & Babu, V. S. (2009). Rough-DBSCAN: A fast hybrid density based clustering method for large data sets. *Pattern Recognition Letters, 30*(16), 1477–1488.

115. Viswanadham, N., & Samvedi, A. (2013). Supplier selection based on supply chain ecosystem, performance and risk criteria. *International Journal of Production Research, 51*(21), 6484–6498.

116. Wasserman, S., Faust, K. (1994). *Social network analysis: Methods and Applications* (Vol. 8). Cambridge University Press.

117. Walter, F. E., Battiston, S., & Schweitzer, F. (2008). A model of a trust-based recommendation system on a social network. *Autonomous Agents and Multi-agent Systems, 16*(1), 57–74.

118. Wan, Q., Xu, X., Chen, X., & Zhuang, J. (2020). A two-stage optimization model for large-scale group decision-making in disaster management: Minimizing group conflict and maximizing individual satisfaction. *Group Decision and Negotiation, 29*(5), 901–921.

119. Wan, S., & Dong, J. (2020). A group decision-making method considering both the group consensus and multiplicative consistency of interval-valued intuitionistic fuzzy preference relations. *Decision Making Theories and Methods Based on Interval-Valued Intuitionistic Fuzzy Sets* (pp. 271–313). Springer.

120. Wang, J. Q., Yu, S. M., Wang, J., Chen, Q. H., Zhang, H. Y., & Chen, X. H. (2015). An interval type-2 fuzzy number based approach for multi-criteria group decision-making problems. *International Journal of Uncertainty, Fuzziness and Knowledge-Based Systems, 23*(4), 565–588.

121. Wen, S., & Guo, G. (2020). Sampled-data control for connected vehicles with markovian switching topologies and communication delay. *IEEE Transactions on Intelligent Transportation Systems, 21*(7), 2930–2942.

122. Wu, J., & Chiclana, F. (2014). A social network analysis trust-consensus based approach to group decision-making problems with interval-valued fuzzy reciprocal preference relations. *Knowledge-Based Systems, 59*, 97–104.

123. Wu, J., Chiclana, F., & Herrera-Viedma, E. (2015). Trust based consensus model for social network in an incomplete linguistic information context. *Applied Soft Computing, 35*, 827–839.

124. Wu, J., Chiclana, F., Fujita, H., & Herrera-Viedma, E. (2017). A visual interaction consensus model for social network group decision making with trust propagation. *Knowledge-Based Systems, 122*, 39–50.

125. Wu, J., Dai, L., Chiclana, F., Fujita, H., Herrera-Viedma, E. (2017). A minimum adjustment cost feedback mechanism based consensus model for group decision making under social network with distributed linguistic trust. *Information Fusion*, 232–242.

126. Wu, X., & Liao, H. (2019). A consensus-based probabilistic linguistic gained and lost dominance score method. *European Journal of Operational Research, 272*(3), 1017–1027.

127. Wu, T., Liu, X., & Liu, F. (2018). An interval type-2 fuzzy TOPSIS model for large scale group decision making problems with social network information. *Information Sciences, 432*, 392–410.

128. Wu, T., & Liu, X. W. (2016). An interval type-2 fuzzy clustering solution for large-scale multiple-criteria group decision-making problems. *Knowledge-Based Systems, 114*, 118–127.

129. Wu, J., Xiong, R., & Chiclana, F. (2016). Uninorm trust propagation and aggregation methods for group decision making in social network with four tuple information. *Knowledge-Based Systems, 96*, 29–39.

130. Wu, Z., & Xu, J. (2016). Managing consistency and consensus in group decision making with hesitant fuzzy linguistic preference relations. *Omega, 65*, 28–40.

131. Wu, Z., & Xu, J. (2018). A consensus model for large-scale group decision making with hesitant fuzzy information and changeable clusters. *Information Fusion, 41*, 217–231.

132. Wu, Z., & Xu, J. (2015). Possibility distribution-based approach for MAGDM with hesitant fuzzy linguistic information. *IEEE Transactions on Cybernetics, 46*(3), 694–705.

133. Wu, T., Zhang, K., Liu, X., & Cao, C. (2019). A two-stage social trust network partition model for large-scale group decision-making problems. *Knowledge-Based Systems, 163*, 632–643.

134. Wu, Y. Z., Zhang, Z., Kou, G., Zhang, H. J., Chao, X. R., Li, C. C., Dong, Y. C., & Herrera, F. (2021). Distributed linguistic representations in decision making: Taxonomy, key elements and applications, and challenges in data science and explainable artificial intelligence. *Information Fusion, 65*, 165–178.

135. Xiao, J., Wang, X., & Zhang, H. (2020). Managing personalized individual semantics and consensus in linguistic distribution large-scale group decision making. *Information Fusion, 53*, 20–34.

136. Xu, Z. (2009). An automatic approach to reaching consensus in multiple attribute group decision making. *Computers & Industrial Engineering, 56*(4), 1369–1374.

137. Xu, Z. S. (2009). An interactive approach to multiple attribute group decision making with multigranular uncertain linguistic information. *Group Decision and Negotiation, 18*(2), 119–145.

138. Xu, Z. (2007). Multiple-attribute group decision making with different formats of preference information on attributes. *IEEE Transactions on Systems, Man, and Cybernetics, Part B (Cybernetics), 37*(6), 1500–1511.

139. Xu, Z. S. (2005). Deviation measures of linguistic preference relations in group decision making. *Omega, 33*, 249–254.

140. Xu, X. H., & Chen, X. H. (2005). Research on the group clustering method based on vector space. *Systems Engineering and Electronics, 27*(6), 1034–1037.

141. Xu, W., Chen, X., Dong, Y., & Chiclana, F. (2021). Impact of decision rules and non-cooperative behaviors on minimum consensus cost in group decision making. *Group Decision and Negotiation, 30*(6), 1239–1260.

142. Xu, X. H., Du, Z. J., Chen, X. H., & Cai, C. G. (2019). Confidence consensus-based model for large-scale group decision making: A novel approach to managing non-cooperative behaviors. *Information Sciences, 477*, 410–427.

143. Xu, X. H., Du, Z. J., Chen, X. H., & Zhou, Y. J. (2017). Conflict large-group emergency decision-making method while protecting minority opinions. *Journal of Management Sciences in China, 20*(11), 10–23.

144. Xu, X. H., Du, Z. J., & Chen, X. H. (2015). Consensus model for multi-criteria large-group emergency decision making considering non-cooperative behaviors and minority opinions. *Decision Support Systems, 79*, 150–160.

145. Xu, X., Zhang, Q., & Chen, X. (2020). Consensus-based non-cooperative behaviors management in large-group emergency decision-making considering experts' trust relations and preference risks. *Knowledge-Based Systems, 190*, 105108.

146. Xu, Y., Wen, X., & Zhang, W. (2018). A two-stage consensus method for large-scale multi-attribute group decision making with an application to earthquake shelter selection. *Computers & Industrial Engineering, 116*, 113–129.

147. Xu, X. H., Zhong, X. Y., Chen, X. H., & Zhou, Y. J. (2015). A dynamical consensus method based on exit-delegation mechanism for large group emergency decision making. *Knowledge-Based Systems, 86*, 237–249.

148. Yager, R. R. (1996). Quantifier guided aggregation using OWA operators. *International Journal of Intelligent Systems, 11*(1), 49–73.

149. Yager, R. R., & Filev, D. P. (1999). Induced ordered weighted averaging operators. *IEEE Transactions on Systems, Man & Cybernetics: Part B., 29*(2), 141–150.

150. Yager, R. R. (2001). Penalizing strategic preference manipulation in multi-agent decision making. *IEEE Transactions on Fuzzy Systems, 9*(3), 393–403.

151. Yager, R. R. (2002). Defending against strategic manipulation in uninorm-based multi-agent decision making. *European Journal of Operational Research, 141*(1), 217–232.

152. Yang, Y., Tan, W., Li, T., & Da, R. (2012). Consensus clustering based on constrained self-organizing map and improved Cop-Kmeans ensemble in intelligent decision support systems. *Knowledge-Based Systems, 32*, 101–115.

153. Yang, C. L., Zhang, C. F., & Xu, W. C. (2010). A model based on similarity degree of interval number for uncertain multi-attribute decision making. *Mathematics in Practice and Theory, 40*(21), 148–154.

154. Yu, S. M., Du, Z. J., Zhang, X. Y., Luo, H. Y., & Lin, X. D. (2021). Punishment-driven consensus reaching model in social network large-scale decision-making with application to social capital selection. *Applied Soft Computing., 113*, 107912.

155. Yu, S., Du, Z., & Xu, X. (2021). Hierarchical punishment-driven consensus model for probabilistic linguistic large-group decision making with application to global supplier selection. *Group Decision and Negotiation, 30*, 1343–1372.

156. Yu, S. M., Du, Z. J., Zhang, X., Luo, H., & Lin, X. (2021). Trust Cop-Kmeans clustering analysis and minimum-cost consensus model considering voluntary trust loss in social network large-scale decision-making. *IEEE Transactions on Fuzzy Systems.* https://doi.org/10.1109/tfuzz.2021.3089745

157. Yu, S. M., Du, Z. J., Lin, X. D., Luo, H. Y., & Wang, J. Q. (2020). A stochastic dominance-based approach for hotel selection under probabilistic linguistic environment. *Mathematics, 8*(9), 1525.

158. Yu, S. M., Du, Z. J., Wang, J. Q., Luo, H. Y., & Lin, X. D. (2021). Trust and behavior analysis-based fusion method for heterogeneous multiple attribute group decision-making. *Computers & Industrial Engineering, 152*, 106992.

159. Yu, S. M., Du, Z. J., & Zhang, X. Y. (2022). Clustering analysis and punishment-driven consensus-reaching process for probabilistic linguistic large-group decision-making with application to car-sharing platform selection. *International Transactions in Operational Research, 29*(3), 2002–2029

160. Yu, S. M., Wang, J., Wang, J. Q., & Li, L. (2018). A multi-criteria decision-making model for hotel selection with linguistic distribution assessments. *Applied Soft Computing, 67*, 741–755.

161. Yu, S. M., Wang, J., & Wang, J. Q. (2016). An extended TODIM approach with intuitionistic linguistic numbers. *International Transactions in Operational Research, 25*(3), 781–805.

162. Yu, S. M., Wang, J., & Wang, J. Q. (2017). An interval type-2 fuzzy likelihood-based MABAC approach and its application in selecting hotels on a tourism website. *International Journal of Fuzzy Systems, 19*(1), 47–61.

163. Yu, S. M., Zhang, H. Y., & Wang, J. Q. (2018). Hesitant fuzzy linguistic maclaurin symmetric mean operators and their applications to multi-criteria decision-making problem. *International Journal of Intelligent Systems, 33*(5), 953–982.

164. Yu, S. M., Zhou, H., Chen, X. H., & Wang, J. Q. (2015). A multi-criteria decision-making method based on Heronian mean operators under a linguistic hesitant fuzzy environment. *Asia-Pacific Journal of Operational Research, 32*(5), 1550035.

165. Zhang, G., Dong, Y., Xu, Y., & Li, H. (2011). Minimum-cost consensus models under aggregation operators. *IEEE Transactions on Systems, Man, and Cybernetics-Part A: Systems and Humans, 41*(6), 1253–1261.

166. Zhang, H., Dong, Y., Chiclana, F., & Yu, S. (2019). Consensus efficiency in group decision making: A comprehensive comparative study and its optimal design. *European Journal of Operational Research, 275*(2), 580–598.

167. Zhang, H., Dong, Y., & Herrera-Viedma, E. (2017). Consensus building for the heterogeneous large-scale GDM with the individual concerns and satisfactions. *IEEE Transactions on Fuzzy Systems, 26*(2), 884–898.

168. Zhang, B., Dong, Y., Zhang, H., & Pedrycz, W. (2020). Consensus mechanism with maximum-return modifications and minimum-cost feedback: A perspective of game theory. *European Journal of Operational Research, 287*(2), 546–559.

169. Zhang, Z., Gao, Y., & Li, Z. (2020). Consensus reaching for social network group decision making by considering leadership and bounded confidence. *Knowledge-Based Systems, 204,* 106240.

170. Zhang, Z., Guo, C., & Martínez, L. (2016). Managing multigranular linguistic distribution assessments in large-scale multiattribute group decision making. *IEEE Transactions on Systems, Man, and Cybernetics: Systems, 47*(11), 3063–3076.

171. Zhang, N., Gong, Z., & Chiclana, F. (2017). Minimum cost consensus models based on random opinions. *Expert Systems with Applications, 89,* 149–159.

172. Zhang, H., Palomares, I., Dong, Y., & Wang, W. (2018). Managing non-cooperative behaviors in consensus-based multiple attribute group decision making: An approach based on social network analysis. *Knowledge-Based Systems, 162,* 29–45.

173. Zhang, H., Kou, G., & Peng, Y. (2019). Soft consensus cost models for group decision making and economic interpretations. *European Journal of Operational Research, 277*(3), 964–980.

174. Zhang, B., Liang, H., & Zhang, G. (2018). Reaching a consensus with minimum adjustment in MAGDM with hesitant fuzzy linguistic term sets. *Information Fusion, 42,* 12–23.

175. Zhang, B., Liang, H., Zhang, G., & Xu, Y. (2017). Minimum deviation ordinal consensus reaching in gdm with heterogeneous preference structures. *Applied Soft Computing, 67,* 658–676.

176. Zhang, B., Liang, H., Gao, Y., & Zhang, G. (2018). The optimization-based aggregation and consensus with minimum-cost in group decision making under incomplete linguistic distribution context. *Knowledge-Based Systems, 162,* 92–102.

177. Zhang, X. Y., Wang, X. K., Yu, S. M., Wang, J. Q., & Wang, T. L. (2018). Location selection of offshore wind power station by consensus decision framework using picture fuzzy modelling. *Journal of Cleaner Production, 202,* 980–992.

178. Zhang, Y., Xu, Z., & Liao, H. (2017). A consensus process for group decision making with probabilistic linguistic preference relations. *Information Sciences, 414,* 260–275.

179. Zhang, Y., Xu, Z., Wang, H., & Liao, H. (2016). Consistency-based risk assessment with probabilistic linguistic preference relation. *Applied Soft Computing, 49,* 817–833.

180. Zhang, H., Zhao, S., Kou, G., Li, C. C., Dong, Y., & Herrera, F. (2020). An overview on feedback mechanisms with minimum adjustment or cost in consensus reaching in group decision making: Research paradigms and challenges. *Information Fusion, 60,* 65–79.

181. Zhang, C., Zhao, M., Zhao, L., & Yuan, Q. (2021). A consensus model for large-scale group decision-making based on the trust relationship considering leadership behaviors and non-cooperative behaviors. *Group Decision and Negotiation.* https://doi.org/10.1007/s10726-021-09723-4

182. Zhao, Y., Karypis, G., & Fayyad, U. (2005). Hierarchical clustering algorithms for document datasets. *Data Mining and Knowledge Discovery, 10*(2), 141–168.

183. Zhao, M., Ma, X. Y., & Wei, D. W. (2017). A method considering and adjusting individual consistency and group consensus for group decision making with incomplete linguistic preference relations. *Applied Soft Computing, 54,* 322–346.

184. Zhong, X., & Xu, X. H. (2020). Clustering-based method for large group decision making with hesitant fuzzy linguistic information: Integrating correlation and consensus. *Applied Soft Computing, 87,* 105973.

185. Zhong, X., Xu, X., & Pan, B. (2022). A non-threshold consensus model based on the minimum cost and maximum consensus-increasing for multi-attribute large group decision-making. *Information Fusion, 77,* 90–106.

186. Zhong, X., Xu, X., & Yin, X. (2021). A multi-stage hybrid consensus reaching model for multi-attribute large group decision-making: Integrating cardinal consensus and ordinal consensus. *Computers & Industrial Engineering, 158,* 107443.

187. Zhou, X., Ji, F., Wang, L., Ma, Y., & Fujita, H. (2020). Particle swarm optimization for trust relationship based social network group decision making under a probabilistic linguistic environment. *Knowledge-Based Systems, 200,* 105999.

188. Zhou, X., Liang, W., Huang, S., & Fu, M. (2019). Social recommendation with large-scale group decision-making for cyber-enabled online service. *IEEE Transactions on Computational Social Systems, 6*(5), 1073–1082.
189. Zuheros, C., Li, C. C., Cabrerizo, F. J., Dong, Y. C., Herrera-Viedma, E., & Herrera, F. (2018). Computing with words: Revisiting the qualitative scale. *International Journal of Uncertainty, Fuzziness and Knowledge-Based Systems, 26*(Suppl. 2), 127–143.

Lightning Source UK Ltd.
Milton Keynes UK
UKHW020828110123
415103UK00002B/32